Youth and Youth Groups

Youth
and Youth Groups

✻

J. MACALISTER BREW
C.B.E.

with a foreword by

SIR JOHN WOLFENDEN, C.B.E.

Revised by

JOAN E. MATTHEWS

FABER AND FABER
24 Russell Square
London

96847

First published in 1957
by Faber and Faber Limited
24 Russell Square London W.C.1
Second impression 1959
Second edition 1968
Printed in Great Britain by
Latimer Trend & Co Ltd Plymouth
All rights reserved

SBN: 571 04629 0

Acknowledgements

✳

In the first edition Miss J. Macalister Brew acknowledged her debt to Mr. Peter Kuenstler, who edited *Social Group Work in Great Britain*, for permission to use much of the material from her section—'Group Work with Adolescents'; to the National Association of Mixed Clubs and Girls' Clubs for permission to use material written for them in *Occasional Papers* 1 and 2 (Girls' Interests and Projects); and to the English New Education Fellowship for permission to reproduce much of the material from her chapter, 'Away from Work' in *Advances in Understanding the Adolescent*.

Acknowledgement is also made to Her Majesty's Stationery Office for permission to reproduce extracts from the Albemarle Report on *Youth Service in England and Wales* in this revised edition.

Contents

✳

Foreword

by Sir John Wolfenden, C.B.E.

✳

It is a melancholy coincidence that this book should appear within a few months of its author's death. But we are fortunate at least in this, that it was finished before she died. For it gives us the mature fruit of an experience which was unique; and we have good reason to be thankful that deprived of her we have not been deprived of it.

Dr. Josephine Macalister Brew was known to thousands. She was absolutely unsparing of herself and her energies, and there can be little doubt that it was her burning zeal for young people that burnt her up. Our compensation is that this book makes permanent what might otherwise have faded as ephemeral, her wit, the precise coherence of her exposition, her philosophic mind, and, above all, her abhorrence of what was pompous or pretentious.

We shall not hear again that precise and lucid speech from the tiny pinched face behind the thick-lensed spectacles. But in every page of this book we *do* hear it.

J. F. WOLFENDEN

11

Preface to the First Edition

✳

This book has been written almost by accident. The original intention had been to revise and bring up-to-date *In the Service of Youth* which was published in 1943. But it could not be done, for the latter was written in the war years and since then we have moved into an uneasy peace and the age of automation. In the intervening years there has been much social legislation, and it would be surprising if an era which has seen the birth of a Welfare State and full employment had not had far-reaching effects on the problems and attitudes of adolescents and, therefore, on the service designed for their well-being.

It soon became evident, therefore, that it was not revision, but re-writing and re-thinking that was required, and this new book is the result of that process. Some of the original material remains, but in the main this is a different book because we live in a different world. Naturally the chapters on youth-group activities deal with the same type of activities—for there is no new subject under the sun; but even here new trends and new adolescent interests have had their influence. The original intention, however, is the same, to suggest to people who are new to youth work a framework for their thinking and doing, and to pay tribute to those who have been in it 'man and boy for forty years'.

Achievement and frustration, failure and fulfilment, have been the lot of all those who have laboured 'in the service of youth', in those arduous years, and without the encouragement and inspiration of those in the field from whom I have received much kindness this book could not have been written.

J. MACALISTER BREW

Preface to the Second Edition

✳

I am aware of two reasons for which I was persuaded to undertake the revision of this book: one is that I was flattered by the request to do it, and the other is that I knew that the book was still widely used in the Youth Service and that therefore there was good reason for attempting to bring it up to date.

I was acquainted with the author, but did not know her very well. I think her educational and social background differed from mine a good deal and although our working experiences touched at a few points, our perceptions must be differently coloured and angled. None of us can know what her reactions would have been to the changing scenes of the years since her death, and I suspect that she would have written a new book instead of revising this one. In any case, I must take responsibility for anything in the new edition which refers to the years after 1957.

When I began the revision the book was eight years old and probably ten years had elapsed since the author began work on it. When the book was first conceived, today's adolescents had not all reached the infant schools; we were still to some extent living in the aftermath of the 1939–45 war; the date was pre-Albemarle, pre-Bessey, pre-Industrial Training Act, pre-Twist and Shake and pre-Beatle. The task, therefore, has been a difficult one for a number of reasons besides the major one of pressure of prior duties.

The author was a highly intelligent observer, who said what she believed should be said with no apparent concern for the results on her personal popularity, and the Youth Service owes much to her.

15

Preface to the Second Edition

She had much to say of importance and was an entertaining talker. Sometimes she wrote as she talked, and this produced an enviable fluency which could cover several pages at a time with comment spiced with a good deal of 'blarney'. The comment was relevant to the time at which it was written, but much of it is no longer so. Consequently several passages of this kind are not included in the new edition, and the 'blarney' has gone with the comment, leaving the book the poorer. Sometimes the writing moves into the first person singular. When this happens in the new edition it is the author, not the reviser, speaking.

The general plan of the book has not changed—no chapter heading has been eliminated and no new one introduced—but some chapters have been entirely rewritten and others largely so. Whenever possible in rewritten sections, passages from the original have been written into the revised text, but about half the new edition is newly written. The first chapter, a first-rate exposition, remains virtually unchanged, but I found that the passage of time had made some change, relatively minor or extensive, imperative in all the other chapters. The rewritten version of the last chapter has not, however, been used, as the publishers wished to retain the reflection of the author's particular approach and charm which the original last chapter contained.

I do not expect the revised edition to be judged as good as the original, but I hope it will be of some use. If there are any who feel it is quite unworthy of its predecessor, I ask them to accept my statement that the work has been done in good faith.

J.E.M.

September 1967

I

Birth into Adulthood: The Nature of Adolescence

✴

At best it is astonishing, at worst it is exceedingly wasteful that when so much care and attention has been given to the problems of physical birth, when ante- and post-natal care have paid such rewarding dividends and when paediatricians and a knowledge of psychology have done so much for the happiness of nursery school children, the second birth of the individual—adolescence—the birth into adulthood, has as yet received so little sympathetic consideration.

We know that although physical birth is a perfectly natural thing, yet if we give the mother extra care and attention during pregnancy the chances are (and we have figures to prove it) that she will produce bigger, better and bonnier babies. In the same way if adolescents are given the necessary care and attention during 'birth into adulthood', there is more likelihood that they will become responsible and mature adults. Statistical proof is not as easy to come by, and those who have most proof to offer, the leaders of the various youth organizations, are not, on the whole, the kind of people who are accustomed to the scientific method. If they keep records at all they are often but sketchy and intermittent, but the combined and continuing evidence of hundreds of such people whose integrity cannot be called into question, bears most convincing testimony to the value of paying special care and attention to the adolescent years. After all that is what all youth movements have recognized and what dictatorships have not been slow to turn to their own ends.

Birth into Adulthood: The Nature of Adolescence

One of the main difficulties of adolescence is that on the one hand we are hampered by the various theories which have been advanced by psychologists and sociologists concerning it and, on the other, by the large numbers of people who still regard adolescence as nothing more than the period at which young people enter on the stage of sexual maturation.

Even the analogy with physical birth is not entirely helpful. Both diagnosis and prognosis have now reached a high degree of accuracy and the margin of error concerning the probable arrival of any given baby is normally very narrow, and there is certainly no doubt as to whether a birth has occurred! When it comes to adolescence, however, there is no means of telling how long a period will be involved. One cannot say to the troubled adolescent or his suffering parents 'Never mind, he/she will be better next week', or even 'It will all be over fairly soon now'. The onset of puberty, however convenient it may be as an indication that young people are undergoing those physiological changes which accompany sexual maturation, is only one aspect of birth into adulthood. Even in this field the little statistical work that has been done would seem to show that too large a number of young people menstruate or experience their first emission on either side of the formerly accepted norm of eleven to fifteen for it to be taken for granted. Puberty among quite normal children has been reported to occur at all ages ranging from eight or nine to eighteen or nineteen, and both so-called precocious and delayed puberty are more common than is generally believed.

But the onset of puberty is but one manifestation of adolescence which is concerned with social as well as physiological changes, with increased emotional awareness and with deep-seated spiritual or idealistic development. It can be likened to a bridge connecting childhood with adulthood, and though the onset of puberty may be a convenient method of assessing the time at which many children normally begin to cross the bridge, the achievement of emotional maturity and social poise must all be gained before the adolescent period is over. Many, as we know to society's cost, get stuck on the bridge of adolescence and never grow up, and when two adults 'fixed in adolescence' marry, the prospect of happiness for themselves or their children is more than uncertain. Hence, helping the adolescent to grow up is a vital part of education for family life.

18

Birth into Adulthood: The Nature of Adolescence

Whether one belongs to the school of thought which maintains that there is no bodily change which has not its emotional counterpart, or vice versa, the fact remains that for large numbers of young people and their parents adolescence is a period of storm and stress; whether it need be so is still a matter for conjecture.

It is interesting to note that in most primitive communities which have been carefully studied there would seem to be few manifestations of difficult adolescent behaviour. The child in such societies passes much more easily from childhood to adulthood. It is helpful therefore to consider what may be the reasons for the difficulties which seem so common in more civilized communities.

In the first place, in primitive society there is never a period at which there is any doubt as to the status of any given member of the community. A boy is either a boy with all the natural freedom and duties of obedience to his tribe, or a man with all the privileged freedom of the adult and the corresponding duties to the tribe. The girl is either a girl with duties to the younger children and the duty of obedience to her elders, or a woman with the privileges of her sex and her duties to her mate and her children. There is no time, as there is with us, when one's status is uncertain.

In the primitive community the transition from one status to another may be sharp and sudden, but there is no doubt about it, since in nearly all cases it is heralded by initiation ceremonies of varying length and elaborateness. The child is admitted into the rites and secrets of the adult community and the formal initiation gives him a feeling of importance and responsibility; he is never in doubt about the side of the fence on which he is standing. In our society the period of initiation into the mysteries of adulthood varies according to the company the adolescent keeps, while the date of his assuming adult duties and responsibilities varies according to the income of his parents, his own social status and earning capacity, and the exigencies of the state. In the majority of homes the boy seems to assume adult independence in the eyes of his mother when he becomes a wage-earner, and this happens at varying ages throughout the social scale up to the vestigial initiation rites of the twenty-first birthday party given for the heir to great estates. Moreover the prolongation of education in a technological age, the very enactments designed for the protection of the adolescent's health, such as, for example, regulations regarding newspaper and milk deliveries and working overtime, the seem-

19

ingly muddled state of the laws relating to the age at which adolescents may do certain adult things seem to those struggling for adult status nothing but an adult plot to keep them in a state of tutelage for as long as possible. Young people may not, for instance, buy intoxicants until they are eighteen, but they may marry (which rightly seems to them a more important transaction) at sixteen, provided that they can obtain their parents' or a magistrate's consent, while boys have long been liable to National Service at seventeen and a half and could, therefore, be called upon to die for their country long before they would be allowed to vote at twenty-one.

'The trouble is I'm neither a kid nor a man,' said the East End boy, 'and I get the fault of being both.' His cry was a statement of fact as well as of desperation.

Nowadays many adolescents are better educated than their parents, most of them have reached mental maturity by about sixteen and they have all the physical potentialities of the adult. '*When* will we be considered grown up?' they cry. The unsatisfactory adult answer is 'These are the happiest days of your life', an answer which it is impossible for adolescents to believe, and which is often manifestly untrue.

The struggle for status is indeed part of the process of birth into adulthood. In the same home boys and girls are often expected to adjust themselves to the mother who insists on her son or daughter remaining a child for as long as possible, and the father who waits expectantly for some small evidence of a 'sense of responsibility'. Indeed, sometimes the very father who demands that his son shall take upon himself the burden and serious outlook of adulthood will fight to the last ditch to keep his favourite daughter 'Daddy's little girl' for as long as possible. Thus in adolescence young people are never really acceptable. They are always either too grown up or too irresponsible for the taste of the surrounding adults. How, then, can it be expected that the time should be anything but one of extreme discomfort for the boy or girl whose dawning sense of manhood or womanhood seems to them to be alternately insulted, or repressed, ignored or discounted?

Again the primitive community has few adolescent problems because there is no deliberately retarded development. In civilized countries adolescents are physiologically complete long before from sheer economic necessity they can hope to be biologically satisfied. In the primitive community the girl progresses evenly from the family of her father to that of her mate. In our community she has a long period of transition between the one state and the other which for many women proves a veritable 'no-man's-land' of complete frustration. The boy has the same period of waiting when he is neither of the family, nor can he afford to found a family of his own. During the Depression and right up until 1939 the marriage age tended to become further and further postponed and this, in itself, led to great frustration. Since then, however, increasingly, young people are tending to get married in their late teens or early twenties. In many ways this is a good thing but it is not without its special difficulties for girls.

The Victorian miss escaped from home into work, and between the wars young women escaped from work into marriage—but for the modern woman there is no escape. No matter what advice press and radio, pulpit and magistrates' court may give her, the fact is that the majority know that when they marry the custom of the neighbourhood (whether it be a council housing estate or suburbia in Chelsea or Cardiff) is to continue working for at least a few years after marriage, and probably in a part-time job at the very least until middle age, unless great good fortune falls to them. Far from waiting to marry until they can support a wife, modern intellectuals at all events seem to be seeking wives who can help to support them. An increasing number of girls now marry while the young man is still in training—whether he is at the university, a training college, on National Service or working for examinations in the evenings. These young wives are helping to support their husbands and to provide a home and home comforts for them. Even in the artisan groups who, before the war 'thought it shame for a wife to go out to work', it is now socially acceptable that a young wife should continue to earn for as long as possible. How else can the standard of living they now desire be achieved? It is pointless to assert that their grandparents started married life in two rooms with very few household goods. For modern couples even two rooms without a television set and a kitchen cabinet and those electrical appliances which are almost essential if the wife is to continue at work, is almost unthinkable. Who shall say that it is wrong to desire comfort rather than hardship; gadgets to make housework lighter rather than tired-out wives;

21

radio and television rather than evenings with the family separately visiting public-house, whist drive, palais de dance and cinema?

Unless the adolescent is very wisely handled it is natural therefore that in a complex society there should be stresses and strains. They feel within them dawning potentialities, they are at the mercy of physical and emotional urges they cannot understand, and they are worse off than their primitive brothers in that they live in a society where there is a constant conflict between those who are responsible for their welfare and those who offer them commercial entertainment, clothes and holidays. They are frequently left to cope with the question of social adjustment, on the physical and emotional level, with problems of behaviour in work and in leisure, and as though this were not enough, with religious and ethical conflicts, with almost no adult guidance. Meanwhile the Press, the cinema, the club and uniformed organizations, the Church, the dance hall, the pin-table saloon, the public house, and the home are competing for their bodies with all the desire to exploit them which characterized the body-snatchers of a more downright age, when they at least waited for death before engaging in their grim work.

And meanwhile life has not lost any of its old problems, but rather acquired new ones. Women are living in a moral climate completely different from their grandmothers'. They have almost complete sexual and economic freedom, and yet to their eternal honour, with integrity of purpose and added responsibility, they have *chosen*, whatever else they may do, to embark on family life. The adolescent girl looks forward, no less eagerly than a Jane Austen character, to marriage and the bearing of children, and believes it to be a matter of both dignity and honour to contrive to be a successful wife, mother, housewife and wage-earner. She has indeed, as my great-aunt Mary puts it—'brought her eggs to a pretty market'.

This determination to fulfil her destiny however has profound effects upon the patterns of behaviour of adolescent girls. The fulfilment of a dual role in society as housewife and wage-earner is a heavy task (however sweet the bondage of her dreams may be), and her choice of employment and her leisure time are, therefore, made to fit in with this twofold function.

In the past social workers often condemned the mothers of

working girls in that they either kept their daughters too much tied to household tasks or (which was far more common) 'waited on them hand, foot and finger', very often not allowing them to 'soil their hands' as they proudly said, maintaining with unconscious pathos, 'Let them have a good time now—once they're married they'll have plenty of this sort of thing to do for the rest of their lives.' Indeed, much of the early resistance to the teaching of domestic science in the schools, many of the pioneers in this field maintain, came from parents who stoutly asserted, 'Time enough for this later.'

It is the girl herself who now, albeit at the unconscious level, seems to say, 'Not yet—I will work hard enough later, probably for the rest of my life, but now—now let me enjoy myself.' Much of the so-called apathy of the secondary modern schoolgirl, much of the difficulty experienced in 'interesting' the girl in club activities (with the exception of dancing) is perhaps nature's way of insisting that the modern girl shall have at least some years of lying fallow in preparation for the over-full-time job ahead of her.

Undoubtedly much of the highly charged emotionalism of adolescence is rooted in the physical. It always seems unnecessarily hard that in addition to everything else that happens to them boys and girls in the early stages of growing up *look* all wrong—they are either too long and lanky or too short and fat. One has only to consider the nicknames common among adolescents—'Fatty', 'Skinny', 'Squeak', 'Spotty'—to realize how widespread this is. Because of the uneven rate of growth of bone and muscle, which is often characteristic of adolescence, they are awkward and clumsy. It is frustrating and disappointing to many boys and girls to discover that the skill with hand and ball, the ability to perform feats of agility which were formerly theirs when at about eleven or twelve years of age they were well co-ordinated physical specimens, are now lost, and that they frequently feel tired and listless.

But far from having this temporary loss of skill and vitality explained to them, only too many adults are impatient of their failure to exhibit the physical stamina of younger children or of adults, while many people who would handle the small child with infinite patience, even those who at least know that the best way to spoil a kitten or a puppy's temper is to tease it, regard the very

23

appearance of many adolescents as fair material for the exercise of platitudinous witticisms.

The answer to the oft-repeated gibe, 'A great hefty fellow like you ought to be playing football instead of just loafing about,' might often be 'Yes, and it's just because I *am* such a great hefty fellow that I *need* the rest', for during some stages of adolescence the growth of the largest muscle of all, the heart, does not keep pace with the body and the disinclination to do anything is very frequently an unconscious protection against overstrain. 'Haven't you started shaving yet?' to a boy who is late in maturing and who is already concerned about it, is not helpful, any more than the accusation of being 'boy-mad' is helpful to the girl who is beginning to exercise her powers of attraction as nature intended that she should. A great deal of the growth of this period is what is loosely termed sex growth—the hair on the boy's face, the development of the girl's breasts, and the embarrassing changes in the boy's voice. The increased sense of physical awareness that all these developments occasion, is accompanied by definite physical, i.e. sexual, sensations. Many adolescents are entirely unprepared for this and are frightened by it.

In spite of all our sex education, the contemporary attitude to the onset of puberty itself is by no means helpful. We have surprisingly preserved a large amount of Victorian prudery so that menstruation still seems salacious to many men and shameful to many women. Girls are still taught to lie about it, it is still not quite *comme il faut* to admit to a pain below the throat, but many girls, especially city girls, *do* experience a certain amount of pain. We know that they need not and we know that they ought not—but it is no good arguing from what is to what ought to be. The pain, and the shame at feeling the pain, and what is felt to be the shameful cause of the pain, set up a trio of discords in the girl's mind and combine to give her a very unpleasant time whether she attempts either to conceal it, or to cash in on it. There are still a surprising number of girls and boys who are not fully prepared for the physical changes which occur. This does not necessarily mean that they have not been given scientific information about what to expect. But we are all a little like the old lady who prefaced her will with the words 'If I should die, which God forbid'. We do not believe that these things are going to happen to *us*. Hence the first menstruation or the first nocturnal emission or erection,

24

is often both startling and shocking. For the first time too many of them suddenly realize the full significance of all they have been taught as it affects their own parents. When this happens the adolescent often suffers a strong emotional rejection of one or both parents for some little time, a situation which needs very delicate handling. For many, too, the full significance of these changes brings forth the unspoken cry, 'Well, you've told me what will happen, but what do I now do about it?'

Furthermore, some adolescents for a little while, even when prepared for all these changes, still retain side by side with this a belief in old wives' tales, and folklore, picked up often from half-understood conversations overheard. Some of their preparation has been full of inexplicable reticences and omissions, while the question of personal hygiene is almost entirely neglected, so that they lose their self-confidence; they become the victims of unnecessary and avoidable anecdotes and feel themselves untouchable.

The answer to this is only partially that of better sex education. This is now part of the curriculum of most secondary schools and is adequate and often excellent, but while sex instruction certainly relieves pathological curiosity, it does not *necessarily* serve as a guide to personal relationships. Many young people know a great deal about the so-called facts of life (or else they know nothing at all; there are still girls from ultra-respectable homes who have an uneasy feeling that kissing may be dangerous, although they are becoming rarer), but what few boys or girls know is how to behave fairly with one another.

Because girls do not realize their power, they often pass from legitimate attraction to unfair provocation. Many girls would be most upset if they realized the strain and temptation to which they often subject their boy friends. Equally many boys are quite unaware of how little a girl may mean by the exercise of her charm upon him. The girls do not know that they are not being fair, or indeed what they *are* doing; the boys do not know what it all means, and none of them know how to protect themselves. Consequently many young people indulge in foolish experiments and adventures—because they feel they needs must practise somehow. They seldom realize because they are seldom taught that one cannot experiment in physical sensation by itself, but that emotional and spiritual values are soon involved. All sorts of odd theories are still current—silly ideas about periods of safety, about

25

contraception, about masturbation, and about venereal disease. Many of them search vainly for scientific information about all these matters and often obtain, in most furtive ways, anything but 'scientific' answers of an alarming nature.

Adolescence is also a period of tremendous glandular activity. Towards the end of childhood the thymus gland shrinks and practically disappears. The generative glands wage a tremendous battle over this, a battle which gives the adolescent body a great deal of inconvenience. If the man or woman is to develop naturally the generative glands must win, but at the same time there is another tussle going on between the thyroid (just below the Adam's apple) and the pancreas. The thyroid gland is the accelerator, and the pancreas the regulator, with the job of keeping the supply of sugar (energy) from being too great. The change in the functioning of the endocrine glands and the accompanying variations in pulse rate, blood pressure and basic metabolism tend to produce certain nervous symptoms such as blushing, excessive sweating and, more rarely, fainting attacks in adolescence. With most young people, when all these physical changes have been taken into consideration, the so-called 'moods' of adolescence are remarkable for their moderation rather than their frequency. The important thing to remember is that when a balance has to be found between all these glandular changes and the various aspects of their physical growth, adolescents may be prone to difficult emotional outbursts.

Hence a most important phase of birth into adulthood is to 'learn to walk' emotionally, or to live with one's emotions and to make it possible for other people to live with them too. Just as the baby learning to walk reels and staggers like a drunken man, and just as we have learned to accept that as one of the trials of babyhood, so adolescent reeling and staggering in the emotional world must be accepted not as a deliberate policy of annoying the grownups but as the nature of the human being at the adolescent stage of growth.

The point to remember is that emotional instability is a perfectly normal phase of adolescence, and nothing to get worried about provided we know how to deal with it sensibly. In other words, the disturbances of adolescence are not symptoms of disease or evidence of ingratitude towards adults, but just a stage of growth.

Birth into Adulthood: The Nature of Adolescence

This great increase of emotional awareness causes most adolescents to seek after what is socially acceptable among their peers, and to seek after beauty and romance according to the circumstance of their environment and means. Adolescent 'moods' swing violently from gaiety to gloom—at one moment they are convinced that they have been born to set the whole world to rights —at another that only the greatest of the poets have ever been so misunderstood. Unstable, moody, battling with adult authority and with themselves, unpredictable, they lapse into much introspection, use the most childish patterns of trouble-solving, bragging, swaggering, storming, sulking, lying, exaggerating bodily ills—crying themselves to sleep and indulging in day dreams of running away from home and committing suicide. 'Am I physically normal?'—'How do I know I'm not insane?' are questions which haunt many of them. They are fascinated by their own personalities and those aspects of them which they feel set them apart from the rest of humanity. ('I'm crazy about animals'—'I adore flowers'—'I'm quick tempered like Uncle Jim'—'I'm sensitive like Mummy'.) They long for independence of action but often feel victimized if they have to bear the consequences of their own actions. It is unfortunate that this difficult period of adjustment comes in many families when the parents themselves are going through the difficulties of middle life. Most of all it is difficult for parents to accept the fact that at this stage in their children's growth their help is often resisted rather than sought. 'We used to be like sisters'—'She told me everything'—'Tom used to be such pals with his father—now he hasn't a word to throw at a dog'. But the severing of the child's deepest ties with the family (and even the severing of the ties with older relatives and teachers) —this second cutting of the umbilical cord—or second weaning— can seldom be achieved without conflict and confused feelings: moodiness, tiredness and self-doubt. Such conflicts are all the greater because on the whole adults, particularly parents, do not take pride in this second weaning.

But the adolescent struggle for emotional and economic independence from their parents and family often makes young people as lonely and frightened as are their parents. They desire most passionately the independence towards which they are struggling and at the same time the security from which they see themselves being divorced. Like so many of the rest of us they want to have it

27

both ways. Just as most parents, however, now realize that the small child needs security and independence, in the same way the adolescent needs both these essentials for growth. The mistake so many parents make is to administer the mixture as before! If it is right that the baby should have nine-tenths security to one-tenth independence so it is probably right that by adolescence they should have one-tenth security to nine-tenths independence! It is often helpful, too, to remember that much of our dismay at their demand for independence is merely a measure of our concern for them, and that our anxiety is really a failure to believe that we have done our best, and to accept that we cannot live their lives for them.

But in this, as in many other departments of life, the way to lose affection is to be too possessive. Having fitted the child out with a reliable chassis, decent road conditions, a good engine of habits, a safety code of morals, we *must* allow the child to take the journey alone. Emotional maturing must take place and childhood dependencies and ways of life must be abandoned if young people are not to become social liabilities—the eternal Peter Pans.

It is helpful to remember that clashes between the generations are unavoidable and age-old, and that no matter how the adolescent behaves he still needs the adults' trust in his essential goodness and he still needs to be shown *demonstrably* that he is loved for himself and respected even for his very inconvenient demands for independence.

In all countries and in all civilizations adults tend to be not only afraid of adolescents—as well they might be of such unpredictable material—but jealous of them. Mothers see their daughters for the first time in competition with them as women; unconsciously they often resent in them evidences of the youth and good looks they once had, and their freedom from the burden of a family, their pretty clothes, and what seems to them the freedom of an office or business life. The boy has become a wage-earner and is in full competition with his father, and most fathers resent the financial independence of their children even while they boast of it to others. This resentment is seldom recognized for what it is, but it reveals itself in many homes in the ways in which some parents try to keep their children on a very short rein. They are unreasonable about pocket-money and criticize on the moving belt the clothes, taste, friends and spare-time activities of their growing sons and daughters with the acidity of over-anxiety. The young struggling for emancipation resent this treatment bitterly and are neither experienced enough nor patient enough to realize and sympathize with its cause. Hence in a depressingly large number of families there is a constant state of friction between one or both the parents and the children. This friction takes a much heavier toll of the girls than of the boys, since, however strict the home, boys have less restrictions on their comings and goings than girls. The girl in her first venturesome flights towards women's privileges often finds herself up against her father's intense jealousy of other men's interest in his daughter and of her mother's jealousy of her good time. For different reasons it is anathema to both of them that she is becoming attractive to other men. Thus the adolescent is not only on the defensive, fighting against all that seems to restrain, but isolated from the loving security of formerly loving parents. Where parents have long since abdicated from all responsibility the isolation is but more complete. An unresolved conflict of this kind may hurl young people into the very dangers their parents so much fear for them. They rush with avidity to forbidden fruit and hot-headed with defiance they make wild and passionate friendships which would have lasted but a little while had they not been garnished and made tempting by parental opposition. The boy who was only mildly interested becomes 'a great one with the girls' and the girl becomes that difficult young person, a 'boy-mad' female. In the beginning it was all quite normal, since any newly awakened interest is always embarked upon with passionate intensity (even stamp collecting) but unreasonable opposition hardens a passing attraction into a definite fixation.

This period with the boy is perhaps less difficult as it seldom lasts for as long. Many boys have no interest in girls as girls before the age of sixteen and therefore this 'always after the girls' stage begins when they are older and so does not occasion as much disapproval. The chief trouble is that when boys develop this interest they often dissociate themselves from their club, scouts, or even their gang, partly because these former activities do not cater for girls, partly because such friendships are often frowned upon as much there as they are at home, and sometimes because they are treated as a joke by his fellows. Hence, unless a few of his mates have similar interests and they can hunt in gangs,

29

they are left without the brake of their normal friendships and occupations just when they most require them.

Most girls still believe themselves to be living in a world dominated by the male, as of course it often is in the home, factory and in business. Hence it is only natural that her imagination should centre round those three things which her limited experience has shown to be valuable—wages, pretty clothes and men. All these things are interdependent; money means increase of status (though begrudged) in the home, and a measure of independence outside it. For most of them their wages are the immediate means whereby they may secure a good time. Their work usually demands very little mental effort—even in the office and shop it is usually of the routine type that gives ample opportunity for the weaving of fantasies.

Most of them are ridiculously efficient on a small scale and they are going nowhere. At this boy-mad stage, having been dominated by the male at home, at school and in the factory, they realize in a confused instinctive fashion that they can only dominate the male in their leisure, and as compensation for all this submission, how they work to use their new-found power of attraction! This is the reason behind what so often seems the over-erotic attitude of many adolescent girls. Hence their pathetic displays of finery and love of dancing, hence the loud shrieks of laughter at street corners, and the loud and competitive boasting of wild adventures.

In all countries at all times more boys than girls are born, but in the past, because boy babies were 'more difficult to rear', and because wars took a heavy toll of young manhood, by the time young people reached marriageable age, females outnumbered the males. As a result of better medical care, ante- and post-natal clinics, diphtheria immunization and better feeding, boys now have as good a chance of survival as girls. After the 1914–18 war much was talked about the million surplus of women who could not hope to find a mate because of the heavy casualties in men of marriageable age. This meant that for generations, although boys and girls have been cast by nature for the role of hunter and hunted, the girl had to perform the difficult role of retreating in such a way as to guarantee pursuit! For this task the adolescent girl called to her aid all the wiles of inherited patterns of behaviour and all the decoration and care in her adornment that she could

30

afford in terms of time and money. All that the young male needed was to be clean, personable and manly.

The situation has now changed. The last war brought in its train a heavy burden of civilian casualties and large numbers of women and girl children were therefore killed. Hence, unless and until we learn how to control the sex of our babies, or some other circumstance arises, the proportion of men to women would seem almost inevitably to go on increasing.

Already this change is becoming self-evident. In many schools the boys now outnumber the girls in many classes. The position is even more apparent in youth clubs, and adolescents, who are extremely sensitive to changes in the social climate of their age, are subconsciously aware of the problem it presents and this is reflected in changes in modern adolescent behaviour.

In the past some of the bitterest quarrels in youth groups and in 'tough' areas were between girls about their boy friends. Many youth leaders used to say that once a girl was 'going steady' with a boy she tended to leave the group lest her girl friends should 'steal' her boy friend from her. Now the quarrels break out among the boys—'All for the love of a lady'. Any reader of the more sensational press cannot have failed to notice how many of the fights between gangs have broken out about young women. A member of a gang has only to 'steal' a young woman from a rival gang to set the bitterest warfare in motion. Indeed there are some girls who have not been slow to exercise their power in thus setting the young men at one another's throats. The urge to power is, after all, strong in all of us, and for many girls there are all too few ways in which that power can be exercised in a socially desirable way.

The situation for the adolescent male is even more difficult. In a society where they are becoming increasingly anxious to prove their manhood, partly because of the increased publicity given to homosexuality, and partly because of the sheer weight of their numbers, it is as important for them, as it once was for the 'million surplus women', that they shall be helped to live with this situation and adjust themselves to it. It is equally important, of course, that girls shall be increasingly aware of the danger of promiscuity.

On the whole, men would seem to take less kindly to a life of celibacy than do women. Hence, while it is important for the continuance of the race that the best type of male shall marry, it is vital for the health of society that large numbers of boys shall not feel themselves useless and rejected because they cannot compete with their more socially acceptable brothers. War between the sexes has already proved itself a wrecker of homes; war between the sexes in this situation, which is already upon us, might well mean that many more young men will seek to find outlets for themselves which, at best, are anti-social and at worst might wreck much that is valuable in society as we know it.

It is therefore more important than ever that if young people are to be helped to lead satisfying lives they shall be given as much support as possible in their efforts to reach happy relationships, not only with the opposite sex, but with one another, and that they should be given some guidance about the tricks our emotions and our minds may play on us.

It would seem wise to explain to them quite frankly why they are so restless and to explain to them that some sublimation is necessary for all. It is important that one's attitude should be that of complete naturalness and should concern itself with constructive advice rather than social misfits, diseases or illegitimate babies. It is as well if youth leaders would see to it that before they venture to give any help their attitude towards their own sex life is a healthy one. There are too many avowed man-haters and 'men's men' in youth groups for one to feel entirely happy about this. This attitude will do nothing to resolve the situation, particularly for some adolescents who in any case go through a period of sick distaste for and even aversion to the opposite sex. Unfortunately some mothers and many teachers and youth leaders are inclined to encourage the boy who will have nothing to do with the girls and many a girls' club has prided itself on those members 'who haven't any use for the boys'. For these boys and girls, the youth group, while providing a refuge, should not be made a vehicle of escape. The shy and frightened need courage to cope with life, not an excuse to evade it. One of the most unfortunate and certainly the most tiresome consequences of providing nothing but an escape is that the frustrated and frightened, unhappy at home and ill at ease abroad, fall violently in love with the adult shelter-giver.

For a long time the adored adult stands in both the position of parents (the sort they would like to have) and the first romantic love, which they are afraid to embark upon or which they do not seem to be attracting. The adored adult does not demand or complain, and does not even have to be sought out, and therefore becomes a satisfactory love object. Many such adolescents have been starved of those outward manifestations of affection which mean so much to the young, and which the films teach them to expect from personal relationships. Many of them crave these small demonstrative attentions of love which take time and demand sensitivity (all love indeed always takes time and needs to be tended and cherished), but the working mother of a large family, however devotedly fond of her family, often has little time to make the home anything but a place of rough-and-ready kindliness (a very satisfactory atmosphere for the younger children but not satisfying enough for the tensed adolescent).

In the youth group where adolescents are made welcome, where their likes and dislikes are regarded and catered for, it is small wonder that many adolescents out of sheer gratitude elevate the leader responsible for all this into a hero, a phantasy parent or a lover.

Herein lies great danger. We can encourage these 'crushes', batten on them, and let our vanity feed on them; we can repulse them, and exercise our lust for power by making our admirer alternately hysterically happy or thoroughly miserable. We can ignore them, and remain like Tennyson's princess 'icily regular, splendidly null'. None of these reactions are fair to the adolescent, all are fraught with grave dangers, not only to the adolescent, but to the adult concerned. This affection which may be so unwelcome to us is a measure of the difficulties such adolescents are going through.

It is not only the obvious sufferer who hangs on our words, but also the contra-suggestive ones who make a point of publicly disagreeing with us, who have to be helped over this hurdle. For sometimes these unhappy young people, feeling that they can claim more attention from the beloved by being tiresome than by being good, deliberately invite trouble which will focus the attention of the beloved upon them. Extreme examples are those of a girl who cut herself every night in order to be iodined and bandaged by her goddess, and the boy who indulged in kicking and arm-twisting in order to be reproached. There is nothing more delicate, more beautiful, than the touching faith of these young people in their 'god' of the moment. We can explain it by saying

C   33

that the leader is acting as a 'mother substitute' or a 'father substitute', but to give a thing a name has not effected a cure.

Our task, therefore, is not to discourage them but to find a more worthwhile outlet for their emotions and to see that nothing is injured in the process. It is no good showing young people our feet of clay, because when they are in that state they cannot recognize clay when they see it! Johnny may come to the club for six weeks, or if the worst comes to the worst, for six months, for the sake of the leader's beautiful high dive; and Shirley may come for the sight of the dancing instructor's bonny brown hair, but if we are alive to all this, if we recognize this dumb affection (which displays itself just as often in being difficult as in being docile) for what it is, at the end of that time they may be coming to the club for the sake of some absorbing interest in the group itself. 'Don't like me, but like what I like, and something different just for fun', is the unspoken recipe for this situation. It is important to avoid extremes of any kind, words of endearment equally with words of reproach; to avoid at almost all costs the type of heart-to-heart talks which end in the pouring out of basinfuls of life history flavoured with love-sickness, but to avoid also leaving the unfortunate one out of anything, and to avoid above all those scolding scenes which some of them really enjoy. The situation is fraught with much more danger for men than for women, for whether the adorer is a boy or a girl the man who allows himself to be isolated in any way by such adolescents may find himself in a highly compromising situation. Hell may have no fury like a woman scorned, but malice has no fury like that of emotionally disturbed adolescents who, after feeling they are in a privileged position, find themselves repulsed. It is probably no exaggeration to suggest that many of the unfortunate cases of sexual assault in which youth leaders and teachers have been involved have had no more basis in fact than foolish mishandling of an adolescent's emotions.

For the sake of the adolescent too, we must recognize that their personal relations for the rest of their lives may well depend on how we deal with them at this stage, and their attitude towards many problems will be coloured by the opinions we venture to express in their hearing. This would be a heavy enough burden if it meant that people going through this phase of admiration would for the rest of their lives admire what we admire and dislike what we dislike. Alas, if they are disappointed in us, if even un-wittingly we seem to let them down, when they remove those rose-coloured spectacles through which they have been gazing at us, the probabilities are that at the best for a very long time they will be inclined to dislike what we admired, fling themselves enthusiastically into every activity of which we have disapproved, and embrace every opinion which they feel is contrary to our own. With them it is indeed a case of 'Love me, love my dog'. If their love is turned to contempt they will often be unable to divorce hate of our person from contempt for all that we have ever stood for in their eyes.

For example, when one boy whose leader was an ardent naturalist became rightly or wrongly disillusioned concerning him, immediately he gave up all his outdoor activities and plunged into a political organization which he had reason to believe was anathema to that leader. Again, a girl whose leader was a beautiful needlewoman, was put off from all needlework for years when her idol was adjudged to have feet of clay. More serious cases will be familiar to most of us. For our own sakes as well as theirs, we must remember that there is little that most adolescents will not take from us if they believe us to be fair and know us to be almost unfailingly good humoured. It is not impossible to help them to reconstruct these romances nearer to their heart's well-being, and an ability to worship a person is evidence of both idealism and devotion, inestimable virtues if properly canalized.

Again, because of their tremendous preoccupation with them-selves as personalities and because of the physical changes which accompany their birth into adulthood, young people are much concerned about their personal appearance. Hence it is helpful if parents and youth leaders take an interest in their clothes. In the mating season birds put on their plumage, and so do boys and girls. Boys may parade themselves about in the most extravagantly fashionable attire. They have done this in every age—from the days of the Norfolk jacket to Oxford bags, from plus fours to spiv suits with naked-lady ties, from 'drape' jackets to Edwardian suits. All have been derided and abused by their elders in their turn. Girls may now experiment with what they hope are film-star effects, but equally there was a time when no girl with a fringe and an ostrich feather in her hat was allowed in a 'respectable' club. But all this only means that they are groping their way anxiously through the sexual urge to attract, to the spiritual urge towards beauty. If we do not encourage and use this, it may never be directed into channels where their desire for beauty and better things can grow and flourish. In any case vanity is probably one of the greatest aids to self-respect.

Just as we encourage them over their personal appearance, however, it is important that they shall be encouraged to understand something of the nature of their emotional and mental processes. As it seems not unintelligent to suggest that young people should be taught something about the way their bodies work, so it would seem a good thing that they should know a little of how their minds work. The world is in great need of a scientific attitude towards problems of human behaviour. We all know that dissatisfaction, unhappiness, worry, anxiety and fear are part of the lot of mankind; that people were sad, worried, frightened and frustrated long before the psychologists were heard of, and that probably they will go on being all these things for a long time to come. But we now know enough about the science of the mind to provide some help and guidance.

One of the most important things in the world is to be able to get on with and understand one's fellow men. The inability to see the reason for the other fellow's point of view is probably the root cause of every quarrel, and writ large, of every war. The most cheering thing about the science of psychology is that it proves very clearly that human problems cannot be settled by argument and that to see the reason for a person's action, or line of thought, is at least half-way to a situation in which—though not being able to say smugly, 'To understand all is to forgive all'—people will at least be able to say, 'As we partially understand how you have arrived at this situation, while not agreeing with you, we can put forward certain suggestions which may be acceptable to you.'

We attach a great deal of importance to keeping the body in such a condition that its temperature shall be normal, but emotionally there are still so many people whose temperatures are well above normal and rationally so many whose temperatures are sub-normal. We talk a great deal of the poise and balance of the body, and yet contrive to do so little to encourage people to develop a balanced attitude towards their own emotional and rational processes, and those of others. This does not mean that youth leaders should provide academic lectures on psychology, but there should be a great deal of discussion, in club committees, in settling disputes, in talking about everyday problems—about *why* people behave as they do.

Just as the body can be regarded as the temple of the spirit, so the emotional and rational processes must be fitting furniture of that temple. Just as the body must be a poised and willing instrument, so the emotions must not be the response to unexpressed fears, but must be able to hold the balance between hate and adoration, and the mind must be capable of balanced judgments and clear reasoning. Just as the body must be trained to certain unthinking responses, so mentally one must come to the realization that some tasks need blind obedience and others need initiative. If our aim is to educate, not fitting subjects for group uniformity, but independent personalities with powers of judgment who will indulge in group living in the service of a social ideal, the desire for a healthy mind in a healthy body requires that we should know ourselves, and encourage adolescents to know themselves.

Finally, adolescence is the age of 'immortal' longings and therefore it is only natural that many of them are deeply concerned over religion, using that word in its widest meaning. Their heart searchings are profound and all the more urgent because of their emotional longing to be at peace with themselves. A small proportion of them 'get religion' and are frightful, a still larger number 'get atheism' and are frightened. Their first ventures into the world of employment set up a series of conflicts, and the conflict of values is the most important of these. In church, in school and in youth groups they are taught that certain things are valuable, but the factory, the street, the films and, quite often, the home, teach them by implication, if not by precept, that quite other things are valuable. Probably one of the greatest difficulties which we all have to face is this conflict between our attitude towards life and our behaviour in life. 'Do not do as I do, but do as I tell you' is the favourite gibe thrown at the parson, but the extreme difficulty of reconciling what we feel we ought to do, what we would like to do, and what we in fact actually do, is too much for most of us. The adolescent frequently gives it all up and just fights for those things which seem to him valuable—amusement perhaps, pathetic attempts at elegance, philandering maybe, aping adulthood's independence by drinking, smoking, gambling and swearing. This in itself would perhaps matter little, as he would 'grow

37

out of it', but all the time the adolescent feels guilty. He feels guilty because of the school which he has so recently left; he feels guilty because he is aware of the disapproval of his parents, of officials at work and others whose good opinion he in his heart of hearts values. Even the films leave a general impression of guilt, since they nearly always have a moral and the really bad usually suffer the most appalling fate, even if only in the last few minutes of the film.

All these authorities combine to assert that really solid virtues count, but boys do not want to be 'sissies' and girls tell us again and again that 'you'll never catch a feller that way'.

If we can persuade girls that there is now no need to be anxious about this since there are more than enough men to go round, and if we can persuade boys that bravery and bravado are not at all the same thing, we will be doing them a great service.

Since 1945, both boys and girls have in their various ways found it difficult to come to terms with a new world. The boy has been brought up on tales of violence and disaster and it is small wonder that some of them take to violence almost with relief and that unorthodox weapons such as coshes, sharpened bicycle chains and knives have a fatal fascination for them. In all civilizations any series of profound crises is reflected in exaggerated form by the adolescent since his sensitivity to stresses, conflicts and unbalances is at its most acute. It is youth which pays the heaviest price in war, and also in peace when values succumb to hypocrisy or when social institutions change. When distrust and fear are the climate of the age the uncertainties of youth are but made more uncertain.

If, however, they can be persuaded to come into any organization with a strong community feeling they gain some comfort and consolation and are provided with a stable atmosphere in which they can work out their problems with their fellows and with the help and encouragement of understanding adults. Youth leaders can give them affection untinged with sentimentality and through that a love and tolerance of their fellows. At the very least they provide a thread to hang on to in a frightening and incomprehensible world. They can also provide a confidant *outside* the family—'Ooh, I couldn't worry Mum by telling her that' is about the finest compliment we can have.

The modern Jack and Jill are breezy, casual and very tough indeed, harder, cooler, and often much more truthful than their parents. They are hard-working and courageous, with the gay uncertain courage of a generation growing up in an uneasy world, a world in which there are no certain landmarks and there is no certain future. They have lost all sense of security and they are not at all sure that they will know how to survive or how to protect themselves, but they pretend all they know. They are spendthrift and prodigal, and, like a small boy whistling as he goes up the dark stairs to his bed, they move forward cheerfully to see what the world will do to them. They are hard-boiled realists who are greedy for life, because life itself has become uncertain, and they are incurable little romantics at heart. They are also the fine raw material of a New Order; they are looking for a way out through their difficulties to a purpose in life. To point the way is the true service of youth.

Much of Jack and Jill's attitude towards home, marriage and children will depend on how they are trained in adolescence. Excessive popularity is a nuisance, and wallowing in emotion is a menace, but brutal stamping on the spiritual gropings of the adolescent is an unforgivable sin. Much modern social work is ruined by too much restraint and has become a purely negative social science. Too much ill-digested psychology has made people afraid of showing disapproval, and afraid to 'influence' people. But while we are alive in the company of others we cannot avoid influencing people. We cannot abdicate from this, and we cannot help young people to become 'persons' in the fullest sense while withholding our own personalities. It is no good having right feelings and the right ideas unless we are prepared to risk acting on them.

Because it is in adolescence that the personality begins to take final shape, young people need variety to satisfy the changes within themselves; opportunities for self-expression to try their wings; and they need to be wanted. Since they are groping for some status in society they need to be helped through the period when their youthful dreams of the glories of adulthood are beginning to give way to a sense of failure; they need friendship to compensate for the possible friction at home and at work; they need something to satisfy their ardent desire for beauty.

Birth into adulthood is the stage of finding one's legs emotionally and spiritually, just as infancy is the stage of finding them physically, but true health and poise and joy are found in forgetfulness of self. Maturity is only reached when one learns 'to measure one's life not by the wine drunk but by the wine poured forth'. Unfortunately it is hard to lose oneself (it is such an interesting subject!) but we all have to choose between barren ease and rich unrest. If, however, adults can take upon themselves the responsibility for an environment in which young people may make their choice so that they may, at a later stage, go out to face life rather than be content to live it at second hand, they have done all that can reasonably be expected of them. They will have given young people the opportunity to find their happiness and wisdom for themselves.

It is small wonder that in the words of the McNair report they need a 'guide, philosopher and friend', and the companionship of their own age group. Joining a social club of suitable young people with common interests often does more good than anything else. Frequently, like the very old, all that they need is an outsider with whom they can talk out their problems and difficulties. For the rest, perhaps, Dr. Adler's customary reply to his more voluble patients—'All that you feel is very natural, but need you feel it quite so much?'—is the only possible advice, though if one can help them to believe that such feelings will pass and to suggest better methods of handling personal relationships the 'feelings' may pass more speedily. It is always worth while to assure adolescents that many of their fears are groundless, and that though there is no such thing as a life without tears, there are still many joys, mysteries and wonders in the world around us, and many years in which they may hope to enjoy them.

2

Adolescents at Large

⁎

The popular image of teenagers in our society is now that of the 'young affluents'—those who fall within Alan Little's definition of the post-pocket-money, pre-marriage group coming from the working and lower middle classes. They have money and few responsibilities. They are unrestricted by education or professional training and unhampered by domestic and family responsibilities. None of them are under fifteen years old and some of them are over twenty years old, so that 'teenager' is really only an approximate label to give them. But they are a very large proportion of the adolescent and young adult people who are over the minimum school-leaving age—probably about 70 per cent of their age group. The minority is a growing minority, and they are those who continue in full-time education until the age of sixteen, seventeen, eighteen and, if they proceed into higher education, until twenty-one or later. Until the age of eighteen years, most of these remain financially dependent upon their parents. If their full-time education continues beyond that age the majority of them are then at least partly supported by grants from the local education authorities or other public sources.

Only a generation ago, those who continued full-time education beyond the minimum school-leaving age, and certainly those who received full-time higher education, were usually considered to be, and often were, the materially better-off young people, in spite of the fact that they were not earning. It was taken for granted that their families were higher up the income scale than the families of young workers. Now, among their own age group the students are the poor who have to eke out their money and carefully calculate

41

its use. The students are an increasing number. Somewhere between the young affluents and the students is a much smaller number of apprentices who are learning their trade in return for a low wage.

Since 1938 the real wages of teenage workers have increased by something like 60 per cent. The number of teenagers in the population has also increased, and it has been calculated that the average teenage worker now has at least twice as much money (calculated in 'real' terms) to spend as he chooses as did his counterpart in the 1930s. It is no wonder, therefore, that young workers have, in the post-war era, become the focus of much interest on the part of commercial enterprise. Manufacturers, entertainers, advertisers and market researchers are all conscious of the teenage market and take it seriously. This market deals particularly in records, record players, transistor radios, clothing, cosmetics, hair styles, scooters and motor-cycles. In the matter of hair styles, the use of cosmetics and clothing, the teenagers have even become fashion setters to the older generations and within the age group fashion-consciousness has vastly increased.

For many generations our society has failed to give its adolescents any clearly defined role to play. They have emerged from childhood but their entry into adulthood is delayed—they may not vote, marry without parental consent, drive motor-vehicles or do a number of other things in their own right, for some years after childhood has been left behind. They have found themselves suspended in some 'anti-sphere' to real life, where adults criticize them sharply if they behave like children, refuse to treat them as adults, and fail to identify them as any other kind of beings.

The growth of interest on the part of commercial enterprise in young people has caused misgivings in the minds of some adults whose worry is that young earners have little discretion of their own on which to base their spending, and that they are therefore the victims of those who would manipulate their taste in order to persuade them to part with their money. This may, in truth, be happening, and may even be detrimental. But on what are our adult tastes based? What makes them change? On what criterion can they be pronounced better or worse? Moreover, one way to learn the value of money, and of what it will buy, is to discover that one has wasted some, according to one's own values.

Whether grown-ups are happy about it or not, and whether the growth of commercial interest is really exploitation or not, it has offered young people one thing which they have been quick to seize—an identity within this society—an image—something to be. Being a teenager meant little, except being between the ages of twelve and twenty years, until the post-war era. Now, besides meaning older than a child and younger than an adult, it signifies a recognized range of interests, behaviour, standards and values, which every young person can measure up to or diverge from, in large or small degrees.

Young people, then, are significant spenders, and for most of them, until they begin to think seriously about marriage, money is for spending and enjoying. Hence they often spend in a way that would have left their counterparts of thirty years ago astounded, but they can still end up 'skint' at the end of the week. They have grown up in a world very different from that of their parents' adolescent years, when the livelihood of so many families was usually precarious, and the economics of Carnaby Street would have seemed utterly fantastic. Not that all, or even most, of the young affluents are irresponsible about spending, at least according to their own standards. Their spending is far from inconsequential. Many of them budget their wages in some detail; having paid over their housekeeping contribution at home, they allot so much to the hire-purchase payments due on motor-bike, guitar or record player, something for buying a new record, so much for stockings, make-up and hair-do, or ties, socks and other items of casual wear, and hair-cut, sometimes something is 'put by' for the next suit or coat, and often something is put towards the next holiday. The rest is available for coffees, cigarettes, dances, films—in fact, for 'going out'.

To the younger teenagers particularly, 'going out' is a significant exercise of their freedom as people who are no longer children. If 'mum' asks 'Where are you going?', the answer is frequently 'Out', and if she persists in trying to find out more, the subsequent answers are often vague: 'Oh, just out', 'Might go to X's', 'Might meet Y' and so on, and this is not usually evasion. What they will do when they are out is often of no great consequence to the young teenagers at the beginning of the expedition. The thing that matters is that they will exercise their own judgment about what to do. They are going out of the direct influence or compulsion of home, school and work, to take responsibility for themselves in their leisure, and to gain experience at first hand. Investigation suggests that young people go out, on an average, four or five evenings a week. They go out rather more in summer than winter. The number of evenings they go out is sometimes limited, and limits are imposed most often for girls by their parents and most often for boys by the requirements of evening classes and study. For girls the amount of going out tends to decrease somewhat, around the age of eighteen years.

What do they, in fact, do when they go out? They meet each other, and not infrequently just walk around together, particularly if there is somewhere congenial or interesting to do this, like a town centre with well-lit shop windows, or a riverside. The boys often go around in small groups, the girls frequently in pairs. Sometimes small mixed groups form, from which boy- and girl-friend couples may later emerge. They visit each other's houses, spend time in coffee bars or go to bowling alleys or skating rinks, and occasionally to the cinema. In all this meeting together they show each other their latest hair styles, accessories and gear for appraisal. They talk about experiences at work and at home. Boys talk about girls and girls about boys, and from time to time they set the world right. Conventions change and the resources available to young people vary from place to place and time to time, but the biggest task that confronts young people remains the same. They have to come to terms with their own newly emerged sexuality and other people's responses to it, with their own new emotional experiences which often make them unpredictable even to themselves. They are now young adults instead of children, and they have to handle the inappropriate responses which some adults will inevitably make to them. They have to establish their independence from parents. Since they can no longer play as they played when children, they have to find new recreational experience. In all this meeting with each other, whether with adults present or not, they are learning about themselves.

Against the unchanging tasks of growing up, there are interests, pursuits, modes of expression and subjects upon which young people form and voice opinions which are particular to the present day. Some of these are only variations on age-old interests of young people; some are especially well marked because they are amply catered for commercially and young people are able to take advantage of this; some are no more than reflections in the younger generation of changes that have come about in this society as a whole. Most young people go away from home for an annual holiday now, and as with the population in general, an increasing number go abroad. Few, if any, of them do it quite in the Cliff Richard's *Summer Holiday* style, but many of them go in groups of teenagers and young adults, rather than with their families, and their approach to these expeditions is often enterprising and adventurous. Music and dancing are, as they nearly always have been, real passions of young people. One wonders if their almost phrenetic desire for music in particular, is for many young people a way of escape, not only from the clatter of workshop and typing office, but from the boredom and the worries which accompany the business of growing up, from their impatience to be grown up, and the difficulty of trying to make sense of the world into which they have to grow. The juke box in the pub or the coffee bar, the record player or the transistor radio in the club or the home, the canned music in the café, the quiet confidential guitar-playing vocalist in the restaurant, or the ear-splitting electric-guitar group, can all, in their various ways, fill up the spaces in the mind and crowd out the less pleasant thoughts that may otherwise find room. (The 'tele' does much the same thing for some of the older generation.) But music is not merely a space-filler for young people. It is something in which they actively participate in various ways. Jazz clubs became popular in the 1950s, and most of them were organized, administered and financially supported by the young people themselves. Some members have always gone to such clubs to listen and not to dance because 'you cannot dance and concentrate on the music properly', and concentration is undoubtedly the right term in these cases. Jazz lovers are either 'mod' or 'trad' fans. The modern style developed out of the traditional via the swing of the 1930s, and one can argue that the division is meaningless, but the argument is senseless to a 'trad' type. The followers of each have their own conventional dress, and, if they dance, their own style of dancing. Each school of thought regards jazz as a serious activity, and each has its own aesthetic rules. Ten years ago the younger generation were consumed by the argument between 'trad' and 'mod' fans. Now the jazz group has become mainly nostalgic. As a social force it has been ousted by the pop group.

Many pop groups begin through listening to records. Many young people spend a fair proportion of their time listening to records in the discothèque. They may do so for the purpose of deciding what record to buy next for themselves, and from this they may go on to save the down payment on an instrument. Some are taught to play it by a teacher and others teach each other with the help of a self-tutor. One grammar-school boy, for instance, started listening to records with three of his friends at home. They then saved up enough money to buy their own instruments, taught themselves to play and were joined by two others. When 'mum' objected, not so much to the noise as the number of complete strangers who came knocking at the door asking if they could come in and listen, they moved to a church hall and then to a room over a pub. They became unpopular there and went to a small ballroom, but got turned out, because some hooligans who attached themselves to the group against their wishes 'broke the place up a bit'. By then they had a following of about a hundred people who came every week to hear them play. So they formed a private jazz club, hired a hall and soon had 200 members.

West Indian immigrants introduced steel bands and skiffle groups to this country, and because these used numbers of improvised instruments the number of young instrumentalists increased noticeably. These bands played mainly folk songs and industrial songs. The jazz and jive fans and the skiffles evolved their own language, well illustrated by a jazz club news-sheet: 'In a hall lit by flickering candles stuck in the necks of old wine bottles a "hep" audience was soon "stompin" with the "trads". Through the blue haze of a hundred glowing "weeds" the sound was coming through loud and clear. The band took the devotees from the early beginning of jazz among the New Orleans negroes, through the dimly-lit cafés and bars of the riverside cities, "Stateside" revelling in the uninhibited airs of true "Dixie", and on into the heady glories of "blues" and "Boogie" where the persistent throbbing of the bass line sends its followers into raptures.

'No liquor was needed to put these modern followers of the jazz idiom in the right mood for dancing and listening. It only took music to really "send" them. All the old favourites among the jazz classics came up just as fresh as ever in slick interpretations. The "horn" and the "liquorice stick" could change from mellow mood to the triumphant glory of *Oh When the Saints Come Marching In* at the mere shake of a shoulder. The advance "spiel" instructions followed to the very letter. The male of the species outshone his

46

mate. Among the outstanding examples of sartorial art was the "City Gambler" with shoes with thick crêpe soles and a coat almost reaching to the floor, his collar and cuffs trimmed with velvet. Most of the "cats" were attired in so-called Edwardian fashion and a "Tony Curtis" was their crowning glory.

'The kittens favoured black sweaters and tight calf-length jeans that did not hamper them in the free-for-all display in which they interpreted the music of the masters. It was no place for "squares" and, when asked what he thought of this latest contribution to the cultural life of the city, a "cat" replied that it was "Crazy man, crazy".'[1]

That was in the 1950s, and they were dancing Rock 'n' Roll. Fashions in clothes, hair styles, language and dances change. Beat groups largely superseded Skiffle bands, and when the Mersey sound broke over us they sprang up all round the country. Some make the headlines, some make the local dance halls, some continue to enjoy themselves without getting anywhere in particular. Pop singers are for the modern young generation what film stars were for the youth of the 1930s. Rock 'n' Roll has been followed by the Twist, the Madison, the Shake and others in quick succession. Whether it is dancing, listening or playing, the desire and ability to lose oneself completely in it—to be 'sent'—is strong, and being 'sent' is approved of in an open and healthy way.

There can, of course, be excess, and being 'sent' can spill over

[1] Cool	= Top Grade
Cats	= devotees of jazz
Kittens	= their feminine counterparts
Groovy	= in the groove—also top grade
Spiel	= publicity
Hep	= understanding the jazz idiom
Stompin	= dancing
Trads	= followers of traditional jazz
Weeds	= cigarettes
Stateside	= the United States
Dixie	= Dixieland jazz
Boogie and Blues	= two jazz forms
Horn	= trumpet
Liquorice stick	= clarinet
Send	= put in a trance by the music
Tony Curtis	= a hair-style affected by a popular film star
Crazy	= top class
Square	= the lowest form of animal life in the jazz world—includes anyone who needs to read this footnote.

into mass hysteria. Enthralled girls scream at the personal appearance of a pop star, and among youths a tense moment at a football match may trigger off mass hysteria.

Although nowadays it is probably true that only very few young people pass through puberty without learning the facts of life, because adults still often fail to do more than pass on the cold biological facts, many young people continue to have considerable anxieties over their own sexuality and over relationships with the opposite sex. They still can find themselves lost over what to expect of the behaviour of members of the opposite sex towards themselves and what the expectations of others are about their own behaviour. Girls may, therefore, pass from legitimate charm to unfair provocation without realizing the strain and temptation they are putting on their boy friends, and the boys may be quite unaware of how little, in terms of real sexual desire, a girl may mean by the exercise of her charm. The girl may then be disturbed and shocked by the strength of the boy's sexual demands. Neither of them understands the sexual feelings of the other or how to protect themselves from being hurt. What they are still too often not taught is that emotional and spiritual values are involved in every personal relationship. Friendly and unshocked adults who are manifestly successful in their own personal relationships can help young people over these anxieties towards the realization and joy of fully adult love and affection, if they are willing to talk informally and frankly to young people about their own and young people's experiences with genuine respect and concern. The vast majority of young people respond readily to the idea of treating each other well, and earnestly want to know how to do this.

Beliefs about the propriety of sexual behaviour and 'how far one should go' and when, vary from place to place and time to time. If boys feel the need to brag about their sexual conquests, real or fictional, and girls about their 'experiences', it is because they feel this is part of being grown up and because to them it appears to be necessary to be able to do this in order to be accepted as adults. If this is a distorted view of the community's expectations culled from popular entertainment and magazines—if it is—it behoves the adults, through their own relationships with the younger generation, to convey a more balanced understanding.

Young workers were, at one time, an important part of the cinema's mass audience. For many of them it was surely the 'quickest way out' of whatever urban industrial oppression they lived and worked in. They went to the thriving local cinemas regularly two, three or four times a week, indiscriminately. But the mass cinema audience has vanished. The film industry has had to try to woo back its customers by special appeals to various groups of people. It appears now to regard teenagers of all classes as one of the minor groups worth specially catering for. Young people respond critically to the appeal made, as indeed they do to the efforts made by television to capture their attention. They have a particular interest in films in which pop stars appear, but beyond this, if they go to the cinema to any extent, their tastes seem not markedly different from those of other cinemagoers, many of whom are knowledgeable and discriminating.

To say that class distinctions in this country have lessened in recent years is trite and over-simple, but one facet of the change that has taken place shows young people of varying social backgrounds making common cause over enthusiasms and convictions which are shared to an extent that would have been unusual twenty or thirty years ago. Pop music, folk singing, holiday travel, leisure-time sporting activities and Aldermaston marches have all demonstrated this. Differences of outlook and attitude do, of course, still persist. They persist partly because they are learned from older generations, and partly because experience, particularly working experience, is often different and engenders different expectations. In the leisure section of life, however, which has become markedly more significant since the end of the Second World War, young people share more experience and interests across class frontiers than did their parents or grandparents. Youth, the world over, is forward-looking, optimistic about new things, revels in physical exhilaration, loves life and strains at the leash to live it to the full. In this country now, happily, privilege and underprivilege no longer select so crudely the ways in which these urges shall be gratified.

There is, of course, the lunatic fringe of youth—the 'ton-up kids', the seaside fighters, the purple-heart brigade, drug addicts and pedlars and other delinquents, who, from time to time, command far more of the public's attention than all the multiples of ninety and nine non-trouble-making young people. It is not this book's task to examine this problem in detail, but not to recognize it for what it is would be courting criticism. Those responsible for

D   49

the Youth Service have become more and more concerned about it in the post-war years, and some of its critics have implied that the service is failing because it has not removed the problem of juvenile delinquency. It is, therefore, worth remembering that the Youth Service was never designed to cure delinquency or even primarily to prevent it; that it does not have within it the skills required for the treatment of serious delinquency; and that in very many cases the apparent causes of delinquency operate long before the young people concerned reach Youth Service age. Among this fringe of the younger generation are some who are mentally and emotionally sick and socially maladjusted. These form the more serious problem—serious for themselves as individuals who suffer, and serious for society because of the disruption and suffering to others that they cause in their efforts to escape from, or work off their own torments. Around these are others whose difficulties are less serious and whose problems are mainly boredom and a feeling that they count for very little. Neither of these groups is readily attracted to the normal Youth Service provision. Some youth workers set out to contact them, and having succeeded in doing so, find themselves criticized for not being able to display a membership of socially competent and responsible beings. We cannot have it both ways, and sponsoring agencies still often fail to think and state what it is they do want. In any case the Youth Service has not the resources to treat the seriously disturbed group, but it can, and sometimes does, given the forbearance and skill required, help some of those on the fringe of this disturbed group to find more acceptable outlets for their active needs, and above all to begin to feel recognized as people that matter. The extent of the Youth Service's effectiveness in preventing delinquency is unknown and unknowable, but it does help some youngsters away from the brink and it may prevent others from ever joining a socially disturbed group.

Some adults seem to see young people with a hostile eye. To them, anyone in a leather jacket is a young criminal, and long hair on a male is a sign of decadence. Yet the psychological gap between today's young generation and the adults seems to be particularly marked. The world has, as it were, spun faster in the lives of the last two or three generations, and happy is the parent who recognizes and accepts with composure that his children live, and must be helped to live, in a world different from his own. Teenage affluence is perhaps one of the juicier bones of contention between the generations, and the manifestations of this, particularly if they are noisy, seem often to raise the hackles of the elders. (Incidentally, it takes only a week or so in a place where space is no problem and the climate does not require most events to take place in a closed building, but where young people are as fond of motor-cycles and electric guitars as anywhere else, to realize how much sheer overcrowding aggravates the difficulty in urban Britain.) The middle-aged generation of today recalls its own youth and young adulthood spent in the inter-war slump and the austerities of wartime and the post-war years. It prayed when its children were born that they might grow up into a better world. Now it sometimes finds it hard that the children do not know how much better off they are than their parents.

To charge young people with a materialistic outlook on life because of the way they enjoy their affluence, is scarcely justified. The space between leaving school and getting married is a short one for most people. The average age for leaving full-time education is rising, though it is not always of the young people's choosing, but marriage continues to be a highly popular institution, and young people are choosing it earlier and earlier, and marriage generally brings affluence to an end.

3

The Adolescent and Work

✳

One of the most striking and delightful things about the
majority of school leavers is the eagerness and excitement
with which they look forward to joining the ranks of the
world's workers. One of the depressing things about some of them
after they have been working for six months or more is their
disappointment and frustration. Most of them do settle into work
quite quickly and well, in spite of all the difficulties that those who
study the transition from school to work become aware of, for most
of them are very resilient. Many of them suffer some measure of disillusionment after a time, and the fact that most of them get over
it again without much help is no good reason for ignoring it. Some
of it may be inevitable, but some of it could be avoided by more
realistic preparation, and wiser counsel over the choice of work.

Disillusionment arises from a number of sources. One of them,
of course, is the discovery that money spent in imagination is far
more elastic than the money in the hand from the wage packet.
Most of us continue to make this discovery afresh each week,
month or year, but young workers who have already discovered
how much or how little can be done with the proceeds of holiday
and week-end work and morning paper rounds are often more
realistic in their expectations and their plans. New recruits to the
working world are more worried, very often, by finding that they
feel insignificant in the working situation—that they are still not
doing a 'man's job', and that they are being weighed up by older
workers and not immediately accepted as one of them. Even so,
acquiring the status of a worker is important to most young people,
especially boys, whatever frustrations it may bring.

The Adolescent and Work

In a highly industrialized society where none of us is willing to forgo the benefits of mass production, it is sheer hypocrisy to suggest that the majority of workers can get creative fulfilment in their work, though there are boys and men who love their machines and glow with enthusiasm as they show them to us, and there are also thousands who do not want 'interesting' jobs, who shirk responsibility, or, more commonly, are not capable of much responsibility. The great majority of young people do not look for creative fulfilment in their work. They do not think of work as something to be enjoyed and for most of them it is something they neither like nor dislike in any conscious way—they just do it. It is a means and not an end in itself. In this, as in many other things, they begin to reflect adult attitudes very early in their careers.

The level of wages is fundamental to most young people and it is an overriding concern for a few of them. Since work is a means to ends which usually cost money, wages must be reasonable and can seldom be compensated for by other advantages. The consciously ambitious youngster may be willing to defer immediate satisfaction in favour of greater prospects. Although he, like most of us, would prefer to have it both ways if he has the opportunity to follow his ambition, he usually regards the comparative hardship of his early working days as an inevitable and necessary frustration.

Present hours of work are not usually objected to by young people. As the working week gets shorter, and as Saturday work becomes less usual in many occupations, so longer hours and Saturday work will be seen as an imposition; but in this, young people are no different from the rest of us.

For those who choose to leave school and go to work at the earliest opportunity, the main concern seems to be to have a job which is within their capacity but does not leave them with nothing to do. On the one hand they do not want their work to be difficult so that they worry about it, and on the other they do not want to be bored. To have congenial company at work is also important. This means people who notice the young person and include him or her in the working group. For girls especially, it also usually means that at least some of the others with whom they work must be below middle age.

The influence of the family and social background is still paramount in the young person's choice of work and his aims. Whether

53

young persons think of themselves as people who work in factories, shops or offices; as operatives, technicians or professionals; whether they are ambitious or not; whether they think of work as something you do with your physical strength or your mind or both, depends on the attitudes these young people have learned from their experience of life so far, and most of all from their families. Boys will not all take up the same work as their fathers and daughters of mill-girls will not all be mill-girls, but the breadth of their view of work opportunities will be conditioned by the outlook of their families and general social milieux. Those whose families see the world as limited to their immediate environment are likely only to think in terms of the work available in the locality; those whose parents consciously wish to give their children 'better opportunities than they had' are more likely to have had their attention drawn seriously to newer modern opportunities; those whose families jealously guard hard-worn middle-class status are more likely to see themselves in offices rather than in factory workshops; those whose fathers and elder brothers consider the apprentices who go round the works with slide rules in their pockets as 'toffee-nosed', are less likely to think of themselves as trained technicians; unless there are strong counter-influences, those whose families think in terms of 'we the workers' and 'them the bosses' are not likely to see themselves as potential business managers.

At a time when the country's economic position demands considerable change in industrial patterns, when the need is for more skilled and fewer and fewer unskilled workers, and readiness to accept change involving re-training at least once in a working life is becoming important, an over-conservative influence in the home can be a considerable disadvantage to the young worker and the community at large. Teachers and the Youth Employment Service can, and in many cases do, achieve a great deal to widen the work horizons of young people and their parents. If the recommendations of the Newsom Report (*Half Our Future*) are imaginatively carried out with the co-operation of employers, young people may really move towards their school-leaving dates with realistic pictures of their own capacities and of the opportunities that exist.

There has been a mounting shortage of skilled workers at all levels in industry in this country for the last twenty years or more, and the Industrial Training Act of 1964 was a determined, if belated, effort to overcome this. Firms have for a much longer time been urged to set up training schemes for young workers, and some have had excellent schemes in action for a long time, but these have been the minority. Many firms have been loath to enter the training field and have hoped to 'get by' either by recruiting workers trained elsewhere or by letting them learn 'the hard way'. Others, mainly the small firms, have genuinely found it too expensive. The Industrial Training Act aims at providing enough skilled workers at all levels, improving the quality of training and spreading the cost of training more fairly. All firms except the very small ones have to pay a levy on the previous year's wages bill to the appropriate Industrial Training Board. Firms providing adequate training receive back a grant from the board, and the size of the grant depends upon the quantity and quality of training provided. Some firms receive back more than the levy they have paid. Since every firm has to pay the levy, there is an incentive to see that their young employees receive training.

There has, for this reason, been a considerable increase in the number of young people, operatives, craft apprentices, technician apprentices and student apprentices, who receive training for some period of time after starting work, though for the less skilled operative this can be for only a matter of days. This, of course, is quite apart from 'Induction Courses' that many big firms arrange for their new employees, and despite these, it is still possible for beginners to remain in ignorance about why they do whatever they do at work.

In the implementation of the Industrial Training Act, there has been a great extension of co-operation between industry and the Colleges of Further Education, without whom much of the training would be impossible. Patterns of co-operation vary a great deal but most colleges endeavour to include some element of 'liberal' or 'general' studies in the time-table of every young student. The quality of this varies, naturally, as do the reactions of the students to it—from 'thought I'd finished with school' to being carried forward into some new thrill of aesthetic delight at the hands of a first-class teacher of music, art or drama.

Operatives, of course, often get more general education than vocational training, since learning to do the job for which they are employed may take a very short time. They are often, however, given the opportunity, and sometimes compelled, to attend a College of Further Education for one day a week for a much longer period. For some of them this may remain 'a bit of a bore', for others it is 'a change from work', but for some it is a chance to pursue their general education to a higher level than they achieved at school, and this in turn can lead them to the chance of training for a more highly skilled job.

The boy or girl working in the very small concern may be isolated, in need of encouragement and support, and denied training and further educational opportunities. In the small unit the facilities may not be so good, but warm personal relationships may more than make up for this, and it is not unheard of for young employees of owner-manager businesses to be given day-release for further education, even though the concern may be too small for this to be compulsory, and even though the young person concerned is not an apprentice.

While it is true that for many jobs in our present society little or no training is required, it is encouraging to find the idea of day-release for young workers for further education becoming more widely accepted. The joy of craftsmanship and creation does not march with the universal desire for mass-produced goods, but increasing automation can make room for greater educational and recreative opportunities. At the same time it is important that in this third phase of the Industrial Revolution, while we cannot give many the satisfaction of creative work, we must remember that work, whatever it is like, must still seem meaningful. We all need to feel necessary, if not important, and those who do not feel they are performing a necessary or important task are not likely to be industrious. If we are to continue to operate all the benefits of the Welfare State, and to increase them to a greater level of adequacy, an industrious population is a *sine qua non*. Do we always do enough to make sure that the young worker, particularly the less skilled, knows in what particular his or her special piece of work adds to the comfort, dignity or happiness of mankind? People are not necessarily frustrated or wasting their lives because we think so or because we would be bored to tears by their job. Too much has been made of the frustration of the dull job. No matter how exacting and interesting one's job is, there are whole wastes of arid dullness and routine for all of us. The essential thing is not to attempt the impossibility of a 100 per cent interesting job for everyone, but to educate the community so that they may be able to regard the dull part of their work as their contribution to the welfare of their fellow men, and as some payment and discipline for the fullness and richness of their leisure hours. William Morris was once interrupted at his work by a visitor while he was putting in the spotted background of one of his famous wall-paper designs. 'Could you not get someone else to fill in those spots?' said the stranger. 'It seems such a waste of time when with all your talent you could be better occupied inventing another design.' 'What,' shouted Morris, 'do you think when I've had all the sweat of making this design I'd let some other fellow have the fun of putting in the dots?' Much creative work is of this character; the very heavy manual labour of the sculptor, the dull manual labour of writing a book—all work has its dull and monotonous periods which are endured for the sake of the work itself. It is a thousand pities that the ordinary process worker should think his work is to be despised, for we all do our work, whatever it may be, not merely for our daily bread, but to help the wheels of life go round. There is no crime in a dull job; the crime is in underrating, or rather ignoring, the value of any worker to the service of the community.

Because one's personal significance in a vast team of workers becomes increasingly difficult to understand, it is all the more necessary to do so. Unless people feel that their work matters, they cannot be persuaded that their play matters, and since social progress and the benefits of leisure itself depend upon work conscientiously performed, it is important that the young worker shall be convinced that the work he does matters to himself and to the community. Every worker, no matter what his job, produces not only a pay packet but *his share* of social progress. This essential fact, however, must be translated into terms which ordinary people can understand—and it must be restated and reaffirmed at frequent intervals. We are only just beginning to realize that, having (out of well-meant sympathy) spent a considerable amount of time telling people that they are mere cogs in the industrial machine, they can hardly be blamed for refusing to see why they should be anything more significant in the political and social machine, and still less for refusing to exert themselves to be anything more significant than lookers-on in their hours of leisure. This reassurance of personal significance is as badly needed as the opportunities to compensate by the experience of creative fulfilment in their leisure hours. For, on the whole, young people do not appear to want 'work's leisure'. The history of many firms with works clubs and sports grounds would seem to confirm this, and it is probably right that workers of all ages should limit the area in which they are prepared to be 'possessed' by their firms, however good and benevolent.

The universal concern of young people thirty-five and forty years ago on leaving school was whether or not they would find a job—any job, and many of them knew that they had no immediate prospect of finding one at all. It is not surprising therefore that the children of those young people learned to want, above all, a *steady* job within their capacity—one that they could hold down, and one that would last if times got bad again. We have a rising generation entering the labour market in the next few years whose parents did not themselves endure years of depression and labour-exchange queues. They are able, therefore, to take a more adventurous view of work and opportunities. Some of us complain that today's young workers flit too light-heartedly from job to job, moving on for a change each time they get bored or see a chance of higher wages. To attempt to steady them down by telling them in tones of martyrdom or self-righteousness that at their age we knew we had to stick to the jobs we had if we did not want to find ourselves out of work is senseless, because we are living, thank heaven, in a different kind of world, and young people know it as it is. If the purpose of work is to earn a living and opportunities abound, the smart thing to do is to move every time a better chance appears. A more responsible attitude, in this day and age, does not necessarily mean staying with one firm for ever, but it does entail having an appreciation of the importance of one's work for other people as well as for oneself.

Girls, on the whole, still tend to take themselves, and to be taken, less seriously than boys where work prospects are concerned, though the girls no longer look upon work as something (with one or two traditional exceptions) to be done only between leaving school and marriage. Most girls now expect to go on working after they have married at least until they begin to have children, though they do not necessarily expect to stay in the same job. They are, therefore, more concerned to be able to do a job that is local, and when they are married it will need to leave them sufficient time and energy to cope with the home. Many of them do, nowadays, return to work again, part-time work quite often, after the children have reached school age, but the majority of young girls, naturally enough, give little thought to what they will do beyond the time they have children. Even girl students training to be teachers seldom show any concern about whether they will be teaching or not when their own children are of school age. Hardly any of them expect to teach for long after leaving college as most expect to marry soon after qualifying and intend to start having families a year or two later. Going back to work when the children are 'off hand' is a growing practice among married women, but the decision to do it is usually a mature one, and not one taken, or even thought about, at the start of a working life. It does not, therefore, affect the choice of work to any extent.

What then should be the main concern of youth leaders with young people's work? In the first place, they need to know a great deal about the working conditions of the young people. One learns from visits to factories and workshops not so much by watching the wheels go round and learning the technical intricacies, as by watching the faces of the workers, noticing how they respond to each other and to visitors. The very attitude of the doorman who shows one into the manager's office tells one much about a firm. One learns more by listening to adolescents talking inside and outside their work places, and one can see what the physical conditions are like. Are they sitting down to work? Do they have to keep to one position most of the time? Do they have to be silent? Is it quiet or noisy? Is there much standing, lifting, or running about? What sort of things do the young employees actually do?

We can alter few, if any, of these things, but knowing them does help us to understand why they are irritable, tired, noisy or want to rush about. True recreation (in the essential meaning of the word) consists in the judicious appreciation of opposites—or in more homely language, a change is as good as a rest. We can then at least offer appropriate recreative opportunities.

Fortunately, there are far fewer young people in unregulated occupations than there once were—errand boys and domestic servants have almost disappeared. But a youth leader should have a special concern for the young people in his area who may still be 'out on a limb'. Waiters and restaurant kitchen hands may work hours that never allow them to attend the orthodox youth club, and ice-cream sellers and petrol-pump attendants can suffer from the lack of legal protection that many other young workers have.

Youth leaders also have an important part to play in interpreting young people's experiences in the world of work to them. This requires the youth leader not only to be informed about the conditions of work but to be interested in the working experience of the young person. Which part of the job does X like best, and which does he most dislike? Is it what he has to do or the people he has to do it with that matters to him? Are any of these young beginners finding themselves *in* the adult world to which they have looked forward so eagerly, but not *of* it—isolated within the working community, the girl being sickened by the unnecessarily dramatic and obstetrical conversation of older women, and the boy finding himself the butt on which older men sharpen their wits or vent their irritations? Or are some of them among the lucky ones who are working under a foreman or forewoman or office head who is a natural artist in human relations? A youth leader needs to be an intelligent listener first of all, and a sympathetic one. After that, he can often help a great deal by letting the young person know that he is not peculiar because he is worried at the unexpectedness of things, and that he takes the young person's feelings seriously. He can help too by being willing to discuss the ethical difficulties of such things as 'getting ticked off if you work too quickly', and by helping them find their way through the intricacies of trade unions, membership and non-membership, if no one at the place of employment or at home seems to be doing this. Above all the youth leader can assure the young person by his attitude that he or she believes the work matters, whatever the job is. By these activities with young workers he is far more likely to help them develop a responsible attitude to work than he is by moralizing.

A number of people—careers teachers, youth employment officers and personnel officers among them—are concerned in helping young people to find suitable posts, and to settle in satisfactorily, and to make wise moves when advisable. In spite of this, many young people still do not avail themselves of as much help as they might get from any of them. While official reports suggest that the

The Adolescent and Work

Youth Employment Service places between 40 and 50 per cent of fifteen-year-old school leavers in their first posts, other enquiries suggest that the proportion is much lower. Some of this is no doubt due to the fact that when there is full employment and there are long lists of advertisements under 'vacancies', many young people can find work for themselves or with family assistance, at least as suitable as they would have found with this help. Some of it, too, is because firms are not bound to inform the Youth Employment Service of their vacancies and youth employment officers have insufficient time or are not numerous enough, to do enough visiting of firms to acquaint themselves of all the vacancies that exist. Some of it is probably due to lack of confidence in 'official' help on the part of youngsters and their parents. Some, however, still seems due simply to a lack of awareness on the part of some young people that the help is there. Michael Carter in his book *Into Work* quotes the Sheffield boy who after several weeks of unemployment 'finally got "guidance" from a milk roundsman, who suggested there might be a job at the dêpot. The boy thus found himself washing bottles although his declared ambition had been to be a painter and decorator. It did not strike him as either odd or regrettable that his actual occupation was at variance with his avowed aim; and at no point had it occurred to him that the Youth Employment Service might have been able to help—in fact he had forgotten all about the Service'. Youth leaders can, therefore, do much to help young people make full use of the help that exists for them, by reminding them of it when they may have forgotten it, by showing young people by their attitudes that they have confidence in these workers, and by knowing these colleagues, with whom they share the experience of working with young people, and co-operating with them so that the young people are offered consistent help and not confronted with varying or even conflicting advice from different quarters.

These are all unspectacular ways of helping, and perhaps less attractive to some than, for instance, 'landing' a job for a club member by persuading a personal friend to take him on at his firm. But like much of a youth leader's work it is likely to be sounder because it is less spectacular. Most of it is achieved through, or arises from, knowing the young people, being available to them, and being willing to talk with them informally but seriously about the things that matter to them about work. If youth leaders thus contribute to young people being able to make a more informed choice of work, to develop a more responsible attitude to it, and to use the fruits of their labours in ways which give them greater purpose and enjoyment in life, their efforts are well spent.

4

Education in Adolescence

During and after the 1939 war public opinion was ready, as part of the movement towards social security for all, to safeguard the rising generation against social disasters, and one of the main administrative results was the all-party Education Act of 1944 which raised the school-leaving age to fifteen, and made school milk and meals an integral part of the education service. This Act also set out plans for the further education of young workers at county colleges for one day a week, and envisaged annual medical examinations throughout that time. This latter was partly covered, however, by the 1948 Factory Act which made provision for 'young persons' to undergo an annual medical examination until eighteen years of age and at each change of employment. Guided by the Ince Report (1948) the Training and Employment Act of 1948 re-established the Youth Employment Service under the Ministries of Education and Labour in order to build up a system of comprehensive vocational guidance.

The school-leaving age was raised by one year soon after the war and its effects, both good and bad, began to be felt. Employers complained that young people came to them less able to read, write and spell conventionally, but what most critics failed to remember is that the increased social mobility of the previous fifteen years meant that most people were now doing jobs for which they were not naturally competent. Young people who, before the war, went into the lower paid and unskilled branches of domestic service and errand-running began to go into factories, the erstwhile factory worker went into a shop, the shop assistant of pre-war days to an office, and boys and girls who would have regarded this as the height of ambition before the war began to find many branches of technical training and semi-professional training open to them. The national level of intelligence has certainly not risen; consequently, the 'material' in all jobs from factory work to teaching is not uniformly as high as it once was. We all went up at least one rung in the ladder—but the general level of mental ability, if anything, has gone down. How then could employers be other than dissatisfied? Nevertheless, these boys and girls were better physical specimens, taller, fatter and more robust than young people of similar background were twenty or thirty years earlier. Their minds were more lively; they expressed themselves more easily; the school, the press, the cinema, radio and television had all combined to widen their horizon, and the cumulative effect of all our socializing agencies began to make itself felt.

Another change that came about almost without remark was that far more parents became 'education conscious' than ever before. Who, before 1939, would have imagined that the more popular daily papers would carry an 'educational correspondent' responsible for at least a column a fortnight, as nearly all did by the mid-fifties? It is true that some of the popular concern about education resulted from the unexpected results of 'secondary education for all'. Since the grammar school was still the broadest, if not the only, gateway to the professions, and since few but the very well off (among which professional parents are seldom now numbered) could afford to pay private-school fees, the anxiety over the 'break at eleven' became more acute than it was even in the bad old days. Consequently, the sense of failure which many children felt, and were often made to feel by their parents when they were not selected for grammar-school education, was more bitter than ever before. Controversy over the grammar and comprehensive schools mirrors public interest.

The Central Advisory Council for Education made a special study of the problem of early leaving from the grammar school, and the report published in 1954 reveals the disturbing fact that over half the children of semi-skilled and unskilled workers either fail their fifth-form examinations or leave before attempting them. The children who stay the course are, in the main, the children of fathers holding professional, managerial and clerical posts. Although these parents combine to make up a mere 20 per cent of the working population who are also parents, their children make up 60 per cent of all the sixth-formers in all our schools.

As the Advisory Council's Report indicated, the difference in performance of young people is based on an intricate set of social assumptions which affect not only a child's parents but the whole group in which he is brought up and has to spend his leisure time. In some neighbourhoods the child who stays in school after fifteen is regarded by his group, and even by his family, as an anti-social oddity. For such a child a good performance at examinations is far more difficult than for a child from a home where there is informed conversation, where the desire to purchase a book is not regarded as a sign of abnormality, and where every facility is provided for doing homework rather than every inducement for avoiding it. Anyone who really wishes to understand what a toll it takes out of the young to educate themselves without a background of culture ought to read *Daddy Long Legs* again. We are beginning to discover by survey what a number of people have always known by instinct: that the family is still the first and greatest educator and that, though we may test children for age, ability and aptitude, their own 'stickability' and their parents' values are also of supreme importance.

In the early years after the implementation of the 1944 Education Act, the Secondary Modern Schools had a hard time. Most of them occupied the premises of the old Senior Elementary Schools, and were often not believed to be any different from those schools. Many of the children entered these schools feeling they were failures and often their parents, feeling the same way, increased the damage. Many of the children, coming from overcrowded junior schools, or having moved from school to school with no continuity in the unsettled immediate post-war years, had not achieved that grounding in the essential skills of reading, writing and reckoning which are tools which their secondary modern school should have been able to help them to use. Teachers were often faced with the choice of teaching the things which should have been acquired in the junior school, or trying to sow a little culture into ground that was not ploughed for its reception. Much of what was thus sown had a low survival value, and most of what survived at first could not withstand the climate of workshop and factory to which it was transplanted. It was no wonder that some boys and girls in their first year of employment

E

felt their education had been useless, or that employers complained that their young recruits lacked grounding and that the new education turned out people adept in nothing but the art of smattering.

Nor did the experience of the first generation of children who had to stay at school until their fifteenth birthday always help the image of the 'new education'. Too often they had to remain in a school of which they were already tired, which had no room for them, no teachers properly prepared for teaching them, and little of interest in the curriculum to offer them. No wonder some of them would go noisily through the streets after school, shoving their way past other pedestrians, flaunting their physical maturity, thus showing how cheated they felt at continuing to be treated as children and being prevented from entering full-time wage earning.

It was indeed a difficult start. Margery Fry once pointed out that one could not give children love by Act of Parliament. Neither can one give teachers and children in schools parity of prestige by that means.

Yet, even in these early days, great advances began to be made in some places. Some secondary modern schools began to give their young people a first-class social education through the development of high standards, achieved by new methods, in music, dramatic work, art, craft work and physical education. Several authorities were bold in experimenting with new patterns of secondary education so that the country as a whole became richer in experience. Evening institutes and evening work in technical and art schools developed rapidly after the war in spite of often having to manage for many years in dreary premises or in the teeth of day school and caretaking staff who resented their evening occupation of day schools. Evening institutes in some places have given a real second chance to those who had 'missed out' in their earlier education, and in some places they developed a strong non-vocational side, thus becoming, under enlightened head teachers, cultural beacons in what was still something of a waste land.

Since the end of the Second World War, education in this country has been battling with three large basic problems. The first and most obvious is the shortage of buildings—in terms of sheer space for pupils and in terms of the obsolete nature of many of the buildings still in use. The shortage already existed before the war, but became much worse by the end of it as a result of the further ageing of them all, the wartime destruction of some of

Education in Adolescence

them, and most of all through the post-war increase in the birth-rate. With the shortage of buildings there inevitably goes a shortage of equipment and outdoor space. The second basic problem has been the shortage of teachers. This is not an isolated problem, but part of an expanded requirement for workers whose skill and knowledge depends on their higher education and training—teachers, social workers, youth leaders, medical workers of many kinds, technicians and technologists. This situation is a vicious circle—without expanded supplies of teachers and trainers one cannot expand education and other social work services, and without expanded education one cannot expand the supplies of such people. This has meant that all these occupational fields have been competing for a relatively small number of suitable candidates for training, and has resulted in a number of 'bootstring' training operations, often labelled 'emergency' courses. The third basic problem has been the economic need of the country for more people with the educational background which enables them to learn to do more than unskilled work; and since we now admit that there have probably always been more people who had the ability to do this than were given the educational opportunity to develop it, the humanitarian grounds for educational expansion are also strong.

How far have we pulled ourselves out of these difficulties? With the supply of both buildings and teachers we have had to run very fast even to remain in the same place. In the introduction to the annual report of the Department of Education and Science (*Education in 1965*) it is stated '. . . it was nevertheless expected that the increase in the number of teachers would at least match the rise in school population, estimated at nearly 100,000, and that current staffing standards ought therefore to be maintained'. The National Advisory Council on the Training and Supply of Teachers published in its ninth report a forecast of the demand for and supply of teachers for the next twenty years. It showed that for the existing staffing ratios to be maintained, the existing rate of recruitment of teachers would produce a supply that was insufficient by about 20,000 in 1976. For all classes to be reduced to thirty pupils it showed that the supply would fall short by nearly 100,000. The forecast also suggested that by 1986 the present recruitment policy, if continued, would enable all classes to be reduced to thirty; but this will be of little help, of course, to the next twenty years' school

67

leavers. Training establishments were therefore asked in 1965 to do all they could to ensure a more productive use of their facilities, and to raise their output of newly trained teachers still further, and they have responded in a variety of ways. Employing authorities were also asked to do more to increase the employment of married women teachers by making more part-time teaching posts available.

The school-building programme has suffered somewhat from the country's economic instability in the post-war years, but in the five years 1961–6, something like one million new school places were provided. Expenditure on building maintained schools in 1966–7 was £80 million, five-eighths of which was to provide for the increase in the school population and three-eighths to replace redundant buildings.

In the next ten years, therefore, it seems that we shall have our work cut out in order to maintain our present position quantitatively, with primary and secondary education. A number of important changes have come about. From 1970 the minimum school-leaving age was expected, until the present economic crisis, to be raised to sixteen years. The training of teachers is now normally extended over three years instead of two for non-graduate entrants, and a selection of these trainees will now have the opportunity to complete degrees during this period. The pattern of secondary education is changing with the move to comprehensive schools in many places, and the development of junior and senior high schools, or high schools and sixth-form colleges. The wisdom of all these changes is still debated, but casual contact with fourteen- and fifteen-year-old boys and girls now, compared with contact with their counterparts of ten years ago, suggests that, although they are frequently critical of school when given the opportunity, the changes have, so far and in the main, been in a positive direction. No one can seriously mourn the passing of the 'eleven plus', and even in some of the places which have not 'gone comprehensive' there is more co-operation and interchange between the different types of secondary schools, so that the difference between them is less socially significant.

Traditionally our education system has been geared to the production of an *élite* capable of governing the country, carrying on its essential business, planning its campaigns in war and producing the next generation's *élite*. The needs of industry and commerce in the nineteenth century taught us that we had to have at least a literate general population, and although we began to allow some of the most able among the socially non-privileged to strengthen the *élite*, we did little more for a long time. We are only now recognizing that we need an educated general population, and that education proceeds in more ways than the traditionally academic. The Newsom report *Half Our Future* has pointed the way in which secondary schooling needs to go—to become less secluded and more truly connected with the community and the working world into which its pupils have to move. Some efforts to put some of the recommendations into practice are being made, while in some places resistance is hardening. Teachers who themselves have no experience of work outside their profession often quite naturally contemplate the changes suggested in the report with unease. A greater influx of mature students to teacher training, and more whole-hearted attention to the new aspects of education in the training itself, might accelerate the change of attitude needed in the educational world in order to make school a real preparation for life for those entering on adulthood. The universities, colleges of education and technical colleges have been expanding and increasing in number, and are 'bulging at the seams' as the post-war birth-rate bulge passes through their age range. Our 'unrealized potential' is made manifest in the number of young people who in recent years have aspired to higher education and acquired acceptable qualifications for it, but have had to queue up for places, knowing that some of them will be unlucky. Meanwhile, something like a second silent social revolution has been taking place in Further Education (see G. A. N. Lowndes, *The Silent Social Revolution*, for the first). Technical Colleges and other colleges of further education have multiplied their full-time courses, sandwich courses, day-release courses and evening courses. A good deal of this increased work has been undertaken in response to the Industrial Training Act 1964. There has also been a development of advanced courses in Technical Colleges, and although it seldom all happens within a single establishment, the work of the Technical Colleges ranges from courses comparable to those provided in senior forms of secondary schools to those at graduate and post-graduate level, complementary to the provision in the universities. Although the bulk of the work with young people in further education is focused on the acquisition of technical com-

69

petence, most establishments ensure that at least all their full-time and sandwich-course students spend some time on non-vocational general education, including physical education, and the best colleges not only do that, but manage, in spite of all the comings and goings of part-time students, to produce a responsible community in which sound social education takes place.

Whatever young people say about school, statistics show that the proportion of them who stay at school beyond the minimum age for leaving is steadily increasing. In ten years, the proportion of seventeen-year-olds still at full-time school rose from 8 per cent to over 13 per cent. If this trend continues and if the number of young people doing full-time or sandwich courses in further education establishments continues to rise, we may in only a few years' time find that about half of our young people are still in full-time education at the age of seventeen. If girls figured as prominently as boys in further education, the proportion would be much higher, but the unevenness between the sexes in this respect persists. In 1959 while about one-third of the boys under eighteen years who were employed were attending day-release classes, only 8 per cent of the girls in the same group did so. The majority of girls who do attend any further-education classes do so for commercial subjects—primarily typing, then shorthand, and sometimes book-keeping—and to learn the use of various types of office machinery; not very much of this takes place on a day-release basis; some girls take full-time courses, often at private establishments, and many of them attend evening courses.

Few boys and girls positively dislike school. Probably about half of them at the ages of fourteen and fifteen years like it on the whole, and the rest have no very positive attitude either way. Their chief complaint is usually boredom and a feeling that what they are doing at school has little relation to real life in which they are primarily interested. This was recognized in the Newsom Report and it remains to be seen whether the report's recommendations will be implemented and, if so, whether or not this difficulty will be overcome. In spite of having no particular dislike of school, two things seem to urge young people to leave. One is money—'If only they'd pay me to stay on!' said one bright fifteen-year-old boy, torn between the opportunity to go on into higher education and the desire for financial independence. The other is status—'The teachers are nice people, but they only deal with us as though we were still kids, and I'm not,' said an attractive fifteen-year-old girl who loved to dress well, could keep the boys in their places, and dreamed of being a fashion model. Some young people are, partially at least, overcoming the first of these counter-attractions to school by working outside school hours, at week-ends and in school holidays. They are making good use of the fact that labour is short and there are jobs available that they can do in their spare time, and as a group they are physically strong enough and endowed with enough energy to do this and enjoy the results. Being at school has for so long been associated with being juvenile that many parents and teachers find it difficult to adjust. But if our efforts to extend education are to succeed, the community at large has to learn more completely than it has done yet to treat its post-adolescent pupils as the young adults they are, and to think of continuing one's education beyond adolescence as an adult thing to do. At the senior end of some secondary schools an appropriate relationship is achieved between teachers and pupils. Grammar schools have in some cases always managed this with their sixth forms. But whether it is achieved or not depends very largely on the attitude of the teachers concerned. It is perhaps easier to begin the right way in colleges of further education, because most of the young people there are there because they have made, or at least shared in, a conscious purposeful decision to go there, even if it only amounted to accepting a job with a firm that sends you there for one day a week to learn something; they are not there simply because the law says that is where they have to be, as seemed to some of them to be the case when they were in full-time school, and for many of them there is an obvious and accepted purpose in their attendance. There may well be more in common between the attitude of the good teacher of young people of fifteen years and more to their class members, and good teachers of adults, than there is between their attitude and that of those teachers who are moved primarily by the love of working with children as such.

Changes in the more formal parts of the educational field naturally call for change and adaptation in the Youth Service as well. Recognition that a higher proportion of young people are involved in full- or part-time further education, will naturally make a number of youth workers feel that their particular contribution is to be made with young people not in touch with formal education of any kind. If 50 per cent of seventeen-year-olds are soon going to be in full-time school or college, there will be the other 50 per cent who are not, and these young people are equally important. Let no one lose sight of this fact—least of all youth workers. It would be a pity, however, if these young people were seen to be the only concern of the Youth Service, for this would sharpen the division between the one group of young people and the other. Moreover, schools and colleges are in need of the very skill which good youth workers could offer. People with youth-work skills, whether they are part of school staffs, or working in 'youth wings' or not, could do much to help the senior work in the schools to become more closely related to the surrounding community, and to produce the more flexible atmosphere appropriate for young adults in the schools. President Roosevelt, in a speech which he prepared just before his death and never delivered, pointed out that 'the history of civilisation will depend during the next decade or so on education and personal relationships—and even personal relationships are very much a matter of education'. While the great expansion in further education is bringing a much desired increase in educational opportunity to young people, the speed of the expansion has also brought a danger that personal relationships will get scant attention in some Technical Colleges and other establishments. Their very size is threatening to make them impersonal, and to leave their students feeling that they have no significance as individuals within these institutions. Many responsible people in this field of education are greatly concerned about this for they know that while some kind of arid instruction may go on in places which are not human communities, true education will not. Youth workers could offer valuable assistance in counteracting this danger. Their primary skill should be the ability to help the development of personal relationships and to foster groups in which individuals can develop personally through being people with identities in comprehensible human settings.

5

The Approach to Youth Work

✳

Many people still play important adult roles in the Youth Service without having had any specific training for it, and this is likely to remain the case although training facilities have increased considerably since the early 1960s. Valuable people such as coffee-bar servers in very large youth centres, caretakers of buildings used by clubs, activity instructors, and many voluntary helpers in one-night-a-week clubs, are primarily the focus of this chapter, but all the others are welcome to share it too, if they wish. New helpers should always be warned that in any form of youth service, and most of all in group work, they have embarked on something unique—unique in the first place because it demands a totally different technique from any other community relationship, and unique because it competes with every other form of commercial and social attraction.

Let us consider the technique first of all. The relationship of the youth leader with the member is not that of the school—that of the teacher and the pupil; it is not that of the workshop—that of master and man; it is not that of the family—that of father and son, or indeed of elder brother and younger brother; it is fundamentally different from all these because it is of a purely voluntary nature. Indeed in the early days there is not even a code of loyalty or friendship to be relied on; if the potential new member does not like the group, or does not like us, he can, and does, walk out. It is one of the reasons why so many teachers, so many 'motherly women' and so many good and worthy people fail—they rely on a response which the adolescent is not always prepared to make, and will certainly *not* make in the early history of his membership whether the group is long established or not. There are said to be groups which have a waiting list for new members, though one seldom meets one, and in such cases it may be easier to secure a quick response, but even in these it is doubtful whether the new member is ever an easy proposition for the first three months of his association with any new group.

We must remember that some young working boys or girls are coping, in addition to all the other trials and tribulations of adolescence, with a dawning sense of disillusion. One is always deeply touched when talking to group after group of boys and girls in their last term at school, with the eagerness which they display to enter the adult world. They look forward to their first pay-day, they spend their first wages over and over again in imagination, and the first few weeks of their working life are almost invariably full of excitement, even though they may be tinged with disappointment. But if we meet these same boys and girls six months later—what do we find? That the day of frustration has dawned—they are beginning to realize that life in the workaday world may mean a dull job, a robot job, and that in any case when all the weekly dues from the pay envelope have been met, there is very little left. They are at the beck and call of their workmates (as the last one in), at the crucial stage of family adjustments and conflicts which come with every additional wage-earner in any home. The youth group is one of the few places in which they can feel free and important. By virtue of a membership subscription they have a stake and feel themselves a power in the land, even if only to the extent of a few coppers. This was never more vividly brought home to me than in a club on a new housing estate. A member was suspended for having been a general nuisance on the very night he had paid his weekly subscription (in advance). He went, protesting vigorously, and the next day visited the club and smashed a window—with the message, 'Tell 'er I came for my money's worth!'

There is something about free and voluntary association with a club which makes all of us feel important. Professional men and women who ask you to meet them 'at my club', do so with un-conscious self-importance, the social climber will refer with casual conscious pride to 'the fellow I met at my club'.

We all need some sop to our self-esteem. How much does the adolescent need a place in which to be important, a place in which to fling his weight about—a place which he chooses freely and in which he makes free associations? Indeed the more humdrum and repetitive the daily work, the more this necessity for voluntary action becomes. It is evidenced so often—and so exasperatingly for leaders—in the way that, having become members, adolescents will quite often refuse to take part in any of the activities which we provide. We all know the boy and girl, clad in whatever current adolescent fashion adults most disapprove of, who attend yet never do anything, or indeed seldom speak to anyone. Nevertheless the group must fulfil some need or they would never come to it at all. We all know those difficult members who will join nothing, and who complain constantly of what is provided, both by way of entertainment and food; but it will help us a great deal in our more impotent moments if we remember that they are enjoying being important, that they feel that such free expression of opinion gives them a status they have not attained (and may never attain) in their homes or in their work. By bearing with them as they express themselves so self-assertively, by leading them gently along the paths that will enable them to express themselves more sociably, we are fulfilling one of the supreme functions of youth work.

In the second place any youth group is competing in an open field, with the dice very heavily loaded against it, with all the numberless bodies offering commercial entertainment—the cinema, the commercial coffee bar, the dance hall, the bowling alley. All these exist for profit-making, no expense is spared in the lighting, the heating and decoration of the majority. Yet, if we can entice them within our walls, and persuade them to stay for a little while under the right leadership we *do* offer them something of unique importance—a society of people being happy together! The club at its best creates a society of personalities with a community sense, which is the essence of good citizenship.

It is useful from time to time, as one visits clubs, to notice where the leader places the emphasis. Is it on 'classes' or 'activities'? The evening institute provides these and, on the whole, very much better than the average club—which, incidentally, should *feed* the evening institutes rather than compete with them. Is it on entertainment? The cinema and the dance hall do it far better. Is it on keeping young people off the streets? A very negative aim surely, and the public house does no less! No! The test of the good club is the test of fellowship and happiness. 'There is no duty that we underestimate so much as the duty of being happy.' Goodness, truth and beauty flourish in such soil and the provision of a place in which it is possible for young people to be happy is the ultimate test of a good club. But the key word is happiness. Pleasure can be found elsewhere. And it is the group which must be good, not the member. We are not concerned with the making of 'good club members' or 'well-organized youth groups', but with a much wider issue, the making of good citizens. This can only be done in a society where each member is important, where each one is given a chance to contribute something to the life of the group—the leader as well as the member—since, though the talents of the former may be greater, who shall venture to assess respective eternal values?

For countless reasons it is vital that we shall not segregate our young people into yet another body of people seeking refuge from the wider community of their village, town, or city. It was one of the probably unavoidable mistakes made in the formation of so many unemployed clubs during the years of the great depression. In many of these excellent institutions wise people began to notice the evils of the existence of a segregated community, a fourth estate, living side by side, instead of with, the rest of society.

It is for this reason that self-government is so important in youth work. If I had to give the first article of my youth work credo, it would be 'I believe in the club committee'. Not that club committees will help us in our task (in the early years at any rate they will add to our difficulties). The adolescent is much too busy settling his own problems and difficulties to help us very much over ours. In one group where I struggled rather than worked for over three years, my club committee was only beginning to function properly six months before I left. This committee had such internal wrangles that no secretary or chairman ever remained in office for more than two months; but that sort of thing matters little. The young people were learning a lesson that many town councillors have not learnt—that having a good idea is not enough, unless we can convince others that it is as good as we think; and that it is not enough to give in to the majority vote, we must be prepared to be loyal to that vote. In their own committees young people learn the power of the vote and in practising democracy in a miniature society they fit themselves to become intelligent members of a democratically governed country. We have been too prone to think that democracy needed no practice, but just as the heavenly provision of harps, however golden, will not secure a celestial orchestra from those with no musical sense, so the provision of a suffrage, however universal, is no guarantee of civic responsibility for those with no community sense. Above all, we must see to it that our club committee has *real* power and *real* responsibility and be strong enough to let them make their own mistakes and have sufficient faith in their power to put them right eventually.

In our approach to youth work, if happiness is our first law and self-government our second, as time goes on all the other essentials of good group work will be added unto us. Before anyone plunges further into the maelstrom of youth work, however, there are three golden rules of conduct which are well worth earnest consideration: we must try to be strictly realist in our outlook; to see to it that we *know* our members; and to make ourselves socially desirable.

Many a well-meant effort in youth work has been weakened by lack of realism, by a refusal to acknowledge where the young people are, by an effort to take them from where they aren't to where they do not want to go. There are still too many people in youth work who suffer from over-elevated souls. It is undoubtedly a charming picture to visualize hosts of young things sitting in ordered rows nightly listening to the B.B.C. Symphony Orchestra, while others in a quieter room discuss comparative religion; but the fact is that, between fifteen and twenty, adolescents like to dance; the boys like to box and develop their muscles, the girls like to dress and practise their powers of attraction.

The constant criticism levelled at some youth groups that all the boys and girls want is 'to dance and listen to that horrible jazz' and 'mess about generally', merely betrays ignorance of adolescent desires and needs. Of course they want to dance! It is psychologically right and necessary that they should do so, and is there really any greater merit in 'Gathering Peascods' than in jive? If folk-dancing means what I take it to mean, the dancing of ordinary folk at any given period of history, then the samba and twist are folk-dancing of this day and age. By all means Gather Peascods, but let us be quite clear that we are performing nothing *more* aesthetically satisfying than a modern dance. The only *real* sin in all this modern dancing and all this jazz (and by the way, Wagner started it!) is that it is sometimes shockingly badly done. Let young people dance, but let them have a chance to learn to do it well; let young people sing, and sing modern stuff too, but see to it that what they sing and dance is not second-rate, and if we are forced by circumstances to put up with the second-rate, never let us pretend that it is anything else.

Adolescents living in the atomic age are accustomed to all the amenities and slickness of a scientific age. Of course they are interested in films, radio and television, the new arts of the century. Again the only sin is that so often they put up with the second-rate because we have given them no opportunity to discover and talk about the excellent things provided much more frequently than some of us like to admit. Let us start from where the young are. They like dancing—very well, let us give them the best dancing instruction we can find and afford; they like modern music—very well, give them the best. There are hundreds of good tunes, so start their musical education via the dance band or group. I have never yet worked in a club for six months without starting an orchestra. Given dancing, singing and an orchestra, we have all the essentials of a concert party and once we have a concert party it is our own fault if we are not performing straight plays in two years, if we think that desirable. But if we begin with a class on speech training, it is doubtful whether there will be any members left in a month. Let us give them talks on make-up, boxing instruction, and encourage them to make things, but let them all be the best we can provide. Let us beware of making things for the sake of making them, of cheap culture in any form, the arty-crafty decoration of what was better unadorned, the let's-make-every-thing-look-like-what-it-isn't school. True culture is the appreciation of everything, from a plate of fish and chips to a Van Gogh, at its true level.

We have concentrated too much in the past on 'higher taste education'. Of course we must give young people a vision, but it must come by way of co-operation through appreciation to creation, and no other way proves anything but an ultimate short cut to the loss of members. The adolescent may not always know the highest when he sees it, but he has an instinctive suspicion of false values. He knows his own world and his own interests, and he can be led through them along many rewarding paths.

It should not be necessary to suggest to youth workers that they should know their members. But much visiting of groups convinces one of the necessity for making such a plea. I confess to being astonished at the number of times I have heard a helper who has been in a club 'man and boy for forty years' calling to 'that fellow with the red hair', or a teacher who has visited the same club for three sessions asking 'that second girl from the back' to do this and that. It may seem a small thing, but if we wish to establish friendly relationships with anyone it is essential to know his name. There is something vitally important to all of us about this. Perhaps it is the primitive feeling that he who knows one's name has power over one (the legend of Rumpelstiltskin). That it has an important influence is borne out by the fact that 'to be called out of your name' is still the deepest insult, and by the fact that even the most tolerant among us is mildly irritated by even a misspelling of our name. We all know that if there is a large club membership and if it carries a floating population, this question of learning names becomes a serious problem. But there are all sorts of tricks for helping one's memory, even to the humdrum level of learning ten new names every evening! To establish contact we must start with the name, and then we must carry on till we know the circumstances of their lives. It is not enough to know Willy, we must know about his little sister, and Mum who goes out early to work, and whether Willy has a bothering time with questions he can't formulate properly—about religion, perhaps, and sex, or how to cope with the fellow on the next bench at work who gets him down for no reason at all. But these things cannot be discovered in one evening by the question-and-answer method. This method was exploded for me for ever by a dear, good, and very wealthy lady whom I had inveigled into one of my earliest efforts at youth work. She was invited to come to see us because we wanted new equipment very badly and had explored every avenue except that of actual begging. She was warned that the club was not very refined, that we were indeed rather tough—'with jolly comfortable girls who enjoyed a dirty joke'—as Jane Austen expressed it, and boys who liked a spot of horseplay on the stairs. However, all went very well until, in the uncanny way in which such visitors always do, she chose to sit next to the most irresponsive and toughest girl of the lot, and proceeded to attempt to 'draw Eliza out'. The conversation went like this:

'Good evening, my dear.' (Mumble that might mean anything.)

'Don't you want to join in the dancing?' (Another mumble that might mean anything.)

'What is your name, my dear?'

'Eliza!'

'Oh, yes! And have you any little brothers and sisters?'

'Yes, four.'

(Faint, but pursuing): 'And where do you work, my dear?'

'Davy's Bone Factory.'

'Oh, yes! And do you like it there?'

'No!'

(Brightly): 'And how much a week do you earn?'

(Savagely): 'Fifteen bob a week—how much d'you?'

It says much for the genuine interest of the inquirer that we got our equipment after all!

Only by the slow and tactful method of inserting ourselves unassumingly into the life of the group, not by talking to members, but by hanging about and learning from their conversation and occasionally, very occasionally, giving it that twist which leads it to our goal, is it possible to open up a new avenue of thought to them.

We must soak ourselves in the local atmosphere; know current rates of pay, and slang, we must often be prepared to appreciate standards which are not our own while preserving our own integrity. We must know, for instance, that in different localities swearing means one thing and bad language something quite different. As a seventeen-year-old chairman of club committee once said, 'You know we all treat you like one of ourselves—but there's swearing *and* swearing and I won't stand for this being said in front of my sister, let alone a lady.' We must know, if we are dealing with girls, all about the accepted methods of 'getting off', what is said and what is 'not done'. Here again I learned my lesson early and in almost the exact phraseology of the well-known *Punch* cartoon. Greatly daring, I suggested one night to a group of sixteen- to seventeen-year-old girls, with whom I took a drama class, that although the adventures they had when they were 'picked up' by car prowlers were undoubtedly exciting, perhaps after all . . . 'You know, I wouldn't dream of going out with anyone I didn't know.' 'We know you wouldn't—and we're really sorry for you—we don't see how you'll ever catch a feller that way.'

The Approach to Youth Work

Finally, youth workers would do well to consider their own social desirability. Too often people want to help, but are no help. If we cannot play a guitar or a piano, or dance or act, help Carol repair her fancy hair-do, be intelligent about Trevor's motor-bike, discuss the latest trends in 'gear', or new pop records, why in Heaven's name should we imagine we can interest adolescents? We are thereby solemnly demanding, like the Victorian miss, but with less reason, that we should be loved 'for ourselves alone'. Clothes, too, matter a great deal, jeans and pullovers which would revolt the sensibilities of a self-respecting scarecrow, neither help the youngster still in the 'scruffy' stage to get beyond it, nor command the respect of smart young 'mods'. Dowdy hair and the 'same old dress' are no encouragement and something of an insult to 'with it' young ladies.

If we are not in youth work because of our love of our fellow men we have no business there at all. This burning love of humanity always meets with response, though not always in the ways we most care for, but as much youth work is ruined by too much restraint as by too much exuberance. Fear to exert undue influence, fear to assert authority when necessary, conscientious scruples about this and that—are all contributory factors. But young people want to know where they are and they need the friendship of those who have confidence and faith.

Perhaps one's approach to youth work can be summed up in the following Ten Don'ts for club leaders. One offers these apologetically, since the positive approach is always more attractive. Mindful, however, of the young lady's criticism of the Ten Commandments—that they do not tell us what to do, but only put ideas into our heads—they are offered to do just that; and as a basis for discussion:

1. Don't suffer from an over-elevated soul.

2. Don't be satisfied. Keep on taking stock and introducing variety into the pattern. We all know how easy it is to keep on with tried and proved methods, but new youth groups still have much to learn from old-established ones, and these in their turn need to recapture some of that pliant variableness that once attracted the young. In the self-satisfied statements of both the Old Guard and the New Brigade in Youth Service, one is sometimes reminded of the discussion between the Primitive Methodist and the Catholic Priest. After a long discussion on the merits of

F   81 their respective beliefs, at length the Primitive Methodist said, 'Ah well, we both serve God.' 'Yes,' said the Priest, 'you in your way and I in His.'

3. Don't forget details. In youth work we have to think with our hearts and feel with our minds but that need not prevent us from keeping a register to the glory of God and a petty-cash book to the satisfaction of the auditor.

4. Don't stand on your dignity.

5. Don't be sorry for yourself.

There are not only too many pocket dictators in youth work but too many folk who can only have been recruited from the noble army of martyrs. It is equally unnecessary to act as if we were either Sir Oracle or the Club Slave. Let us take our share of the odd jobs, even the washing-up rota in the canteen by all means, but it is no one's fault but our own if we are left surveying a litter of games equipment after the club has closed.

6. Don't nag. The press and the pulpit have quite enough to say about youth—its evils and its perils—without our swelling the chorus!

7. Don't ask questions. Just stick around, as the Americans put it.

8. Don't be ashamed of exploiting your gifts. This is what the parable of the Ten Talents is about.

9. Don't try to do good. No one can do good to anyone, or teach anyone anything, or make people happy. We can only give people a chance to do good to themselves, a chance to learn and a chance to find their own happiness.

10. And, finally, don't expect results. We are dealing with the most mercurial quality in the world, the adventurous yet timid, changeable yet loyal, earnest yet frivolous, adolescent human being. Often these young people will have passed out of the group long before the effect of their membership will be apparent to them or others.

One must always view with caution that type of social work which claims that it has been 100 per cent successful, and which tells, for instance, of hooligans, who in three months turned into refined young ladies and gentlemen, carefully crooking the finger on the coffee-bar cups. Let us not be downhearted if we can never count our successes, they will be none the less real for being dependable rather than dramatic. And for our encouragement let us be mindful of the missionary who went to Fiji. He spoke to the natives of the great power and goodness of God, but they were unresponsive until he asked if they had not felt the power of an unseen Spirit who influenced their lives. 'Oh, yes,' they said, 'there is a Spirit. He walks in the woods at night, but we don't talk of him.' That same night they killed the missionary and ate him, but he tasted so nasty that they never ate a man again. So you see, he did some good after all!

6

The Historical Development
of Youth Service

✳

Most primitive societies pay a great deal of attention to the welfare and education of their young people. As infants their children are usually gently, often indulgently nurtured, but some little while before the onset of puberty, through initiation ceremonies which usually include a period of intensive and often very strict training, adolescents are taught the rules of conduct and skills necessary to fit them for adult status in the community, as hunters or warriors, as mothers and fathers. This training both ensures the well-being and continuity of their society and confers status on the adolescent.

Before the Industrial Revolution, Great Britain was an agrarian community which had grown rich from its wool trade. Like all agricultural communities, young people were trained in the necessary skills. The boys helped on the farm, hunted and fished; the girls helped in the dairy, learnt to cook and preserve and the use of simples, even the toddlers scared birds. Then young people had a well-defined, if not always enviable, place in society, and the status accorded to the place. The Industrial Revolution disrupted the whole of this settled society, broke down communities and caused vast conglomerations of human beings to work in unaccustomed ways and to live in close contact with one another in houses often hastily built by their employers or by speculative builders or else in large houses originally designed for quite other kinds of living. The young were welcomed in the factory as necessary 'little nimble fingers', but the work brought neither satisfaction nor status. Many young people in the larger industrial areas became 'anti-social' problem children—almost all became young workers whose living and working conditions eventually shocked the social conscience of those who, however unwittingly, had thrived on their labour. Far more important, the role and status of the adolescent in our society became undefined.

Piecemeal legislation designed to regulate some of the social evils, such as the Factory Acts and compulsory education, though good in fact and intention, has tended to increase adolescent confusion, since they find themselves at one and the same time children and 'young persons', in a state of tutelage and of independence according to the people who happen to be dealing with them, whether they are teachers, employers or parents. The result is that adolescents increasingly find themselves deprived of any clearly defined status and with very little consistent adult direction at a time of rapid physical and emotional change and stress. This is probably the main reason why youth work has become a necessary feature of all rapidly changing and industrialized societies.

Any study of the historical growth of youth work and the social and economic backgrounds from which such group work has emerged, cannot ignore certain other factors which would seem to be present in any such industrial society. It cannot be without significance, for example, that at the turn of the century, in three countries showing a widely different social pattern, within a space of a few years three great national youth movements came to birth—The Wandervogel in Germany, the High School Movement in Russia and the organization associated with the name of Baden-Powell in England. The two former, after a number of changes of form and policy, became welded into nationalist youth groups of an extremely powerful kind; the latter expanded into an impressive international organization of Guiding and Scouting. What were the circumstances in three such widely different countries which caused these youth movements to spring up within a few years of each other?

It is an over-simplification (but perhaps a justifiable one) to suggest that the first constant, at all events, was social. Each nation was at a different point in its own Industrial Revolution, but in each, working conditions, living conditions, overcrowding and other social evils were pressing especially heavily on young workers, and had reached such dimensions that they aroused the social conscience of many of the leisured and educated classes. Secondly, in each country there had been a history of many years of bitter struggle for popular or universal education as a means to social betterment. At the same time an increasing awareness of the problems of young workers had brought with it an interest in the nature and needs of adolescents and, in some minds at all events, a growth of political conviction that youth was important, a conviction which has seldom been stronger since the golden age of Greece. Finally, the growth of the science of the mind and civilizing influences generally, caused people on the one hand to become interested in the problems of adolescence, always an interesting stage psychologically, while on the other hand the stresses of new methods of civilized living tended to make the adolescent problem acute in a way which it seldom becomes in the primitive community.

It is the presence of these constant factors in the emergence of youth work which may account for the fact that wherever it occurs in any strength, matters of social conscience—and, therefore, very often of religious conviction—a concern for education, a political awareness of the significance of youth in society, and an absorbing interest in adolescents, as political leaders, as potential citizens or delinquents—form some of the main motivating forces of those organizing or sponsoring such groups.

One can conveniently think of the development of youth work in Great Britain in two clearly defined stages—before 1939 and afterwards—the dividing point being the stage at which local education authorities began to take an active part in the field of youth work. But the picture is never static. At one moment one particular kind of youth work, promoted perhaps by a voluntary organization or, nowadays, by a local education authority, may be flourishing. At another time it may have lost its appeal. At all stages, however, the social reformer, the religious reformer and the educationist will be found.

THE ERA OF VOLUNTARYISM

In the main, all group work among adolescents before 1939 catered almost entirely for the 'under-privileged' and was sponsored by people with tender consciences who gave of their time, talents and money to improve the leisure-time lot of the young worker. Sometimes it was a concern for factory workers and attempts were made to enlist young people in a crusade for 'industrious and sober living' as in many of the earlier uniformed organizations. During the cotton famine in the Industrial North, clubs and afternoon classes were started for boys and girls; in the south the needs of 'domestic servants away from home' attracted the attention of reformers; and it is due in great measure to their work that much social legislation concerned with the improvement of working conditions (e.g. hours of work, 'the full dinner hour', the Shop Act, 1912, The Children and Young Persons Act, 1918) found their way on to the Statute Book. Some groups attempted to teach girls to do plain sewing and cooking, to illuminate texts and abstain from 'intoxicating liquor and the reading of foolish books', others were concerned to widen young people's interest generally in crafts, music and drama. Sometimes the stress was on preserving a healthy mind in a healthy body, as in the type of group that specialized in the provision of outdoor games and opportunities for camping; in others the most important element in group activity was considered to be the weekly Bible class.

Some of the earlier pioneers brought young people together to learn to read and in particular to read the Bible, sincerely believing, as many of them did, that people only needed to know what was good in order to do it. Equally influential among the pioneers were those who believed that in order to be good it was necessary to be happy and that happiness consisted in no small measure in education and the promotion of physical health. Among this group were to be found those who agitated for educational reform, notably the raising of the school-leaving age. They were convinced that, as an extension of the franchise brings with it political power, so the youth of the nation must be made aware of its democratic freedoms, guarded from subversive propaganda, and prepared for its responsibilities.

But in its early stages all this work was in the hands not so much of voluntary organizations, as of volunteers, individual men and women who pioneered with small groups of young people in neighbourhoods where overcrowding and disorderly behaviour, poverty and drunkenness most attracted their reforming zeal. Before they began this work, almost the only non-commercialized provision for the leisure time of the poor was made by the Sunday Schools and the Salvation Army.

The Historical Development of Youth Service

Obviously when such groups were financed from private sources, they flourished or decayed according to the merits or demerits of the person in charge at any given time, and naturally those who formed the groups felt, as all do who pay the piper (whether they are ratepayers or subscribers), that they were entitled to call at least some of the tunes. There is no doubt that a great deal of artificiality in the way of religious symbolism, make-believe discipline, melodrama and leader-worship was imposed by the people who financed such groups, and often by the leaders of the groups themselves, who, whether they were paid or did the work voluntarily, were at the mercy of such friends and benefactors as would support them financially.

But this is not exclusive to youth work before 1939. Members of education committees, even teachers and local authority officials, who should know better, are still suspicious of a service to young people which supplies nothing but what they like to call 'mere amusement'—though why it should be less worthy to make people happy than it is to inoculate them with doses of ill-digested information, it is difficult to discover. It is all too common nowadays to hear people discussing the pre-1939 era of Youth Service as though it bore as much relation to Youth Service as we know it today as the amoeba has to the adolescent. But these early pioneers, the great ones such as Sir William Smith, Baden-Powell, Lily Montagu, Alec Paterson, 'The Doctor', Basil Henriques and countless others, set a pattern of work which is still the blueprint of most youth work, and more is owed to them than is ever acknowledged. The inspiration of leadership and love of humanity of one man or woman who gathered a band of friends together and proceeded to attract young people into an aura of friendship and worthwhile pursuits were of the essence of youth work from the beginning. The pioneers often met, as many youth groups still do, in insalubrious and inconvenient premises, they often braved physical danger, as only few of us are called upon to do now, and though they had more leisure they spent freely of that, and of their wealth. It is true that much of the work was often tinged with patronage and flavoured with a kind of piety which is distasteful today, but that it made an incalculable contribution to the lives of many young people in an age when few cared for them is indisputable and should not be lightly dismissed.

It must not be forgotten, either, that a great deal of youth work

The Historical Development of Youth Service

has always centred around schools, university settlements and churches. It could indeed be argued that the earliest youth groups centred round the monasteries where the monks gathered likely lads from the neighbouring village and taught them better husbandry, or to read and write and illuminate. It is certain that many of the old-fashioned pre-1918 night schools were youth organizations of the best kind, while the university settlements did for the slum dweller what the community centre now endeavours to do for the dweller on new housing estates.

The era of voluntaryism was dealt a death blow, however, in World War I, when increased taxation and the beginnings of the social revolution were beginning to make themselves felt. World War II accelerated this change.

In 1916, largely as a result of public concern over a very sharp rise in juvenile delinquency, the Home Office and Board of Education together inaugurated a scheme for building up all over the country organizations for grappling with the causes of juvenile delinquency and suggesting remedies. A central Juvenile Organizations Committee was set up as the parent body for a number of local committees. Their duties, somewhat nebulously defined, were to make suggestions to combat the rising incidence of delinquency, to help and encourage voluntary organizations to see that leisure-time occupations and facilities were provided for young people and to give a general eye to their social welfare. After 1918 the history of these committees makes rather sad reading though; from a welter of committees which sprang up all beginning with 'J', emerged the Juvenile Employment Bureaux which, since 1944, have as Youth Employment Bureaux been so closely welded into the fabric of Youth Service in many areas. But the Juvenile Organizations Committees themselves soon fell into desuetude in many areas, partly from lack of interest and support but chiefly because few authorities made very much financial provision for this service. In common with the other proposals and Bills affecting youth and education, which have been the products of war years, they suffered from economy cuts in the years of depression. A brave attempt was made to furnish some help to leisure-time training for adolescents by the social and recreative clauses in the oft-quoted Section 86 of the Education Act, 1921—but by 1936 only six authorities employed full-time salaried secretaries to Juvenile Organizations Committees and only thirty-six authorities still had a J.O.C. of any kind. In many of these areas its chief function seemed to be the holding of an annual sports day or organizing a football or swimming league.

Thereafter there is a long series of bleak years during which the small units carried on as best they could and the major voluntary organizations continued to plough their particular and sometimes lonely furrows, but in spite of much that was done to try to awaken the interest of local education authorities to their permissive powers to grant aid under the Fisher Act, much was necessarily unachieved. During the 1930s, the bitterest period of economic depression, when youth groups were more than ever needed in the so-called 'depressed' areas, the club groups in particular would have found it difficult to keep going had it not been for the grant-aid of wealthy Trusts—among whom the Carnegie Trust has an honoured place. Much of this grant-aid was expended upon club leaders' salaries and on the salaries of the specialist headquarters staff of the voluntary bodies. After 1935 too, an even greater stimulus was given to youth work by the King George's Jubilee Trust Fund which distributed over a quarter of a million pounds to youth organizations between 1936 and 1939. For the first time youth organizations could look to a fund which would provide not one windfall for one specific purpose in a lifetime, but a grant which might continue over a period of years.

In 1936 the British Medical Association's Report on the disturbing state of the health of the nation's youth, together with eye-witness accounts of the high standard of physical fitness attained in much of the youth work going on abroad (notably in Czechoslovakia in the Sokol, in the Hitler Jugend, and the Norwegian Folk High School), accounted, among a number of other factors, for the setting up of the National Fitness Council. In Great Britain, two National Advisory Councils for Physical Training and Recreation were brought into being by Acts of Parliament, one for England and Wales, one for Scotland. The emphasis was primarily on physical fitness and to many this proved a great stumbling block, even when the name was changed to the National Fitness Council and much made of the all-embracing connotation of fitness. Never in the history of this country was so much public money voted to a department with so few provisos, but unfortunately, in most areas both the local authority and the voluntary agencies were alternately ignored, cajoled and abused. The National Fitness Council seldom seemed interested in anything but large schemes of capital improvement and extensions, and local government officials and voluntary bodies alike were concerned about maintenance. The former considered the latter timid and unadventurous, the latter considered the officers of the National Fitness Council unrealistic; and, for these and a variety of other reasons, the National Fitness Council never made much impact on youth work.

The outbreak of war must have made a very welcome excuse for the Government to put an end to a scheme which had provoked a great deal more acrimonious discussion in local committees and town councils than physical well-being in the adolescent. Never, to parody a famous statesman, was so much spent by so few with so little result. Nevertheless the clock could not be put back. The age of state partnership in voluntary effort envisaged in the Fisher Act was about to begin.

SINCE 1939: VOLUNTARY EFFORT AND STATE PARTNERSHIP

The outbreak of war in 1939 put an end immediately to the raising of the school-leaving age, which was to have been implemented in September 1939. However, the Board of Education, as it was then called, was not unmindful of the problem of the fourteen-plus age group and was certainly, with the memory of 1916 so recent, not unmindful of the additional perils of war in sapping the moral fibre of the adolescent. Hence in November 1939 the now famous Memorandum 1486, *In the Service of Youth*, was circulated to all local education authorities. This was quickly followed by 1516, *The Challenge of Youth*, and together they form the basis upon which youth work has since developed.

Unlike most Government circulars, the two which together form the Bible of Youth Service, had not only a number but a name; Circular 1486, *In the Service of Youth*, had the additional distinction of being a best seller and going out of print in a remarkably short space of time. In spite of those glimpses of the obvious, which are perhaps inevitable in Government publications, these circulars clearly recognized and expressed the view that adolescents have not only bodies to be exercised and minds to be occupied but characters to be formed and that the spirit of youth is something to be both served and challenged.

The Historical Development of Youth Service

For the first time local education authorities were charged with the responsibility of seeing to it that youth work was neither neglected nor unsupported. For the first time youth work was given a place side by side with the other educational services and was to be of equal status. Indeed all the circulars made clear the Government's intention to treat the youth problem in a positive fashion. Circular 1486 states: 'The social and physical development of boys and girls between the ages of 14 and 20 who have ceased full-time education, has for long been neglected in this country. . . . War emphasizes this defect in our social services. . . . The government are determined to prevent the recurrence during this war of the social problems which arose during the last.'

A National Youth Committee was established, including 'Members of local education authorities and voluntary organizations, and also others competent to speak on behalf of industry, medicine and physical training'. 'It will have as its counterpart local youth committees representative of both the local education authority and the voluntary organizations. The Board therefore urges that all local education authorities for higher education shall now take steps to see that properly constituted youth committees exist in their areas.'

Circular 1516, *The Challenge of Youth*, gave more explicit details of the functions of youth committees and how they should try to perform them, and clearly formulated the principle of partnership between the State and the voluntary bodies in the field of group work among adolescents.

These youth committees, when constituted, were to be given the duty of formulating 'An ordered policy, which shall provide for meeting the most immediate needs and which shall indicate the lines on which a real advance can be made under more favourable conditions'. They were to consider not only the use of leisure but also the larger social and economic questions affecting the fourteen to twenty age group. 'It is not the task of the local youth committees directly to conduct youth activities, but to strengthen the hands of local authorities and voluntary organizations. But co-ordination is not enough: a new initiative is needed. Young people themselves must be encouraged to find through the local youth committee new constructive outlets for their leisure hours and for their voluntary National Service.' Even the claims of the young people themselves to have a say in the administration of youth activities were not wholly overlooked. 'In order to ensure that free and direct expression may be given to the views of youth, it may be desirable for some representation to be given, by co-option or otherwise, to young people of both sexes, not necessarily connected with any particular youth organization.'

Local authorities were encouraged to assist financially by the assurance of 50 per cent grant-aid from the Board for all approved expenditure on premises, equipment or leadership. In fact, the whole machinery of youth committees was designed to combine, in the interests of the welfare of youth, the administrative and financial resources of the local authorities with the unhampered, practical experience of the voluntary organizations.

There can be no question therefore that those responsible for the launching of this Government 'Service of Youth' were sincere in their desire that there should be a genuine partnership between the voluntary bodies and the local education authorities, but the whole scheme ran into difficulties almost at once.

In spite of the model constitution appended to Circular 1486, representation on local committees was often the cause of great ill-feeling and much criticism. Obviously all youth units could not be represented if the committees were to be kept within workable limits, but it cannot be denied that in certain areas there was a lack of readiness to take advantage of the knowledge and advice of people who had been actively and honourably engaged in youth work for many years. This not unnaturally planted the seeds of suspicion and mistrust in the hearts of those who felt that all their painfully acquired knowledge of young people was to be disregarded and indeed swamped by a 'soul-less' Government scheme. As always on such occasions, 'the good were so harsh to the clever and the clever so rude to the good', and the younger generation were rude to both—feeling, perhaps justifiably, that a meeting of the youth committee in any area should mean something more than a collection of Rolls Royces and bath-chairs outside the town hall. It is only fair to add, however, that the average age of youth committees went down in the post-war years; but one often wondered whether this reflected a decrease of influential interest rather than deliberate policy. Youth Service was no longer new, and many of those who for ever seek after new gods —many of those who saw in Youth Service a way of making a mark for themselves and a position of influence—passed to other, seemingly more rewarding, aspects of local government or social welfare.

On the whole, in the realm of administration, the view of young people themselves was heard through the formation of separate Youth Parliaments or Youth Councils, but there was much local variation.

The main trouble at committee level, however, seemed to be the liaison with the education committee. At best a Youth Advisory Council was advisory, and not executive, to a Youth Committee, which was advisory to an education Committee, which was under the ruling of the local council. This cumbrous machinery often caused delay and confusion, and robbed Youth Service of that sense of urgency which is all-important, important in dealing with the needs of young people themselves, and in coping with the requirements of voluntary leaders in particular. Many leaders and members had little knowledge of local government procedure and they read into these delays a lack of interest and public support and official recognition of their work—which was not always without foundation. But there are many other reasons why this partnership between voluntary and statutory bodies remained an uneasy one. It is essential to the full success of any form of partnership that each partner shall frankly recognize the powers and limitations which necessarily govern the activities of the other. The voluntary organization has to recognize and respect the conditions which must attach to state action; for example, the obligation to avoid any suggestion of unfair preferences, and to safeguard the tax and ratepayers against the waste of their resources. On the other hand the statutory authority has to recognize and respect the conditions which govern a voluntary community such as a club whose members are free (within limits) to choose the activities in which they will take part, and the fact that any youth group is perforce much less cohesive and more elastic in its programme than, for instance, a school which boys and girls are compelled to attend.

One of the most important elements in the partnership was that the Board of Education (which became the Ministry of Education in 1946 and the Department of Education and Science in 1964) was empowered to spend public money in making grants. But the partnership was uneasy. The partners were in most cases strangers to each other, and to each the ways of the other seemed alien.

The Historical Development of Youth Service

Voluntary agencies felt that some local authorities were far more concerned to foster their own schemes than to help those of others —a feeling not always without justification, and one which is not unknown even in the 1960s. In the early 1940s many of the voluntary agencies' former supporters were engaged in the war effort; much of the private and personal financial aid they had received had been redeployed into welfare schemes for the troops, evacuees and air-raid victims, and much of their work in the field had been disrupted by the blackout, evacuation, and taking over of premises for military or civil-defence purposes, and by air raids. That they were not in an expansive mood towards their new partners was not therefore surprising. The intervention of local education authorities into the field of youth work was experienced by many voluntary agencies as a threat to their very existence because the local authorities could command better facilities and equipment. Local authorities found some voluntary agencies had no understanding of the exigencies of local government procedure, and sometimes failed to recognize the principles governing grant-aid from public funds. At that time the voluntary agencies had most of the experience and the local authorities most of the power. Intellectually the advantages of full co-operation were easily understood, but this was countered by the many factors which produced strong emotional antipathy between the partners. There were those in local government who declared that their aim was 'to wipe the inefficient voluntary organizations off the map', and there were those in voluntary agencies who accused local education authorities of 'knowing nothing and understanding less about youth'. Wild utterances and clashes of personality sometimes turned uneasiness into bitterness. Fear of the control and inspection that the acceptance of grant-aid would bring was sometimes just the fear of the unknown, and sometimes the fear of a deadening influence. Many people, too, were much concerned lest the intervention of the State should be the prelude to a nation-wide youth movement which would be open to the dangers of such movements in dictatorship countries.

In spite of all this trouble, which tended to be felt primarily at administrative levels, much excellent work was being done with young people in this difficult period. The Youth Service not only survived, but it was the only branch of the education service which was able to expand in the early 1940s. There was a sense of urgency. Money and equipment were available, and many very able people were drawn into the field.

One evidence of this urgency and expansion is the spate of Government circulars concerning youth work which is characteristic of the war years. One of these, Circular 1543, *Youth Service Corps,* introduced a new phase. It was issued in March 1941 when Youth Service work had been proceeding with varying degrees of success for just over a year, when after the initial bolstering up of existing schemes and the launching of new youth centres by the local authority, it was found that youth, while needing to be served was also anxious to serve. The Service of Youth, therefore, took on a new angle and in many areas service of youth became translated into service by youth.

One of the first of these ventures was the Youth Service Squads, probably the most loosely administered youth organization ever established. Hard upon this followed the establishment of the Air Training Corps, which gave boys the opportunity to train for future service in the Air Force. At the same time recruitment for the oldest pre-Service organization of all, the Army Cadets, and later the Sea Cadets, was stepped up. The response to all these pre-Service units was amazingly good. The Home Guard opened its ranks to boys, and a new girls' organization—the Girls' Training Corps—was established in order to co-ordinate all the pre-Service work for girls. Circulars 1585 and 1603 dealt with the particular problems that these developments occasioned. It must not be overlooked that at the same time the Red Cross, Saint John Ambulance and the nursing profession, all revised their provision for young people and began an intensive campaign designed to attract those who wished to train for their particular form of National Service.

The public was shocked in the early 1940s by the much-proclaimed fact that after leaving school, between 60–70 per cent of the adolescent population remained thereafter untouched by membership of any socializing influence including membership of a library or a Sunday school. This was often used as a stick to beat the voluntary youth organizations, and both sides seem to have overlooked the fact that, if this meant that the voluntary organizations were doing something when they were alone in the field for 30–40 per cent of the youth of the country, the record was not an unworthy one.

Circular 1577, however, was an attempt to get hold of some of this 'untouched' youth. It provided for the registration of all boys and girls between the ages of sixteen and eighteen. Particulars were to be taken concerning their employment and education. Those who were not attached to any youth organizations were to be interviewed and persuaded to join a youth group. For a number of obvious reasons this scheme was unpopular and did not prove very successful. It was later superseded in some measure by the youth employment officer and the youth organizer's talks to school-leavers on the leisure-time facilities available to them after leaving school.

Much of the development and expansion of this period was motivated, however, more by a concern to ameliorate the effects of wartime conditions than a concern to establish a positive and permanent contribution to adolescent education. Indeed, there were many who genuinely thought of Youth Service as a wartime measure. The fact remains, however, that for twenty years or so from 1939 local education authorities spent approximately £1,250,000 per annum, which attracted a 60 per cent grant, while the Ministry of Education itself spent approximately £250,000 in making direct grants, for example, to a youth organization for a particular project such as the acquisition of a camp site. Finally, the state was assisting directly most of the major national voluntary organizations who received grants for the training of youth leaders and towards the expense of maintaining headquarters, buildings and staff. Local education authorities varied considerably in their encouragement of Youth Service, but this, too, was in accordance with the whole structure of British education. Some local education authorities still assist voluntary organizations and do not maintain any clubs of their own; in other areas they organize their own large clubs or youth centres to the virtual exclusion of any substantial help to voluntary organizations as such, though help is often given over premises and instructors to *individual* clubs and to *individual* leaders and members for training.

It is important to remember that in this wartime period of rapid expansion it was not only the local education authorities' youth work that increased and multiplied. The voluntary organizations, through various forms of grant aid, were able to expand not only by promoting new work, but by employing a variety of expert advisers. It is true that no one ever felt that grants were generous enough, but what department of local government ever felt that their sectional interest has been sufficiently catered for in the estimates?

AFTER 1944: INTEGRATION

One of the important by-products of this period is often overlooked. The attention of the public had been focused on the needs of youth and the results were seen in some of the provisions of the Education Act of 1944 and in such Ministry of Education publications as *Further Education—Youth's Opportunity*, which paid tribute to what the country owed to 'the steadfastness, the enthusiasm and courage of its young people during the war'. The McNair Report was another landmark in the history of Youth Service since it contained a whole section on the training of youth leaders, whose training was thus conceived to be as important and as much a matter for Government concern as the training of teachers.

The 1944 Act charges the Minister of Education with the promotion of the education of the people, and neither age nor form nor place of education are limited by law. It makes it the duty of all local authorities 'to contribute towards the spiritual, moral, mental and physical development of the community . . . by efficient education'. 'Members of the community' may be anything from five to a hundred and five years old, they are all entitled to such education as befits their age, aptitudes and abilities, which of course should mean their leisure needs, in a world where the delights and dangers of leisure are available to all. It was obviously the intention of the Act that such needs should be included, and that the interpretation of 'education' should be as wide as possible.

Unfortunately, Youth Service was not mentioned specifically in the Act and, as many people felt at the time, this was probably a tactical and strategical error of the greatest magnitude. It is true that Section 53 imposes the duty on every local authority to provide 'facilities for recreation and social and physical training', but omission of a specific reference to Youth Service gave an unfortunate impression which has had a most serious effect on the work.

Since 1944 the administration of Youth Service has come under the general umbrella of Further Education, which includes evening institutes and adult education. It could be argued that organized provision for the leisure-time education of young people needed no longer to be operated in a no-man's-land between compulsory education and adult education, and that the development of Youth Service from 1944 could very properly be regarded as one of integration. But the process varied in different parts of the country. In a large number of areas it meant the appointment of Further Education officers with a responsibility for all forms of after-school education. This would have been no bad thing were it not for the fact that unless the Further Education officer so appointed had a real concern for youth work, it was tempting to neglect it for other forms of education, and in particular for adult education in which results are more easily achieved and assessed. In other areas the fusion of Youth Service with Youth Employment has been complete in that Youth Officers fulfil the double role of Youth Officers and Youth Employment officials. In theory this close connection between young people's work and leisure was a move in the right direction. The Youth Employment Officer who sees young people in their last year at school is in an excellent position to advise on their leisure-time activities and to be the person who bridges the gap between school-days and young adulthood. In practice, however, fusion of these two offices was open to criticism on the grounds that if Youth Employment Officers had too heavy a load of work to carry it was inevitable that it was the leisure-time provision rather than the employment side of their work that tended to be neglected. Moreover, it was but natural that unless officials were primarily interested in the Youth Service side of the work, they should tend to give more attention to employment where results are readily assessed, and progress more clearly defined. These two criticisms really boiled down to a question of personality and staffing. Many people prefer to go for the job that shows results 'in the here and now', but an administrative fusion of two offices was not necessarily wrong because it was under-staffed.

There was, however, still some doubt that those in authority, from the Ministry to the local authority, really recognized the conduct of youth groups as bona fide *work*. The tendency was still to think of it as 'messing about with darts and table tennis', and it had yet to be fully recognized that those who work most evenings and the whole of at least every other week-end, should not be expected to work all day as well.

A period of integration is never as exciting as a period of experiment, and the economic blizzard of the post-war years which delayed the raising of the school-leaving age to sixteen, and which transmuted the proposed County Colleges into a pipe dream, meant that Youth Service, instead of being the idolized educational venture of wartime, became, in the eyes of many people, an unnecessary and wasteful expense. The temperature of public regard can be read moderately accurately on the thermometer of fashionable lecture titles. In the 1940s lecturers were asked to talk on such titles as 'The Needs of Youth', 'The Challenge of Youth'. In the 1950s the favourite titles were 'The Future of Youth Service', 'The Way Ahead', 'The Challenge of Tomorrow', and even 'Whither?' —and the invitations seemed to come either from those who seriously questioned whether it had a future or from those with a longing to be reassured.

Nevertheless the cuts in educational expenditure did not press as hardly on Youth Service as might have been expected. But one of the great difficulties which resulted from this period of economies was that at the very time when many local authorities made drastic cuts in their own Youth Service so that voluntary provision was more necessary than ever for filling the gaps, there was less money than ever available for voluntary bodies to carry out their established programme. Since the war the voluntary organizations have found it increasingly difficult to raise funds and, in the 1950s, were therefore faced with meeting increased salaries, rising overhead costs and all the extended commitments of wartime expansion at a time when their grants were cut.

Hence the 1950s were a period of frustration within Youth Service and intensified criticism from without. Between those who thought that Youth Service was at best merely a wartime provision, and those who thought that the advent of the County College would do away with the necessity for Youth Service, the later 1940s were a time for constant reiteration of the needs of youth. Once the economic blizzard occurred and swept away any chance of the early establishment of County Colleges, however, the ranks of the opposition were increased by those who felt that cuts in education should have been confined to the frills, of which Youth Service was the most extravagant and bedraggled.

For a variety of understandable, if unfortunate, reasons Youth Service was not at this time very popular with the teaching profession, nor did it always have the whole-hearted support of local government officials, inspectors or other special-subject organizers. Youth groups were sometimes referred to by people who should have known better as Time Passing Devices, Evening Institute Preventers, Dance Mania Providers, Reading Avoiders, Background Radio Promoters and General Sappers of Standards. There are answers to all these accusations, but there is of course no smoke without fire. It is undoubtedly true that many youth units were and are ineffective and inefficient, but so are some schools, and some evening classes. It is understandable, however, that when one's own educational endeavours are hampered by economics, one should be irritated to see money spent on youth work which has little to show in the way of demonstrable results. It was conveniently forgotten that the standards of some recreational evening institutes, and even some schools were also lamentably low, and in any case, low standards or not, any school was deemed better than no school. Not so any youth unit.

Because many youth organizers in local government service as well as the voluntary organizations felt that their work was disregarded and unpopular, people engaged in Youth Service often tended to behave as though they were the sole saviours of mankind. A too acute realization of the needs of youth caused many of them to overstate their case and ignore or minimize the efforts of teachers, parents and employers. They talked as though no one else ever had such high principles and as though no one else *understood*. This does not help in the field of personal relationship, nor does it make for co-operation and good public relations. Again, many youth organizers and voluntary youth organizations, only too conscious of a field ripe for the harvest, tended to spread their resources and energies too thin. Perhaps the service would have stood higher in public regard if less had been done better. But whether that would have been better for young people rather than reputations is a moot point.

By 1950, or thereabouts, there was a marked paucity of people coming forward for youth work, and the quality of Youth Service had been seriously affected by the fact that from 1939 the voluntary organizations in particular suffered from at least three draining operations of some of its best personnel into other branches of the Social Services. In 1939, Circular 1486 had the effect of transferring many excellent club leaders to the administrative youth work of various local authorities. This was undoubtedly necessary and proper, but the loss of excellent general practitioners is never fully met by the provision of specialists. One of the many effects of the 1944 Education Act was that excellent youth leaders and organizers tended to become Further Education Officers, Youth Service Officers or Youth Employment Officers. The Children Act also drained off both club leaders and organizers into the new profession of Children's Officers. This occurred in a field where there never had been enough first-class club leaders and organizers, where for years there had been more vacancies than suitable people to fill them.

AFTER 1950: THE LEAN YEARS

The result of all this was that a growing concern was felt about standards in youth work, and a large number of individuals and both public and voluntary bodies conducted a spate of 'analyses' and 'surveys', 'inquiries' and the like into Youth Service.

Most of these did nothing to help, and much to increase the insecurity and unhappiness of those doing their best in the field. It is important to recognize that where so much is dependent on voluntary leadership, local management and private subscriptions, or else on the status of youth work in the eyes of members of local education authorities there are bound to be wide differences of standard, and between the good and the bad youth group a great gulf yawns. But since it is not necessarily from the seemingly most efficient or the most well-equipped group that adolescents may get what is most valuable to them at certain stages of their development, it is almost impossible to make any judgment on a group's effectiveness without having a very intimate knowledge of the work of that group over a period of at least months and perhaps years. In any case, constant changes of leadership made it very difficult to create or maintain anything like an even standard of efficiency.

Whether they agree with the phrase's political inferences or not, those who worked in the Youth Service through the 1950s have their own understanding of 'private affluence and public squalor'. While the community at large was becoming rapidly accustomed to living with television and cars, to eating out, and to taking holidays abroad, the Youth Service was indeed poverty-stricken.

The Historical Development of Youth Service

'. . . the Youth Service is at present in a state of acute depression'.

'. . . during the ten years up to 1958 the Ministry have not issued a single circular devoted solely to the Youth Service. During the same period there have been ten circulars which have some bearing on it; . . . and seven of them imposed restrictions . . .'.

'. . . lack of finance is at the root of several shortcomings we have noted; clubs that frequently have to function in dingy drab premises: lack of equipment for the job; insufficient provision for outdoor recreation; and a failure to measure up to the needs of new towns and housing estates . . .'.

'. . . leaders feel unsupported and unappreciated; they look for some sign that their work is nationally recognized as important, but find it neither in official expressions of policy nor in the rewards of a salary scale for those who are full-time which would put the work on a level with cognate professions'.

'. . . recruitment is still haphazard, salaries and conditions of service have never been agreed, and professional training is producing only a trickle of full-time leaders'.

These are some of the reflections of the state of affairs which appeared in the Albemarle Committee's report which was published in 1960. It is no wonder that a service in so depressed a state exhibited many short-comings, for which it was often criticized—some overlapping in the field, and no doubt some leaving of gaps; publication of training courses and of literature in pamphlet form; the use of too much time and energy by some agencies in justifying their own existence; a general tendency to arrive at an uneasy agreement about spheres of influence rather than the development of optimum use of resources in common purpose. Yet the Service survived the 1950s, and it would be a mistake to assume that it would have died if the Albemarle Committee had not rescued it at the end of that decade, though its life was undoubtedly in danger. Its survival until that time was due partly to the enterprise of young people and partly to a toughness of purpose and a conviction of value which the many part-time and voluntary and the few full-time youth workers had, even though this was sometimes expressed in an understandably cynical 'we-can-take-it-if-we-have-to' kind of way. Side by side with the depression, there remained a firm conviction, in the minds of those who did the work, of the fundamental value of the Service.

Thus, though partnership had not become worthy of its name, parsimonious provision remained the order of the day, and few new avenues were opened, many units of work continued to offer a wide range of membership experience to young people, and young people joined them voluntarily. L. T. Barnes at one time during that period (*The Outlook for Youth Work*) estimated that the Youth Service was in regular contact with something like half of the adolescent population of the country. Youth work, by this time, had ceased to be thought of, by those who thought about it at all, as something for the underprivileged. Adults, though usually quite vague about it, regarded the Service as 'presumably a good thing', except when they were taking exception to the behaviour of particular people; most young people knew something of the Service, and regarded it as normal, or at least not eccentric, to belong to some part of it.

AFTER 1960: THE ALBEMARLE ERA

That the Youth Service was in a depressed state had already been pointed out in the Seventh Report of the Select Committee on Estimates for the session 1956–7. In that report, attention was also drawn to the lack of clear policy for the Youth Service on the part of the Ministry in the use of even the little money that was available, and to the resulting confusion and dissatisfaction. The post-war rise in juvenile delinquency had been checked, but a new rise was apparent by the end of the 1950s. There was consciousness of the fact that the number of young people reaching school-leaving age was about to rise sharply as the 'population bulge' was entering adolescence. Teenagers had become a significant part of the spending public, and perhaps because the commercial world was not slow to take advantage of this fact, the arc-light of public attention glared upon young people even more fiercely than it always did. Their manners, spending habits, tastes in music and dancing, their hair-dos and their fashions in clothes all became the subjects of public comment which was usually disapproving and not infrequently abusive. Conscription for National Service was to end in 1960; the school-leaving age had not been raised; County Colleges were a lost cause. Should the Youth Service be left to languish further?

The Committee on the Youth Service, under the chairmanship

The Historical Development of Youth Service

of the Countess of Albemarle, was set up in 1958, to 'review the contribution which the Youth Service of England and Wales can make in assisting young people to play their part in the life of the community, in the light of changing social and industrial conditions and of current trends in other branches of the education service; and to advise according to what priorities best value can be obtained for the money spent'.

Some of the Committee's findings have already been quoted, and because of what their investigations showed, the Committee worked with a sense of urgency. In its report, presented to Parliament in February 1960, the Committee conveyed its strong conviction of the need for an adequate youth service, and put forward recommendations about how adequacy should be achieved. In spirit the Report is very much a reavowal of the concern for and belief in the youth of the country that had been expressed in Circulars 1486 and 1516 twenty years earlier. In substance it was concerned with conditions in the 1960s. While it was forthright in its insistence that the Youth Service be taken seriously and that government action should be speedy, the immediate demands it made were comparatively modest. Perhaps because of this, it was immediately accepted in principle and action was speedy. The Committee reaffirmed the belief in partnership and in variety of provision by voluntary agencies and local authorities. The detailed recommendations are best read in the Report itself. They centre round a ten-year development plan for the Service, in which opportunities for association, training and challenge are to be offered to all young people from fourteen to twenty years old, to be initiated by the Minister, and they include a training programme for youth leaders and 'a generous and imaginative building programme'.

In the five and a half years that have followed the publication of the Report, how far have we moved?

To advise the Minister in carrying out the ten-year development plan, the Albemarle Committee recommended the appointment of a small advisory committee of men and women 'with special qualities and experience'. This committee, known as the Youth Service Development Council, was set up in February 1961. After a year or two, this Council set up a sub-committee, known as the Review Committee, to do what is probably the most important part of its present work—to review the first five years' progress, and chart the way for the second five years of the development plan. Some of the most important answers to the question just posed must inevitably await the forthcoming reports of this committee. Since this was written the Review Committee has been discontinued and other Youth Service Development Council Committees are at work.

Meanwhile, those who are in the Service know that development has been taking place. The new financial support which the Service has been receiving centrally and locally has put new heart into the work and done much to convince those who work in the Service of the country's serious and honourable intentions.

There is as yet no up-to-date estimate of how many young people are in contact with the Service. The Albemarle Committee estimated that perhaps one-third of the age group were in contact, and casual observation suggests that the proportion has risen, though probably not dramatically, since then. This is not an easy estimate to make; separate membership units can count their members, but what constitutes membership varies from unit to unit; some units do not operate on a membership basis; duplicate membership is difficult to trace. One of the Albemarle Committee's recommendations was that the Service should offer help to 'self-programming groups' of young people who are not part of any officially recognized youth organization. The more effective the Service becomes in this aspect of its work, the more difficult it becomes to estimate the number of young people in contact. Some estimate should, however, be made from time to time since the country has the right to know how many of its young people are participating in the results of public expenditure on the Service. Quantitative evaluation, however, is not everything, and qualitative assessment of the work done by the Service remains as difficult to make on any objective standard as it ever was. We are probably never going to know with any degree of certainty just how much or how little any young people have been helped towards more complete maturity through the Youth Service than they would have attained without it. We do, however, have a clearer understanding than once we had, that this is what the Youth Service exists to do, and of some of the implications of this fact. That the young people's participation should be a happy experience for them is essential if our purpose is to be achieved. There are more youth workers now who accept also as a cause for rejoicing the fact that, for instance, some of the older and most capable club members are beginning to spend less time in the club and more time as effective members of groups in the community at large. The club may be 'back at square one' in terms of its internal social competence because of the absence of those members, but if in a year or so a few more members have, through their membership experience, gained enough poise and self-confidence to go forth in the same way, the club will indeed have served them well. The unit organization in the Youth Service is not an end in itself, but a means to helping young people in their task of growing up and becoming more effective members of the adult community. This, with all its implications, is still not fully understood in all the quarters in which it should be, but it is more generally accepted.

To make generalizations about the state of partnership between statutory and voluntary organizations is still difficult and liable to be misleading. At the national level a good deal is being achieved, but the channels of communication between each partner and the Department of Education and Science are different, and there is no regular forum in which both partners and the Department talk together. That this is so is simply the result of historical accident, but that it should be left so may well be hindering the development of full partnership since however scrupulous everyone may be, one partner may easily be left wondering what is going on between the Department and the other partner, and an atmosphere of competition and scheming can easily be generated instead of one of whole-hearted co-operation. At local levels there is great variation, partly due to the inevitably varying incidence of voluntary sponsored work, partly due to the past policies of local authorities, and partly to present attitudes on both sides. But on the whole it would be fair to say that attitudes have eased and co-operation has increased, and in some places the advance has been marked. The effect of positive government policy and a more widespread general recognition of the value of youth work has made it possible for both sides of the partnership to raise their sights from the stunting business of keeping their own ends up and justifying their own existence against great odds. Thus they can now regard each other as co-workers, and are in most cases manifestly glad to do so.

If in the course of an evening one visits three youth clubs of the kind which are open most nights of the week and have week-end programmes, they may well be about fifteen miles apart, and it is quite likely that two of them are still in inadequate, inappropriate, dull or even 'tatty' premises and the third is in a modern, purpose-built place of attractive design. As working buildings, these new additions vary in efficiency, but together they give some concrete expression of our belief in and respect for the younger generation. From 1960 to 1965, £16,000,000's worth of Youth Service building projects were authorized to start. By December 1964, 968 projects worth £8,100,000 had been completed, 112 projects worth £1,829,000 were under construction, and 252 projects worth £2,106,000, though not at that time started, had been approved.[1] When the whole £16,000,000 has been spent, the Youth Service will have something in the region of 1,600 additional buildings designed for its purpose. The average cost will have been in the region of £16,000 but the spread around this average of actual costs is considerable as the buildings vary in size and design. Looked at in the context of the country's total capital spending on education during the same period, this is still modest, but it is far beyond anything the Youth Service has experienced before; and it is not a farthing too much.

The number of full-time leaders in the service has increased substantially during the period. No exact figure is available, but a careful estimate suggests that there were, in 1966, about 1,200 full-time employed leaders in the Service, as against the estimated 700 at the time of the Albemarle Report. The number of part-time leaders and assistants must also have increased substantially. Again no precise figures are available, but a new departure has been taken by the acceptance of the idea that part-time workers should be employed in the Service, not exclusively as activity instructors, and that they should, as far as possible, be trained.

The pay and conditions of work for full-time leaders meant for a very long time that only those who had private means, and those who had no family responsibility and were prepared to accept a lower standard of living than most of their peers enjoyed, could take it up; and of those only a tiny minority made a career of any length in it. The Albemarle Committee recommended that the Minister should appoint a committee representative of voluntary and statutory employing bodies and leaders employed by both types of bodies to negotiate salary scales and conditions of work. Accordingly, the Joint Negotiating Committee was set up and

[1] Cmnd. 2612, 'Education in 1964', H.M.S.O.

made its first recommendations in 1961. These recommendations and subsequent ones have been accepted, and although some difficulties still arise from uncertainties about starting points on the scale and special responsibilities, this has meant that trained full-time leaders now have some security and that they are paid on a scale approximately parallel to that of trained teachers of similar age.

Since 1961, encouragement has been given, through the offer of substantial financial assistance, to those who would break new ground with experimental youth work. The response was at first disappointing, but some substantial experiments have now been carried out and written up and others are in progress. There appear at present two main foci for experimental work—working with the 'unattached' and counselling services.

Among those young people who are not attached to any recognized unit of the Youth Service are many who, as far as one can tell, do not especially need it. There are others who are unlikely to join any established youth organization but who, it appears, could benefit from adult help of the appropriate kind. There are others, who are also unlikely to approach any established youth organizations, who need highly specialized help, usually of the psychiatric and rehabilitative kind. Efforts to work with the 'unattached' range from the running of a teenage coffee bar in which young people who do not avail themselves of more orthodox youth service facilities may meet, to the kind of project in which workers make contact with the young people concerned in a variety of ways, and follow up the contacts in order to study these young people and their lives in some detail and offer any services or facilities which appear helpful and possible. At the time of writing there seems to be some difficulty in following up the implications of the experiments once these have been made.

The interest in offering counselling services to young people is not a new one among youth workers. The role of personal counsellor has always been one which youth workers have been called upon to play by some members of their organizations, though there seems to be, even now, uncertainty in the minds of a few employing bodies about the propriety of this. Some agencies have recently set up counselling services open to any young people, and the use that has been made of them suggests there is a need for them, at any rate in some places.

The Historical Development of Youth Service

Both these new departures have, of course, implications for training which have yet to be thoroughly examined. The findings of both kinds of work point quite often to failures in other parts of the community—to difficulties whose beginnings in the lives of the young people concerned occurred long before they approached Youth Service age.

It would be wrong to suggest that the Youth Service has never before offered anything to those outside its organizations. Some County and County Borough Youth Services maintain youth orchestras, choirs, outdoor pursuits, centres and other things, which are open to all young people of Youth Service age. That the new experimental efforts are also being carried on outside organization walls encourages one to think that the Youth Service is now beginning to think of itself as no longer almost exclusively 'organization bound', and truly as a Service for young people.

7

The Infinite Variety of Youth Groups

✴

Because of the similarity of aim and purpose of most youth groups in Great Britain, and because of the way in which until recently most grew up around persons rather than ideologies, it is almost impossible to classify them and certainly impossible to evaluate them. Most youth organizations would maintain that their aim is to plan and carry out a 'balanced' programme of activities which should cater for the physical, emotional, mental and spiritual welfare of the adolescent. Their method of carrying out that aim may differ, one seeking, for example, to inculcate a sense of leadership and responsibility through a strictly devised code of training, others through encouraging a large measure of self-government among the members of the group themselves. Nevertheless, allowing for the fact that some groups have uniforms while others do not, that some march while others dance, in actual fact the drama done, for instance, by an Air Training Corps group to raise funds for its annual camp, is much the same as the drama work done by a club which is raising funds for the local church. Whether a group 'does' music or crafts will depend very largely on whether the adolescents concerned can be interested in such an activity and whether a suitable leader of such a group can be found and if necessary paid.

Many inquiries, some more scientific than others, have been carried out from time to time in an effort to discover the trend of adolescent interests; the fact remains that, if the right person undertakes to interest a group of young people in the right way

111

for that group, there is nothing from chess to archery, from photography to the making of a film, from holidays abroad to learning a foreign language, that cannot and has not been carried out successfully in one group or another.

All British youth groups would, however, probably stress their efforts to enable or encourage their members to learn the arts of citizenship and to apply themselves intelligently to the duties and responsibilities of adult citizenship. The members themselves are for the most part unconscious of this, but it does represent, even if they do not know it, the purpose and objective of their organizations. To the members themselves the direct appeal may be any one of a great variety of interests—Christian fellowship, rolling bandages, or breeding rabbits. Solemn dissertations on 'citizenship' and 'obligations' are seldom heard, but in practice most members of youth groups respond readily to calls for service and responsibility when those calls are to do definite, clear and concrete jobs.

Most of the national youth organizations began as small local units, which at some point 'federated' or 'associated', or united with other like-minded groups in their region which later formed a National Association or Council. Most of these national youth organizations had emerged well before 1939.

They differ considerably one from another but their unity of principle is symbolized nowadays in their membership of the Standing Conference of National Voluntary Youth Organizations. They range from the Girls' Friendly Society to the Welsh League of Youth, from the Young Women's Christian Association to the National Federation of Young Farmers' Clubs. Each has its distinguishing characteristic, its own motif or ethos, its own distinctive appeal. All, as a body, show at its best that British spirit of initiative, independence of State control, and self-government, which has been the inspiration of so much that is valuable in our national life and, at their worst, all show the principle of fragmentation seemingly inseparable from a democratic way of life.

But it must not be forgotten that even today, in countless towns and villages in the United Kingdom, there are youth groups which owe affiliations to no local education authority or national agency and which have flourished for decades. Others spring up and flourish for a year or so and then die away. There is nothing to stop anyone starting a new type of youth group—or opening a club for boys and girls—and it would, of course, be impossible to control or to enumerate the so-called 'spontaneous groups' into which adolescents themselves collect from time to time.

Broadly speaking one can classify the various youth groups into the uniformed groups; those sponsored by the Churches; the undenominational groups, who work through what has become known as 'the club method'; and those whose approach is through some specialized activity. But immediately one's classification breaks down for some church groups wear uniforms and some uniformed groups are geared to one special interest.

Classification on the basis of sex is not easy or very helpful. Most of the uniformed organizations cater for one sex only, but beyond this it is difficult to make clear statements. The Young Women's Christian Association organizes youth clubs mainly for both sexes together; church clubs, fellowships and guilds tend to be mixed and single-sex clubs; the National Association of Boys' Clubs affiliates clubs for boys only and boys' sections of mixed clubs. There has been a trend for some time towards mixed work, and the number of units for girls only has probably decreased considerably. No account, therefore, of the kinds of youth groups to be found in Great Britain could possibly be exhaustive. All that one can hope to do is to pick out some of the main trends in some of these organizations, most of which have their own literature which is readily available for those who wish to make a more careful study of their work.

UNIFORMED ORGANIZATIONS

The oldest of these is the Boys' Brigade, founded in 1884 by that great pioneer, Sir William Smith, though it was closely followed by the Church Lads' Brigade. The former has close affiliations with nonconformity, as the latter has with the Anglican Church. In most of these units Bible study is still a compulsory activity, as is also attendance at church parades. Their declared aim is to ensure that by the promotion of habits of obedience, reverence, discipline and self-respect, their members may become responsible, self-reliant and useful men and women.

The most celebrated uniformed organizations, of course, are the Scouts and Guides, because of their world-wide affiliations. It would be impossible to do justice to all that youth groups owe to

Baden-Powell's ideas on informal education, and impossible to praise too highly their excellent outdoor activities and their work in the pre-adolescent age groups.

The pre-service organizations, as their name implies, owe their allegiance to three various parent bodies of the Armed Services: the Army Cadets, the Air Training Corps and the Sea Cadets. All the pre-Service organizations were in existence long before 1939. Their expansion was deliberately undertaken for the purposes of war, to make boys into better sailors, soldiers and airmen when their time came to join one or other of the Services. The appeal of uniform, the glamour of sharing in the lives of the adult Services, the genuine eagerness to do a job of work for their country, all had an effect in attracting boys and girls. But this was a wartime appeal and, as might be expected, as the urgency of the training for the war effort disappeared membership declined. This does not mean that these organizations do not make an important appeal to certain types of boys and girls but it is so specific as to be obvious, so that all who run may read. On the whole their training and discipline are good, they teach young people something very definite and valuable, and it is one of the few forms of youth work in which one can see demonstrable results. Even in the matter of improving the posture of boys and girls, uniformed organizations have probably made an enormous contribution to the physical well-being of the nation. As long as a pre-Service unit is directed by men and women with breadth of vision and understanding, there seems no need to worry about excessive militarization. Moreover, experience has shown that where the pre-Service unit does not cater for some social life, the adolescent's first flush of enthusiasm tends to wane: a tacit proof that though the glamour of the uniform—and 'playing at soldiers'—has its fascination, something more is needed to hold all but the more serious-minded young recruits.

CLUB WORK—CHURCH GROUPS

The Churches have every right to maintain that they were among the first in the field in any form of group work. But Church Clubs or Youth Fellowships and kindred organizations also vary very much from Church to Church and from place to place. They may take the form of 'open' clubs, i.e. clubs open to young people in the neighbourhood whether they are members of the Church or not, so that, in a sense, they are undenominational; or they may be 'closed' clubs for Church members only. Whatsoever form they take, however, they still play a prominent part in the life of the community.

Unfortunately the necessity to make money to pay for the up-keep of the Church as a whole has frequently meant that its youth work has been sacrificed to adult interests and to more financially profitable undertakings such as the weekly whist drive. Even among Church groups who pay lip service to youth work, there is only too often a tendency to make the youth group 'give up their night' if other groups need the premises periodically, and as everyone knows, a youth group which cannot rely on its regular evenings, is a youth group which soon disappears. Another unattractive feature of some Church groups is the tendency to exploit their youth. While it is right and proper that young people should give service to the Church that houses them, many young people have been made increasingly restive and eventually embittered by the constant pressure that their major interests should be sacrificed to the sort of craft work suitable for the church bazaar, and the sort of drama suitable for the Nativity play and the Christmas carol service. This, of course, is not Church policy, but the fault of individual clergy or their congregations who are out of touch with the needs and temptations of modern youth, people who seem to have become experts in sinless existence, and who are viewed by all but the most priggish young people with either uncomfortable awe or irreverent impatience. These are the people who are not slow to reproach the young when they find other interests and other accommodation, and who lament the decline of Church-going. These are the people who are quick to blame the schools for the quality of their religious education. But it is only when we admit once and for all that we cannot teach religion, any more than we can teach anything else, and that we can only give people the opportunity to live a religious life, and that a religious life is by no means divorced from a joyful life, that such Churches will begin to regain their hold on the adolescent. In the early 1940s quite a number of such Churches 'took up' youth work, seeing in it a method of increasing their Church membership, but when they found that such work is demanding of time and often destructive of property and that Church membership did not always increase rapidly, enthusiasm quickly waned, and a fresh opportunity to make the Church the neighbourhood community it was in medieval times was lost. Happily this sad picture is not universal; Church youth groups have increased and multiplied since 1939 and some of the best youth work is done under the auspices of the Churches.

SETTLEMENTS AND COMMUNITY CENTRES

In the slum the Settlement was often the social centre of the whole neighbourhood—educational, recreational and religious; the headquarters of such organizations as the Charity Organization Society and the Poor Man's Lawyer, and more latterly the Citizens' Advice Bureau and the Ante-natal Clinic. The Settlements (originally a house in a slum area, where young men and women with a desire to do social work lived with the people they worked for) at the turn of the century were almost entirely staffed by university men and women and they still obtain a great deal of their finance from universities and public schools. They are still excellent training-grounds for various branches of social work, but as the slum clearance programme has advanced, and as material poverty has happily declined, much of the old urgency disappeared, as did indeed a large proportion of the population which formerly crowded in upon them. In some areas a new population is growing up around the settlements as new housing developments are completed. Some settlements which in the late 1950s had given up youth work in favour of other neighbourhood services, have started youth work again usually employing full-time trained youth workers.

Since the 1930s the Community Centre movement has received fresh impetus. Before the war slum-clearing housing estate schemes very seldom catered for anything other than re-housing, and throughout the country thousands of houses were built without any consideration for social amenities. In some notorious cases no site was prepared even for a school, and there were many such arid wastes as Dagenham and Becontree up and down the country with miles and miles of houses and no shops, no churches, and not even a public house. Many Community Centres started in the houses of tenants themselves, and are as much centred round an individual personality as any of the older groupings. In some places a house was made into the social club of the neighbourhood and in many cases since the war premises of a semi-permanent or permanent nature have been built in a creditable number of cases by the tenants themselves with the assistance of some grant aid. The Community Centres cater for every variety of interest and the only criticism one could offer is that some of them stress the adult side of their work at the expense of the adolescent. Education authorities have power to give grants to community associations, and in the new towns community centres have been recognized as desirable and necessary for the growth of community life. Many community associations have always sponsored and supported their own youth organizations, and since 1960 some combined community and youth centres have been built. These usually have some shared and some separate facilities, and though there can be difficulties, there is much to be said for not isolating youth from the rest of the community in social life. In some of these combined centres a community Warden and a Youth Centre Warden or Leader have been appointed. In others a joint appointment has been made. Neither of these arrangements has proved always to be a happy one, and it seems likely that this is more often due to lack of careful thought and planning before appointments are made, and to lack of confidence in their positions on the part of the persons appointed, than to anything intrinsic in either situation. There is a case for training at least some people for both these positions together and the short-comings in the present training of both community centre wardens and youth workers are very probably responsible for difficulties that either may have in appreciating the work of the other and in co-operating with him.

CLUBS AND YOUTH CENTRES

Apart from the youth organizations attached to churches, settlements and community associations, there are others sponsored by the local education authorities, or by local voluntary committees. They may have their own premises, or use hired accommodation or school buildings. They may meet once a week only or be open every night of the week and week-ends, or anything in between these two. They may be staffed by one or two full-time, employed leaders with some part-time paid staff and some voluntary workers; by part-time and voluntary workers; or by voluntary workers only. Membership may be anything from thirty to about five hundred, and a few centres have memberships of up to 1,000. Some of these clubs and centres are set up by the Young Men's Christian Association and others by the Young Women's Christian Association. In such cases the club members are offered opportunity for associate or full membership of the association, but they are in no way obliged to take either. Any of these clubs and centres, like the church clubs, settlement clubs and community association clubs, may, if they choose, and if they fulfil the minimum conditions, become affiliated to the National Association of Youth Clubs, or the National Association of Boys' Clubs, or in some cases both, either directly or through local associations.

The number of youth clubs and ventures sponsored by the local education authorities has increased since 1960, but policy varies from authority to authority. In some places increased activity is represented by an increase on the part of the voluntary organizations financially aided by the authority. The majority of the clubs and centres mentioned in the last paragraph receive financial aid in some form from their authority.

Since the number of full-time leaders has increased there have been some new developments in rural areas where only small numbers of young people can get together in any one place with any regularity. In one place, the pattern has emerged of one full-time leader in a larger town, in charge of a club there and responsible for the supervision of voluntary or part-time paid leaders of small groups in surrounding small villages. In another area, 'peripatetic' leaders have been appointed, each to the leadership of four or five separate small clubs in different villages in an area.

SEPARATE OR MIXED MEMBERSHIP

During the 1940s there was considerable heated discussion about the wisdom of single-sex or mixed youth groups. Most of the heat has now died down, and not surprisingly it is generally accepted that the Youth Service should offer young people opportunities to mix with the opposite sex, and to be only with members of their own sex at times. Whether this is done by means of separate clubs which on occasion meet together or bring in their girl friends or boy friends or whether it is done by means of mixed clubs whose members sometimes meet separately, is largely a matter of personal preference, expediency and, to some extent, historical accident. The recent trend has been markedly towards mixed membership groups. Statements that used to be made about girls of sixteen years only being interested in boys of eighteen years, and boys of sixteen years not being interested in any girls, have been rendered manifestly untenable by young people themselves. Far more of them now than formerly have been in mixed classes at school, and it is fashionable among quite young adolescents to be at home in mixed company. A number of them do go through a phase of feeling a little awkward in each other's company, but those who feel that way need not, in most youth organizations, go any further than be in the same room or building with each other, and if they can learn to do this without fuss and without behaving artificially, they are making progress in their social development.

SIZE OF MEMBERSHIP

The large youth club or youth centre with several hundred members is, with a few exceptions, a development which came after 1940. There was some misgiving about this development in its early days because of the need for a youth leader to know members individually if he is to do anything significant with them. Even so, the fact that young people flocked in their hundreds to these places, even when they were uncomfortably housed in unsuitable premises, was indisputable evidence of the need for them. The intricacies of manning a youth centre with sixteen exit doors, three helpers and 600 members has to be endured to be understood, and the most vociferous criticism of large centres was made at a time when premises and helpers were in very short supply. In suitable premises and with adequate staffing, however, much good work can be done in large centres. It is not simply the number of helpers that matters, but the quality of their work. If staff members are no more than 'club minders' commercial enterprise can offer better facilities than the Youth Service, but if the staff members really understand that the personal development of the young people is the first priority, and if the leader is not only skilled at working with young people himself but also in working through his helpers, good large-scale work is possible.

The Infinite Variety of Youth Groups

AGE RANGE

The official Youth Service age range is fourteen to twenty-one years but many organizations have always catered for a wider range than this. The Y.W.C.A., for instance, has always worked with 'young marrieds' and other young adults, and many voluntary youth organizations have always had their junior sections which usually cater for boys and girls between ten and fourteen years. The uniformed organizations in particular have done this. Community Associations and Settlements have traditionally worked with children's and adult groups as well as with youth groups.

Some youth workers seem particularly prone to the temptation to try to be all things to all men, and this can easily end in their being nothing to anybody. To attempt to serve all these age groups in the same place at the same time is usually disastrous, for their needs and interests are almost certain to conflict with each other. Some division of either time or space is necessary. If this is possible (and sometimes we have to admit that it is not) there need not be over-rigid boundaries, and some crossing over for particular purposes can be advantageous to all concerned. Drama and music can, for instance, successfully span all the age groups, and some social events can embrace all members and include parents. The age at which a member moves from one section to another need not be rigid either. A span of, say, eighteen months, before which a junior may not move into the Youth Section and after which he may not remain in the junior section, can accommodate a considerable amount of variation in individual development and the natural desire to wait for one's pal who may be a few months younger.

SPECIAL INTEREST GROUPS

Just as youth centres, and many Church fellowships, are mixed, so are many Young Farmers' Clubs, many Cycling Groups and many of the groups who visit the Youth Hostels as a party. All these have a definite and specific aim but, on the whole, they cater for those young people who have a definite hobby, be it walking, cycling, keeping bees, or camping, and their chief difficulties seem to be those of finding suitable meeting places in winter where they can keep their summer enthusiasm alive.

Even in the 'special activity' organizations, however, classification is not easy; the Junior British Red Cross and St. John Ambulance Cadets wear uniform, while the Young Farmers' Clubs and the Co-operative Youth Groups do not. These, as their names imply, come together because of an interest in some special subject towards which the whole of their programme is orientated.

Unlike continental youth work, youth groups in Great Britain are seldom politically conscious, perhaps because as a nation the British are not politically minded. The three main political parties have their own youth organizations but these, like political groups abroad, cater on the whole for an older age range and are mainly special interest groups. During and since the war a great deal of excellent work has been organized by the Co-operative Youth Movement but, by and large, although some young people have become more politically minded, the political group as such still attracts the young intelligentsia rather than the rank and file of British youth.

SPONTANEOUS YOUTH GROUPS AND YOUTH SQUADS

A great deal of attention has been given to the so-called 'spontaneous' youth groups, by which is meant those groups of young people who go off on their own and do certain things or who meet 'the gang' just in order to sit and talk, or watch a sporting or other event. Like all groups they tend to throw up a leader who is usually the ideas' merchant or the general organizer of the events, the rank and file members and the hangers-on. They usually possess the inevitable 'funny boy' of adolescent gangs, and the girl who is seldom addressed except in terms of 'Oh, you *would*, Mavis'. Nearly all such groups have their hangers-on—the fringe members who are not part of the inner circle and whose attendance is more erratic.

On the whole, 'spontaneous' youth groups tend to be special interest groups—cycling groups which may or may not seek the advantages of affiliation to the Cyclists' Touring Club, groups of hikers—young people who meet to go together to speedway racing —dirt-track events—ice hockey—or even to local dances, cinemas, espresso cafés, coffee bars or record dives.

121

The Infinite Variety of Youth Groups

But there is never any knowing when one's classification of a spontaneous group may break down. For instance, a 'spontaneous' group of cyclists may evolve their own uniform—and would consider themselves a uniformed group. Again spontaneous groups can be composed of one sex or they may be mixed groups. It would be equally wrong to assume that a Church or a Community Centre, a Settlement or a club does not have within it a 'spontaneous' group from time to time. For instance, in the 1940s, one of the most interesting forms of these spontaneous groups developed a loose tie with local education authority Youth Organizers. These were the Youth Service Squads. They were started in East Suffolk, an area where the population is scattered over many small villages.

The original idea of the youth squad was that young people should band together and do definite jobs which were of some urgency owing to war conditions. For example, boys were enlisted to fill sand-bags, girls to distribute A.R.P. animal discs; kerbs were whitened, allotments taken over, gardens kept in order, A.R.P. posts swept and garnished, and many other varieties of work that appeared of moment in the area were undertaken by these groups, who elected their own leader and secretary, and registered the group under the local Youth Committee. A great deal of extremely valuable work was done in this way; for after a little while squads from various villages met one another, and it was possible to arrange for inter-village matches and competitions, leadership courses, and so forth. In this way the country squads developed naturally into social and recreative units. In the towns the squads had great success with the 'tough guy' who felt perfectly happy if he could meet his friends and discuss plans for constructive, or even destructive work, such as killing rats in a surface A.R.P. shelter.

Unfortunately, rather too much was claimed for the scheme in some places, and the enthusiasm of the first years was not always sustained. It was difficult to find fresh activities for them, especially since they were not always encouraged when they offered their services to adult groups. Nevertheless the experiment was an important one and it is regrettable that the lessons learned from it have not been incorporated into some present-day scheme. It was a useful method of coping with the rural problem and of coping with the boy in urban areas who has to be tamed before he can enter even the roughest of clubs, and where the taming has perforce to be the work of his group rather than the work of an adult, however sympathetic. One of the most valuable principles of youth work was maintained in Youth Service Squads in that emphasis was placed on doing for others and feeling for others rather than on talking, or even 'training', while in organizing their own squads the members themselves learned to use their own initiative and to develop responsibility. They elected their own leaders and submitted reports of their activities. All administration was effected by guidance rather than direction.

IN AND OUT CLUBS AND TEENAGE CANTEENS

In some cases young people too wary or shy to be attracted by the more orthodox youth group have been attracted to what during the war were called 'In and Out Clubs', later were called 'Teenage Canteens', and more latterly 'Coffee Bars'.

In and Out Clubs were started in London and other large towns during the war. They were intended for young people who were drifting about in the blackout, often getting into very undesirable company. They were intended as a bright and safe meeting place for young people who were not evacuated with their families and who were at a loose end, since many of their normal entertainments had closed down. An entrance fee of a few pence was payable at the door and the club was yours for the evening. Various table games and a radiogram for dancing were provided and refreshments were usually available at slightly less than commercial prices. The games and dancing rooms were usually in a space separated off from the café tables in another room. There was no membership card and no loyalties were expected or demanded. In most respects the Teenage Canteen of the 1950s was much the same, though the entrance fee was waived in most of them, which is probably not a good thing. Leadership of such groups should be in the hands of the 'manager of the coffee bar' and 'waiters' and 'waitresses' should be helpers, but few groups seem to arrange this in a really imaginative way.

It is indisputable, however, that such places do cater for boys and girls who are suspicious of joining anything which means giving your name and address and binding yourself to a certain regular attendance. The young people come and go but such ventures can surely not be regarded as altogether a failure if they give them a refuge when it is needed and one or two happy evenings. In common with many of the patrons of the In and Out Clubs and the Teenage Canteens, the coffee bars find that once a friendly relationship is established some of the young people demand something 'more like a real club' and in quite a large number of cases a club is eventually found or founded for some of them. It is the old story of first catching your hare and then doing something about it, but if in one's attempts to cater for these difficult people known as 'unorganized youth', one displays a desire to cook the hare too soon after catching it, one only has oneself to blame if one is left stewing in one's own juice.

There is probably room for at least one of these youth cafés in every large town; it does a very useful piece of work for those young people who are very diffident and very unwilling to come out of their reserved anonymity. Such 'clubs' are of course costly and it is difficult to produce the quick and tidy results which many people demand. There is a regrettable tendency to measure the success of such ventures by the number who are transferred to 'the club proper'. And yet it is difficult to see why young people should always be under the burden of improving themselves in their meeting places. After all, the responsible adult members of far more celebrated and indubitably respectable clubs are not considered unworthy because they merely go in and out, using them as meeting places without making many contacts and certainly making no contribution beyond their membership fees.

THE UNATTACHED

In addition to these varied youth groups with their clearly defined aims and objects, many attempts have been made to capture the interests of those young people who were once called, usually unfairly, 'unclubbable', sometimes erroneously assumed to be 'toughs', and now usually labelled 'the unattached'. The label tends to be used indiscriminately and, for those who work in the Youth Service, too easily suggests that all young people who are outside it are of the same kind. This, of course, is not so, nor is it true that all the young people who do not use the Youth Service are in some kind of difficulty. There are certainly some adolescents who are of the breed of Kipling's Cat Who Walked by Himself—

The Infinite Variety of Youth Groups

boys and girls who prefer to 'gang their own gait' and keep rabbits, watch birds, make things or go places, all on their own or with a carefully selected mate—mates and girls who will resist all our efforts to 'take them out of themselves', or who will maintain as one did when pressed, 'they like to choose the company they keep'. It is salutary to remember that many such 'isolates' have contributed some of the best gifts to mankind.

It is salutary to remember, too, as one investigation shows, that there are other normal, socially healthy young people who spend a good deal of time in small groups, who know about the Youth Service, but who do not consider the units of it which are available to them worth their while to join.

Those upon whom the interest really centres are those young people who are in difficulties because of their own social incompetence or their own anti-social attitudes and behaviour. The task is to identify them and to learn to work with them. Working with them requires considerable skill and patience. A certain amount of experimental work of this kind has been going on, from early efforts such as the Barge Club to a number of more recent efforts including the Y.W.C.A./L.U.Y.C. (London Union of Youth Clubs) Coffee Stall Project. Experience is now beginning to be accumulated, and from it we should begin to learn more about the possibilities of serving the needs of these particular young people, and about the kind of training that those people who will work with them require. Accounts of some of this work are now available in published form and the details will not therefore be retailed here.

Youth workers are liable to be caught between the devil and the deep blue sea because they are either accused of wasting their time and public money on 'ne'er-do-wells' who do not appreciate what is done for them, or of working with the respectable youngsters who are in need of much less help than the 'toughs' and the anti-social youngsters who in fact seldom go near established youth clubs or other officially recognized organizations. Both these accusations betray an incomplete grasp of the purpose of the Youth Service, and a lack of understanding of the nature of the work. The Youth Service exists for young people, not just those young people who are found wanting, or not found wanting, as the case may be, as judged by some other members of the community. There is no sharp division between the respectable young people and the anti-social, and in any case who is to say that the respectable youngster did not become or remain so partly because of his youth club experience, or on the other hand that the anti-social would become respectable if they had youth club experience?

Conceptually, one could arrange all the young people in a community along a continuum with the most anti-social at one end, the most socially acceptable at the other, and all the rest in order of respectability in between. A youth organization made up of members mainly from one half of the continuum would produce a certain kind of ethos which would in the main be unattractive to those who were placed on the line some distance away. The youth leader, whose concern is the further social development of members, has to start with them at whatever stage they have reached. Individually, of course, they will all be at different stages, but groups who are approximately at the same stage will tend to come together as they will naturally find each other's company satisfying. The needs of the more advanced and the socially backward can seldom be met at the same time and place, and a youth leader must have extensive premises and staff if he is to do this—more extensive than most youth organizations have at present. It is legitimate for a youth worker to work with any group and he usually wants to work with as many young people as he can. The members of any well-established, socially advanced club are not themselves very likely to welcome the introduction of people whose interests and standards would interfere with and possibly destroy what they have built up; nor incidentally would all the parents of these members approve of such a move. An established group of less sophisticated and less socially acceptable young people would view with suspicion the suggestion of joining or being joined by a group of socially advanced young people, who would appear to them to be associated with adult authority, with which they have not yet come to terms.

CONCLUSION

This is by no means the complete picture. In youth work as in all fields of human endeavour the pattern is constantly changing, and it would be a mistake to imagine that because the life of any group is short, or because various types of group gain and then lose their popularity, they have therefore failed in their purpose. It is safe to believe, what is usually the truth, that any given youth

The Infinite Variety of Youth Groups

group flourishes for as long as it fulfils some adolescent need. It is also wise to reflect that the greater the variety of choice with which the adolescent is confronted, the greater the chance that he will find a group particularly suited to his needs. In that variety of choice lies the greatest safeguard to all the dangers of one national 'youth movement'. The critics can point to much overlapping and consequent wasted effort in a field where the labourers arc still too few, but on balance it is believed by most people that uniformity has greater dangers than variety has disadvantages.

8

Youth Leadership

✳

There is no greater indication of the social changes that have occurred over the last three or four decades than the changing pattern of youth leadership; and nowhere is the change of emphasis displayed more than in changes in the wording of the aims of various units. Over a half-century they seem to have moved in this kind of progression: 'To *give* whatever is most lacking . . .'; 'to *broaden* their lives . . .'; 'to *provide* advantages . . .'; 'to *help* those who have not had the advantages . . .'; 'to *help* the members *themselves* to obtain . . .'; 'to *offer opportunities* for . . .'.

Such differing phraseology indicates not only changed views about the functions of the leader, but changes in attitude towards the members. The function of the nineteenth-century youth group was to make young people respectable citizens; standards were to be improved and authority imposed. Now the function is expressed in terms of offering young people opportunities through which they may develop more their potentialities and therefore become more effective adult members of the community.

In the early days the word 'leader' seldom occurred. The phrases used changed with the years from 'Lady in Charge' to 'Lady Superintendent', from 'Manager' to 'Skipper', and the members were almost invariably referred to as 'my girls' or 'my lads'. The pronoun indicated a degree of possessiveness which had its endearing and its domineering qualities. The term 'leader' seems to have been established at least by the mid-1930s, and it may well be that we were comfortable with its connotations at that time, but certainly from the early 1940s onwards we have from time to time been troubled about it. It suggests too readily that the part of the

128

young people is merely to follow—passively or submissively. It suggests also that the leader always knows where the young people are going, want to go, or should go. Sometimes we try to overcome our difficulty about the idea of leading by saying that the leadership comes from behind, but if the leader is behind, is he leading? And may he not sometimes be driving? The term 'youth worker' has become much more prevalent in the 1960s because it avoids these difficulties, but the official title is still usually Youth Leader, or Warden of a Youth Centre. Social change is also reflected in the change of mode of address between members and workers. Not so long back, it was usual for women to be addressed by members as 'Miss' and occasionally 'Miss or Mrs. X', and for men to be called 'Sir' or 'Skip', while the workers invariably used the first names or nicknames of members. Now it is far more usual for first names to be used in both cases.

At first, all youth work was unpaid and was headed by a lady or gentleman of private means who quite often undertook practically all the financial responsibility entailed and arranged a rota of friends to help. Since that time the number of youth groups has increased, and a social revolution has taken place, and by the late 1940s and 1950s the problem of finding enough people to do youth work had become almost intractable. This was not solely because people were less willing to give their services, but because the whole condition of our living had changed. As we happily no longer have a massive underprivileged class called 'the poor', neither do we have any more a leisured class in the old sense of that term. But people do have leisure, and between us all it may be that we have more leisure than our counterparts two generations ago, and although it is impossible to calculate even approximate figures or proportions, it is still true that a very large number of people still do give voluntary service to youth work. This is particularly true in the uniformed organizations and the smaller one-night-a-week clubs.

The work is now too extensive for it all to be done by interested people in their spare time. This change has been a gradual one. By the end of the 1914–18 war many of the larger clubs already had paid leaders, even if it was only in the sense that the secretary to the committee, who also took on most of the duties of leadership, was given an honorarium or a small salary. This was often merely intended to eke out the private means which were still almost a *sine qua non* of youth work. But even in some of the smaller clubs an 'honorarium' was often given to a 'leader', who was very much the servant of an active working committee which, nevertheless, no longer had the time to do the day-to-day work of running the club.

This process was accelerated in the 1930s and much of the grant aid which came from the Jubilee Trust fund during the years immediately before 1939 was expended on club leaders' salaries. The expansion of the youth service after 1939 and the increased pace of the social revolution combined to make youth leadership at one and the same time a profession still struggling for professional status, and a vocation shared by many men and women from all walks of life, ranging from agricultural labourers to retired generals, from the village postmistress to the squire's lady.

The publication of the McMair Report—*The Training of Teachers and Youth Leaders*—in 1942 was a great step forward in that it embodied recommendations for the training of professional youth leaders and for the recognition of youth leadership as a professional career. Its recommendations were never implemented, but it did make it clear that the fact that most youth work was voluntary was no good reason for thinking that youth work was something for which training is neither demanded nor deemed necessary. Several universities provided training for full-time youth workers for a time after 1939, but very few candidates indeed came forward for it in any one year. Professional training therefore ran down almost to a standstill, and status, salaries and conditions of work remained indefinite.

At the same time there were interesting developments taking place in the effort to 'train' voluntary or part-time youth workers, to give them some of the confidence which comes from mastering some, at all events, of the techniques of the job. In this the voluntary organizations were the pioneers before 1939, and were greatly helped by the Jubilee Trust, and later the King George VI Memorial Foundation Fund. In the 1940s and 1950s most local education authorities and national voluntary organizations were engaging in a great deal of part-time, *ad hoc* and in-service training for their voluntary and part-time paid workers. This took the form of conferences, week-end training courses, residential summer schools, or a series of evening lectures and demonstrations. It says much for that array of volunteers, as it does for their present-day counterparts in 'Bessey' courses, that in addition to giving time to youth work, they also give up many week-ends and evenings to training.

During the 1940s and 1950s, short courses, drama and music festivals, sports, galas and exhibitions became almost part of the stock-in-trade of the local education authority and voluntary association organizers. Undoubtedly such work helped leaders to improve standards, and encouraged new work. Above all it gave everyone a chance to learn from others. Such events also had great merit in that they worked both ways; one can learn from both good and bad work. As an awkward club member once put it, 'Well, whatever you may say about our club, we're at least not as bad as St. X's. . . .' But one did begin to wonder whether some of those in administrative posts were using the 'event' for producing results for public admiration, or for justifying their own positions, rather than as a method of training. In some areas leaders became so encompassed about by extra-curricular events and short 'trainings' that one wondered if the ordinary programme of the unit ever materialized. Loyalty to the organization or considerations of efficiency, rather than concern for the needs of the members, seemed to make leaders feel morally bound to enter for everything. When 'events' are designed to raise standards, and short courses are planned with some element of progression, they are obviously helpful, but it is undeniable that a great many of the same people seemed to keep on being 'introduced' to adolescent psychology or 'youth drama' year after year.

Though full-time training was nearly at a standstill through the later 1940s and the 1950s, there was some debate and a good deal of uncertainty about what the training ought to consist of. Since 1939 when the Board of Education (later the Ministry and later still the Department of Education and Science) became actively concerned with youth work, much of the thinking about youth work had an 'educational slant', and a significant proportion of the new full-time leaders who came into the Service at that time, came from a background of teaching experience and training. In an older tradition the basis of a full-time worker's training had been social science rather than education, and the work was associated with social work in the minds of many. Though the full-time workers in the Service were not very many, there were among them people with both these backgrounds, and there was some conflict of opinion about which training basis was the 'right one', neither side of the argument knowing very much about the training background of the other, and both, no doubt, feeling insecure in a new situation.

Training was, therefore, no new subject for the Service to be concerned with, either in respect of full-time or part-time and voluntary workers, when the Albemarle and Bessey Reports appeared in the early 1960s. But this time the need for action was seen as urgent. The need to ensure that there would be reasonable salaries and conditions of work for those recruited to the service was also recognized, and the first report of the Joint Negotiating Committee for Salaries and Conditions of Work appeared in 1961. The old argument about the basis of training for youth work became very largely irrelevant since those concerned with social work and those concerned with education are now finding a great deal of common ground and training for youth work gains from both partners. The main concern about training for full-time youth work is now the extent to which the training needs to go. The McMair committee, reporting in the third year of war, could not hope for immediate extensive action. It saw some action as immediately necessary, but beyond this made little concession to the exigencies of its time. The wisdom of the Albemarle committee's training recommendations is to be found mainly in the restraint exercised in making demands. This at least meant that the proposals were seen as possible, and action was not, therefore, delayed. Compared with the McMair proposals made twenty years earlier, however, the training which the majority of recruits to full-time leadership now receive is short and, though intensive, scarcely adequate. The conflict now is between the desire to train adequately and the desire to train quickly in order to answer the call for more and more trained leaders. The short (one-year) training was envisaged by the Albemarle committee as a five-year emergency measure, but the rate of expansion of the Service and the consequent demand for leaders has already meant the retention of 'emergency' training beyond that span of time. Whether or not full-time youth leadership is a lifetime career is still an unanswered question. At one time it was generally assumed not to be, and the assumption is still held by many people. The establishment of reasonable salary scales and conditions of work have made it more possible, and at least some full-time leaders appear to think of themselves remaining in the work until retirement, but there is at present no career structure in the field of leadership.

Being a youth leader (not a helper or assistant) can mean many different things. It may mean being a voluntary leader in one's spare time, with a unit which perhaps meets regularly only once a week, and sometimes engages in week-end activities. It may mean being a part-time paid leader in one's spare time with a full-time job outside the Youth Service. The part-time paid leader is often in charge of a unit that operates two, three or four evenings a week, and possibly some week-ends as well. Many voluntary and part-time leaders undertake training for the work, and this can vary from the '*ad hoc*' day course to one evening a week over two years, plus a number of residential week-ends, and practical work in a club other than one's own. It may mean being a full-time leader, and this term itself covers a multitude of variations. There are some whose unit is based in a building of its own, some whose unit operates in a school, some in 'youth wings' attached to schools and some in other, usually hired, premises. Some leaders are mainly occupied directly with members of the unit; others are primarily occupied with administration and organization for education or recreation, for very large numbers—occasionally between 500 and 1,000; some are managers of coffee bars; and some work with 'unattached' groups with no permanent location or formal membership basis. There are those who work only with a youth unit; those who are 'teacher-leaders' whose duties include some work in a school; those who are also in charge of a community centre, and those who work in partnership with a community centre warden; leaders may be members of the staff of a Y.M.C.A. centre or settlement; and in some rural areas there are 'leader-organizers' who have a unit for which they are directly responsible together with supervisory duties with smaller units in the surrounding area. There are also 'peripatetic leaders' with direct responsibility for a group of units in neighbouring villages. Some leaders are employed by local education authorities, with or without a management committee, others by voluntary agencies, but their salaries are usually heavily grant-aided by the local authorities. Some are employed by local authorities and seconded to work for voluntary agencies.

Even this is not an exhaustive catalogue, but it demonstrates that the term youth leader is by no means self-explanatory in terms of function. Is there a common denominator of purpose and function for the full-time worker in all these varied situations? In order to get on with the job in hand, training agencies are bound to make assumptions about how to interpret the generally stated aim of the Youth Service—'to help young people to make the best of themselves and act responsibly . . .'. They have to decide what understanding and skills the full-time worker receives and to design an appropriate training programme. The Youth Service as a whole cannot reasonably be expected to make one definitive statement about the function of its full-time workers, at any rate at present, but there needs to be orderly, realistic, on-going discussion between the training agencies and employing agencies, in which purpose, function and training requirements are seen as common concerns. Initial training is not something which produces 'finished products'. It can only prepare beginners. With such a wide variety of demands being made by the field on full-time leaders, it seems important that the Service as a whole should consider what the common elements are in its views of the functions of these employees. Training agencies might then be better able to serve the field by concentrating on these. Even with longer courses, the training agencies are unlikely to be able to go much further than this. The rest is a matter for in-service training in the field, and the Service needs to be structured in such a way as to provide for this.

9

Youth Group Organization: Management, Helpers' and Members' Committees

✳

There are moments when we all feel the truth of the famous definition of a committee—'A group of people who individually can do nothing and collectively decide that nothing can be done'—but the fact remains that although their nuisance value is often great, a committee can, if properly educated, give any official the moral support and encouragement which is so sadly needed from time to time.

Ideally all clubs should have two committees to attend to the internal organization (the members' and the helpers' committees) and all youth clubs should also have a management committee.

When the group is financed and controlled by the local education authority, the management committee is often the Youth Committee or some section of it, and need concern us little here, though its duties and responsibilities should be much the same and it should give just the same support to the warden as the management committee of a voluntary club. When the club is financed and controlled by a voluntary body a management committee is essential, not only because it is responsible for raising at least some of the money needed to finance the club but also by virtue of that very elementary law that he who pays the piper has the right to call at least some of the tunes that are being played.

Time and time again one hears complaints from leaders about their management committees—'they take no interest', or 'they

135

are only interested in the balance sheet', or 'they never come to the club except on gala occasions', 'they won't *come* to committees'. Probably half the trouble is that the club leader or secretary does not make the meetings interesting enough, and that there is not enough careful preparation beforehand, and not enough sympathetic understanding between the only three officials it is necessary to have on such a committee—the chairman, the treasurer, and the secretary-leader. I am unrepentant in believing that this last is ideally a combined office. Difficult as it is if the leader is a paid officer of the management committee, it is much easier in the long run for all concerned if these two offices are combined.

It is part of the business of the club leader or secretary to make friends with the chairman and the treasurer. He or she should be prepared to assume full responsibility for carrying into action the decisions that have been made. The chairman is responsible for the order of the meeting, for protecting the officials and guiding discussion, but unless we take our chairman into our confidence we must not be surprised if from time to time we do not find it easy to get the support we wish from our committee. No chairman can guide if he has no guidance from those responsible for the actual organization. Management committees need not be the dull matters they sometimes are, or eternal wrangles about money (what we cannot afford or what we could do if we could afford it). The committee should get a full and interesting picture of the life of the group. We should not lay ourselves open to the reproach a councillor once levelled at his education committee: 'I wangled myself on to the education committee,' he said, 'because I am interested in education, and I served on it for six years before I even heard the word education mentioned!'

Management meetings should be called regularly and the statutory ten days' notice should be given. People involved in what has become known as 'the youth field' often lose both sympathy and support because they seem unable to grasp the fact that the sort of people who sit on management committees usually sit on many other committees (that is why they are so useful to us). They are much tried if, in a busy life, we seem to expect them to lay everything else aside at a day or so's notice to attend to our affairs to the neglect of their many other commitments.

No management committee ought to find it necessary to meet

more than quarterly, so there is no reason why a fixed meeting for the first Monday, Friday, or second Thursday, whichever it is, should not be adopted to give people a chance to get the 'X-Club Committee' habit. This question of regularity matters for our helpers' and members' committees too, but here one is helped by the greater frequency with which they should meet.

Again, one can never take too much trouble over an agenda. It is not simply a jumble of items but a recipe for a good meeting. Even the order in which items appear is important. We have all experienced the intense irritation of making a special effort to attend a meeting because of a particular item on the agenda, a really interesting and constructive item, but placed just before 'any other business'. The minutes, the various reports and financial statement are listened to with growing impatience and just as one's foot is in the stirrup of one's particular hobby horse, one catches sight of the time and is faced with the stark fact that one must go or else miss bus, friend, or next engagement. When a committee is faced with a controversial subject it is usually a good idea to put it on fairly soon, when people are fresh and tempers less ruffled. Human nature being what it is, if there are *two* controversial subjects, one can, by tactful planning of the agenda, often arrange it that they weary themselves so much over Item 4 that they are in no mood to battle again over Item 7. This is a much fairer procedure than that of springing something on them unexpectedly under 'any other business' (when we hope half of them will have left, anyway!) because there *is* a sporting chance that having won, or lost, Item 4, they may be prepared to forgive Item 7.

Another useful thing to remember is that one can obtain subjects from the committee which they wish to discuss and give them a place on the agenda. It does not seem to be appreciated always that any member of the committee has a *right* to send in items for the agenda.

The Clerk of the House of Commons once gave some very wise advice about committees; he said that only three rules need ever be strictly adhered to in order to secure smooth functioning. In the first place the chair must be the sole authority, and enforce order and decorum to avoid waste of time; secondly, it is for the convenience of members that they should know what business to expect, and they should not be taken by surprise; and lastly, although the unforeseen will happen, in the House of Commons as elsewhere, there ought to be no unnecessary departure from the programme.

Minute-keeping should be *accurate*, but most amateurs make the mistake of making the minutes much too full. It is not really of world-shattering importance that Mrs. Jones proposed and Mrs. Smith seconded the proposal that the caretaker be paid 2s. 6d. extra for his services at the jumble sale and that it is carried unanimously. 'Resolved that the caretaker . . .' will do just as well and save time in both the wording and the saying.

It should not be necessary to say so, but it is just as well that both chairman and secretary should have some knowledge of committee method and procedure. It is wiser *not* to surrender to the vanity of having an elaborate constitution if one can possibly avoid it. Constitutions serve very little purpose except that of providing additional argument; they are alleged to make matters business-like but as they are always being amended or rescinded they certainly do not save time. When one remembers that Britain managed fairly well for all those years without a written constitution, it is surely not beyond the bounds of possibility that the Little Slowcombe-under-Mud youth club can manage with something fairly simple.

Lastly, one should encourage all the members of the committee to say what they have to say *in committee*, and not afterwards. As long as we believe in majority decisions each member of the committee is in honour bound to be loyal to the decisions of the body. One of the reasons why democracy is such a difficult thing to work is the fact that too many of our self-styled democrats, both in local government and in voluntary associations, feel that if they fail to get their own way in committee they owe it to their principles to sabotage the policy of the majority. By what underhand methods this is done from time to time could only be adequately dealt with by one who has served on many a town council, man and boy, for forty years.

The assistants, voluntary helpers, instructors, part-timers—all kinds in fact, including caretaker and cleaners—together with the youth leader, form the staff of the youth club or centre. One important task of the youth leader is to lead this team of adults, who, with him, are committed to carrying out the policy of the management committee in helping the young people to develop their potentialities and to grow into effective, responsible members of the community. Sometimes a helper may also be a member of the management committee, and may even be Chairman. This should not affect his attitude to the leader when performing his duties as helper, but the need to play a dual role can create difficulties for one or both of the parties. Where this happens, it is probably better for the member of the management committee to cease acting as a helper as well. Some helpers may be instructors, coming to teach a particular activity to a group at a regular weekly time. These are probably employed for the purpose by the local education authority, and the club or centre that receives their services is expected to provide a reasonably regular group of members to form a class and adequate space and equipment. Some may be employed by the local education authority as assistants to the leader though this normally happens only when the leader himself is a part-time or a full-time employee of that authority. Some may be interested people who are giving voluntary service, and these sometimes include ex-members and parents of present members.

Organization of staff duties is of course simpler in the small club, but it is of importance whatever the size of the unit or the situation. It should hardly need saying, but the leader should ensure that every helper knows what his function is—what area of the work is his particular responsibility and care, whether it be the embryonic guitar group, the boys who tinker with motor-bikes in the shed, the coffee bar, or the group that plays records and likes dancing. A helper's work may entail a fairly concrete job like teaching dancing steps, playing an instrument for a music group, or keeping a register, or it may involve only being available to and interested in a particular group of young people while they relax informally. The vital thing is that every helper should be clear about what he is doing and to what purpose.

The leader and his helpers stand, organizationally, between the management committee and the members. They need to be in communication with both sides. They must know what the management committee's policy is, and they must know what the members, through their committee or representatives, decide within the area of their competence. They should also be able to contribute ideas, suggestions and observations to both sides. At one time, ensuring that helpers knew their role and understood how it fitted in with general policy seldom presented much difficulty or required any organization. For instance, Miss Smith, the local solicitor's daughter, came down to the club from seven to eight and 'took folk dancing' (it was sometimes very open to conjecture where she took it!) and the leader, or one of the members if it was that sort of club, played the piano for her. Miss Smith knew the leader and her mother was on the committee, and though she went at the end of the hour she did in fact know quite a great deal about the members. She, and most voluntary helpers of her day, went *down* to the club to give their welcome and often popular services, irrespective of the geography of the area. Nowadays, however, the Miss Smiths, our solicitors' daughters, are most probably qualified teachers of physical education in some other town, and the club obtains a trained and well-qualified keep-fit teacher from the local education authority who is paid by that body. It is significant of the social change that has taken place that he or she does not automatically go '*down*' to the club, may well go 'round to' or just 'to' it, and sometimes goes 'up to' it. Much the same thing has happened with the woodwork class. In the old days the Canon's gardener, who was a *very* handy man, took the class and knew the leader and half the boys. Now, boys and girls often learn all kinds of crafts in finely equipped school workshops with highly skilled teachers, and if the Canon had a gardener-handyman, and we persuaded him to take the class, it would not last long because the boys, and probably some of the girls, would know more about the job than he did. So instead, we have Mr. Jones provided and paid by the local education authority, a handsome young man and a most superior craftsman, who welcomes the chance to put in a few extra hours at evening institute rates, since he wants to get married next summer.

Clubs are often much larger now than they used to be, and some are open five, six or seven evenings a week as well as having additional week-end programmes. This can mean that no member of the staff except the leader has a picture of the whole of the club's life, from the one part of it in which he plays his role, nor can all the members of the staff know each other, let alone work co-operatively, unless some deliberate means of doing these things is established. The situation is occasionally even more difficult still, when a full-time club has no full-time staff, and the leadership (as well as the staff-membership) is divided between two or even

140

three part-time workers. It is not impossible to maintain a club or centre this way when there is no full-time leader available, but it inevitably means that the programme has to be 'laid on' by 'the authority', and the result for the members is a set of facilities—perhaps very good facilities—being offered to them for their use, rather than the experience of being involved in the management of their own affairs.

There is, of course, nothing wrong in the offer of good facilities, particularly if the human relationships that these bring are sound. If this were all the youth service set out to do, it could be reasonably argued that the job could be better done by commercial enterprise. But in the Youth Service the quality and use of human relationships should be more than just a matter of chance. Hence the importance of all the staff members consciously working together as a team. This means that the leader needs to see all the members of his staff at regular intervals, when the club is not in session. At these staff meetings the helpers should be kept informed of management committee policy and of members' decisions, interests and suggestions. They should have the opportunity to ask questions and make suggestions; then they can discuss what they have been doing and how they intend to proceed in order to carry out their helping functions co-operatively and in a way which will, for the members, be consistent.

However, the opportunities which staff meetings provide for communication between leader and helpers need supplementing if the leader is to pass on to his helpers the full benefits of his own training, skill and experience. The leader will also need to see his helpers individually; sometimes, too, discussions with two or three of them at a time will produce useful results. This form of supervision constitutes a valuable part of a helper's training and enables each to absorb at his own pace the information and advice that the leader has to impart. In this way, he will gain in time an objective and enlightened view of the club members and of his own particular bit of work. The leader himself will benefit from discussions of this kind and this will help him to maintain a good relationship with each helper and to get from them all a complete picture of how the club is working and of members' reactions.

All this, of course, takes up time outside club hours, and all helpers should know about the meetings and the reasons for them from the start. If part-time helpers are paid by the hour for club work by the local authority, it is fair that they should be paid for the time spent on staff meetings and supervision. Since there are limits to everyone's time, it is important to be realistic about these demands, but regularity is important. Monthly staff meetings to which everyone comes will be far more productive than weekly ones attended by only a few people each time. Supervision sessions need to be more frequent, at least to start with, but can be kept short and well disciplined.

Training for helpers is not a new idea, though in the past it usually took the form of occasional training days or week-ends, run by voluntary youth organizations at local level. In the last decade, and especially since the publication of the Bessey report on the Training of Part-Time Youth Leaders, training schemes have blossomed all over the country. These are usually run by local education authorities, but sometimes by the joint training agencies suggested in the report. The schemes differ considerably in content and duration so that no general comment would be valid. Since the Youth Service now needs far more part-time paid workers it is obviously a good thing that those who pay them should demand that those they pay should learn about the work they are employed to do. Training schemes in some places are admirable and have generated a new source of enthusiastic help for leaders, where the supply had seemed to have run dry. Some part-time leaders in charge of their own clubs have certainly become able to do far better work because of the local training provided for them. In other instances, however, the quality of the training schemes is suspect. The weekly lecture on adolescent psychology attended at the end of a day's work, and perhaps without having had time for a meal, may fail to stimulate the trainee. Yet in some places considerable pressure seems to be put on part-time workers to attend such forms of 'training'. One wonders sometimes, too, whether sufficient thought is given to the different needs of part-time leaders in charge of their own units and part-time workers who are helpers, and whether sometimes helpers are being pressured into attendance at training courses when they would gain more from spending the time on good supervision from the leaders with whom they work.

Great effort has been made to develop training for part-time workers, and although the development over the country as a whole is somewhat haphazard, one is often filled with admiration for the determination and devotion of part-time workers who, while doing a full-time job outside the Youth Service, are giving two or three evenings a week to the club or centre, and devoting one evening weekly and several week-ends a year to training. At this stage it is obviously all-important that the leaders with whom these helpers work and the authorities who employ them on a part-time basis carefully co-ordinate their demands and ensure that altogether these demands make sense to the helpers and are of real benefit to them and to the Service.

The most important part of the youth club organization is the members' committee or whatever other form of machinery for self-management the club has. A club that has not, as one of its first principles, that of making good citizens, is not fulfilling its most important function, and for this reason the sponsoring body, whether voluntary or statutory, must have some area of freedom within which the members can practise managing their own affairs. No art, whether it be that of playing football or painting pictures, writing poems, making dresses or friends, can be achieved without practice, and this is no less true of the art of citizenship. If democracy can be said to have failed in this country, it is because most people do not realize the power the vote gives them and are, therefore, neither interested in using it, nor in using it intelligently. Through being involved in the management of their own affairs as a membership group through some form of committee, adolescents learn, however painfully, *how* to use a vote, and most important of all how to abide loyally by a majority decision or to seek to alter it by constitutional means.

But none of this is learned by members who are carried or pushed through the motions of democratic management by adults who never allow them to carry real responsibility and to do things in the way they want to, in spite of having been told why it will not work. By facing up to the consequences of their decisions with the support of sympathetic adults who are not interested in saying 'I told you so!' young people will learn lessons they can never learn in any other way. This means that the role of adults within this area of freedom is a subtle and difficult one, for while their function cannot be fulfilled by despotic means, neither can it if they dissociate themselves from what goes on. Adolescents will often enough learn only 'the hard way', but the art of democratic self-management will seldom be learned at all without the help of more experienced people being available. Help will be needed over how to do the endless number of things that have to be done in order to make and carry out a group decision—how to prepare for a meeting; how to conduct it; how to write letters of invitation and thanks; how decisions may be arrived at; when it may be better to defer decisions; what some of the implications are that the young people may not have thought of. The help must be offered but cannot be forced and the adults concerned need the kind of patience that enables them to 'show young people how' rather than to 'do it for young people', for the club is run for the benefit of members, not as an arena for the display of adult powers of organization. The adults need to be unshocked and personally unoffended when their help is rejected, and able to go on offering it again and again to the same young people and to successive groups of them.

The area of freedom needs to be defined for the young people, and from time to time re-defined. Some of its limits may be fixed by circumstances. If, for instance, the club meets in the primary school hall, neither the members nor the management committee have the right to redecorate or refurnish it to suit their own purposes, as they might do with their own premises; if a local authority directly sponsors and finances a number of clubs, fixes the membership subscriptions and rules that these shall be paid over to the local authority office, neither the management committee nor the members can have any hand in deciding what the subscriptions should be or how the revenue derived from them shall be used, though they may be able to raise some income besides the subscriptions, and use this according to their own plans. These kinds of restrictions have some obvious disadvantages and in particular tend to make a good many people feel less responsible, because for them this kind of financial arrangement denotes that the club is something which 'they' organize rather than something which is 'ours'. The post-Albemarle development has produced a good deal of this type of Youth Service organization, and much of it may be inevitable, but one could wish that in some cases county and area administration could be made to serve the units in the Service more realistically in this respect. Public money must, of course, be responsibly handled and accounted for, but young people do not learn to do these things by having the finances kept beyond their reach. Other limits are usually set by the management committee through its policy. That committee, or the leader on its behalf, may specify some regulations as a result of policy, but it is usually best to keep these ready-made specific regulations to a minimum and to have the young people, or their elected committee members, work out for themselves with the help of the leader such rules as are required. It is the members who have to keep them, and they are more likely to learn that rules are things intended to make life work better and not just arbitrary restrictions placed on 'us' by 'them', if they have had a hand in formulating them. The adult's job is usually that of showing young people that it is better to keep rules to a minimum, and no more severe than necessary, than to have so many that few people can remember them all, and to make them so severe that either they cannot be enforced or everyone decides it is not worth being a member. A good many young people tend to want to go too far in the matter of rules—perhaps reflecting their own experience with authority— and they can often be somewhat self-righteous about them. At the same time, adolescents are naturally exuberant, undisciplined and to some degree destructive. Equipment and premises are likely to be damaged on occasions and rules of behaviour broken, and on such occasions offenders have to be stopped and persistent offenders may have to be penalized. The leader is, of course, the ultimate authority as far as the members are concerned, but as much of this authority as possible should be delegated to members in positions of responsibility. Members in these positions cannot always enforce the rules they have made, even when these are entirely reasonable ones, without a good deal of support from the leader and helpers, and even with this they may be powerless if they are in a neighbourhood where local loyalty demands that members turn on each other, but close the ranks against authority, be it policeman, school attendance officer or youth leader. The leader has, then, to use his authority directly, but he can and should always associate the members with his actions. When repeated experience has taught committee members that the leader uses his authority on behalf of the membership group and not for his personal satisfaction, they begin to be able to associate themselves with this authority and to be able and willing to exercise it for themselves, though the leader should be sensitive to the strangeness that this role may have for some of them. When members have had the experience of raising their own money and buying some coveted piece of equipment with it, they are usually very careful in guarding what they have acquired from their own and their fellows' mishandling.

It usually takes two or three years to develop a good working members' committee in a youth club, and leaders and helpers seldom have the satisfaction of working in a club that has such a committee for any length of time, if at all. This could be disheartening for anyone who did not realize that the job of the adults is to help the young people *discover how* to run their own affairs. If the young people were already skilled at doing this the adults would be largely redundant. In most cases the young people who have become really effective club members and officers are those who are on the point of leaving the youth club. This is as it should be, for having had the freedom to make their mistakes, and learn from them, in a small, and to some extent protected, democratic unit, they are ready and able to take their places in the larger democratic units of adult life.

IO

Youth Group Activities I:
Programme Planning[1]

✳

The difficulty about programme planning is that no matter what activity or method is suggested there will always be those who declare, 'It can't be done in our group.' Indeed one is often forced into believing that all youth groups work under a Statute of Limitations.

Firstly, there is the limitation of finance. 'We can't do crafts, because we can't afford the materials and the members won't buy their own.' Or, 'We can't do that sort of discussion, we haven't a radio or a television set or a film projector.' The hard answer is that lack of money seldom stops people from doing anything. It is usually possible to do most things as long as one does not lack persistence and imagination. The thing to be clear about is what we want to do, how much work will we do to further that desire, and what we will give up if necessary for its sake.

Frequently youth leaders suffer from too grand ideas, or are too lazy in demanding that a grant from somewhere or other should be forthcoming for almost everything. They do not see that part of the very education of their members is in working to obtain their equipment, in saving up for it, in making some of it, and in discovering the infinite resources of the second-hand and junk shop, for the necessary repairs and renovations are an additional activity. Money-raising efforts for equipment should be part of the activity of the group, and it is just that extra penny or

[1] For a fuller exposition of the technique of programme planning, see *Informal Education*, J. Macalister Brew (Faber and Faber).

147

so from the dance or social, just that extra effort to make the canteen pay, that can provide many pieces of seemingly lavish equipment without tears. For instance, a club sited in the middle of a derelict piece of land cultivated it and by selling the potatoes they grew in the first year 'to clean the land', they bought a full set of football jerseys. Since then, it has provided them over the years with a record player and a ciné camera, among many other luxuries.

Many youth groups certainly suffer from the limitations of their premises, but so do nearly all schools and most families. 'But I have only one room.' 'The room isn't our own.' 'We've nowhere to store anything,' they say. But even one room need not be utterly impossible. We have never explored sufficiently the use of portable screens. One of the most successful clubs I ever visited managed three activities each evening by dint of using the stage and by dividing the rest of the room with screens into a woodwork corner, a girls' group activity and a refreshment bar. Such premises demand much give-and-take and there are always the 'funnies' with us who knock the screens over, but they can be educated to social responsibility by their peers, and they are eventually. Rolled hessian can provide notice- and display-boards which are easily hooked on to walls, cushions and curtains are portable, and a good canteen can be rigged up with the aid of two barrels and two planks of wood. Moreover, I have yet to find the owner of premises who will not house an extra cupboard or chest of drawers for one's equipment, provided that the approach is not 'This room is so inconvenient we can't manage without'—but rather 'I know it's not very easy for you, but . . .'. In such circumstances it is essential that they shall be consulted about the size and setting of the cupboard or chest, and that it should match (or be painted to match) the other furniture so that it does not stick out like a sore finger as a constant reminder of our tenure.

Then there is the limitation of time. 'We only meet one night a week.' The answer from many a six-nights-a-week club leader might well be—'How lucky you are—your ideas will last so much longer.' But one of the more practical answers is to make the best use of space in that one night in the week and to discover what groups can meet or what activities can be undertaken elsewhere on other nights. The members' committee, film discussion groups, radio listening, TV viewing groups, play reading, reading aloud, gramophone societies, and the Service group can all meet in the leader's or one another's houses. There are few villages at least that do not possess a disused shed or the kindly owner of a large kitchen, loft or barn. Inter-club visits of observation can always be arranged on other nights, always provided, of course, that the members *wish* to meet on more than one night in the week.

The limitation of leaders and helpers is always with us. 'I can't find anyone to take Keep Fit or Drama or Crafts.' Here we must ask ourselves some searching questions. Must we have them? What kind of drama or crafts do we want? or How much can one learn on one's own—or from books? Do we go out looking for helpers or hope they will fall from Heaven? Sometimes adults, when personally approached, will do for young people what they will not do for adults. Finally, if we fail to get people to help with the usual activities, what about the unusual? How much can we call upon people with fascinating hobbies, how much can our members do to entertain one another?

Then there are those sufferers from the limitation of popularity —'They don't like the club in our village or neighbourhood.' Why is this? Is it our fault? What can we do to alter this? Have we tried to engage in any community service, have we attracted the right people on to our Advisory or Management Committee so that our work is explained and interpreted in the right quarters?

The final limitation is that of personality. 'Our club members aren't interested in anything.' This is seldom true and, if it is, how much of it is our fault—are we too possessive, too bossy or in too much of a hurry?

There are only two essential guiding principles in programme planning. Neither the programme nor the plan is sacred—a great deal of work among adolescents is a process of trial and error and, as we must be prepared to build and plan so we must also be prepared to discard. A youth group is neither a series of individuals attending a series of classes, nor a place for eternal billiards, dancing and bean-bag hurling; nor is a club a club leader. A group is a community engaged in the task of educating itself. It therefore follows that a youth organization can meet anywhere. There are only three necessities—light, preferably the sort that cannot be turned off or blown out by the practical joker—warmth, and if we cater for boys this often means a 'fug'—and comradeship. Given these three essentials, the most important provisions thereafter are games, music and dancing administered in equal doses of variety and dependability.

For those who think of clubs as embryo evening institutes or physical culture palaces or homes for higher taste education, all this may seem rather humdrum. But the very nature of an industrial society demands that for the majority of people leisure-time activity really means doing the things they enjoy, as distinct from the activities they do for money. Moreover, enjoyment itself is a heavenly grace. To the question: What is the chief end of man? the answer of the Shorter Catechism is still one of the best, 'To glorify God and *enjoy* Him for ever.'

Again, how far have we the right to dictate to others what they should do in their leisure time—how they should enjoy themselves? How far is it fair to insist that young people shall improve (or rather do what we think will improve) their minds and their bodies in their spare time? And before answering quickly that it will be 'for their own good', just think for a moment what we do with our leisure. Is it so very cultured and improving, or are we past improving? Four of the most highly respected and worthy friends I have, all of impeccable academic distinction, spend their leisure respectively in reading detective stories, in amateur conjuring, in training performing fleas, and in the ancient sport of lady killing! Mindful of our own leisure-time pursuits, I do not think we dare betray their trust by being too dictatorial about the leisure time of adolescents. One visits club after club where the leader wails dolefully, 'They don't want to *do* anything, except dance and play billiards or dance and just sit or gossip.' What happens in so many clubs for adults apart from sitting and gossiping? And what happens in so many homes? If Mary and Martha, or Johnny and Willie, or even Mary and Willie, want to talk to one another and get to know one another, the club is often the only place where they can do so except for the street. At home there is Father and the radio, or Grandma, Uncle Bert, the rest of the family and the 'tele', mother and the ironing, and young Alf and the baby, and even if you could afford it, you do not want to go to the cinema every night of the week.

We all need to sit, and a comfortable chair to do it in. As one busy and cheerful mother of a large family said to me once, 'You know, luv, what I would do without the pictures I don't know.

Youth Group Activities I: Programme Planning

I know it costs money I can ill afford, but I do get three hours' comfortable sit down!' Hence, just as it is a *sine qua non* of the adult club, so the lounge, with its comfortable chairs, its papers and magazines should be the central feature—the focal point if one likes—of every club and youth centre. It seems very little to ask or provide; yet, in all too many cases, 'Pro Bono Publico' and 'Indignant Ratepayer' and 'Pater Familias', those three hardy annuals, all write intermittently and at length to the Press when easychairs and record players are purchased in extremely moderate numbers for 'the Youth'. But a comfortable chair and papers and a room of taste and dignity and beauty to sit in are among the best methods of teaching the art of social living. I sometimes wonder, when we have to answer for our youth work, whether we shall be blamed most for our failure for so long to provide more than a few such centres or for the fact that they were so appallingly ugly, so badly lit and heated, and so uncomfortable that it is a veritable feat of endurance to work in them. Quite apart from the members lost, were the truth known, it is possible that as many helpers have been lost to youth work from sheer rejection of the unutterable squalor, as have been lost to it from all the other causes put together.

Given the comfortable room, and the opportunity to sit there without being made to feel either lazy or anti-social, there are two other things to remember in planning a programme. In the first place a consideration of the school syllabus and the evening institute syllabus will give us much guidance, as much in what to avoid as in what to include. Secondly, no group on earth will succeed with a programme which bears no relation to the industry, working conditions and economic and social background of the area which it serves.

Let us consider the school first. In most schools boys and girls are grouped according to age and ability. In the club we have perhaps two hundred, or twenty (it is no simpler with either number), of all ages and maybe of both sexes, between the ages of fifteen and twenty-one—with 'gate-crashers' of under thirteen and old-timers of well over twice twenty, if we are not very firm, tacked on either end. In the school there is a teacher for each class, or age group, in the club we are lucky if we have one helper to each fifty and some specialists for occasional classes. Nevertheless, there must be some age grouping, not only for convenience of handling,

151

not only because there is often a sharp cleavage between the tastes of the fourteen-year-old and the sixteen-year-old, but because the dignity of the growing adult demands that he shall be treated differently from his juniors. We can seldom keep our seventeen-year-olds with a programme which they are expected to share with young Peter who has only just left school. Instinctively, adolescents are on their guard against anything which may assault their newly found, and as yet rather unmanageable, adult dignity. There is a gulf between fifteen and fifty that can more easily be bridged than the gulf between fifteen and eighteen, because the eighteen-year-old is not sure enough of himself to be able to give way. Conversely a fifteen-year-old, though never so much a man of the world, must have the opportunity to work off his puppy fat, without earning the scorn and derision of his not much olders, but oh, so much wisers!

We must try, however, to cater not only for different age groups but for different ability and aptitudes. In most schools the A, B and C streams are well known, even if they are not separated. In the club, there may not be many of the A stream, they are probably rightly sacrificing their leisure on the altar of homework, or on the treadmill of the evening institute, but we do have some of those bright ones who developed late so that they missed the first educational opportunities. In the programme we have to cater for them all, remembering that any youth group is not a mass of level uniformity but a widely diversified group of varying talent and background.

At school, the dancing, physical education and craft work are all taken by experts. Therefore, if we are to attract the young worker, we must remember that his standards are high, and that though he was compelled to go to school he is not compelled to come to us. Indeed it is a salutary thought and one that should never be lost sight of, that the standards of our young people in technical ability and achievement are high, and that they value almost everything in terms of entertainment-value, or, as I would prefer to call it, interest-value for money. Some of us might be astonished to realize how they measure everything up in terms of what Winnie the Pooh called 'pounds, shillings and ounces'. They know the exact value for money of all the local dance halls, both the Wednesday and the Saturday dance; they know how long they can sit for a shilling at the local cafés and just what sort of fare to expect at the neighbouring picture houses. They often know, too, what all the Youth Fellowships, Church Guilds and Socials can offer, and reckon it all up in hard cash. Many of them pay their weekly subscription to a youth group because it is open every night of the week, or because it is always there to fall back on if they are short of funds, or if other entertainments do not come up to scratch. It is our business to be worth the subscription and to make the group so much worth while that they will come more often. We must exercise our salesmanship and offer a bargain because we may be quite sure, unflattering as it may seem, that when we cease to be worth the money they will stop coming, and we will be left with only those young things who find in the youth group an escape rather than an adventure—the over-shy and serious boys, or the girls who are not fond of boys.

Our standards must be, as far as possible, as high as those of the schools, which is difficult, and often almost impossible, and therefore we must also offer something *different* from the type of activity offered in the school. This is especially true of the younger members. 'Oh, we did that at school' can still be a term of reproach rather than a paean of praise to the club leader. Nevertheless we can sometimes dance and play songs they have learnt at school to the older members and they will shout, 'Oh, we learnt that at school,' with a mixture of delighted recognition and nostalgic reminiscence which will only be equalled by a group of over-seventies.

This revulsion from the school pattern is no criticism of the school but a stage in adolescent growth, but it makes for great difficulties, especially since a number of our best and most conscientious youth leaders are also day-school teachers. They go, all honour to them, to refresher courses for teachers, to youth leaders' courses, craft week-ends, drama week-ends and so on and so forth, with a devotion and a sense of professional responsibility which does them credit. When they come back full of new ideas and enthusiasm it seems but right that both the school and the youth group should profit. It is not only easier but it often means a saving of materials and equipment. But next year those who have already done this new and exciting work at school greet us with a 'pooh, we did that at school, it's just a kid's game'. For example, in the early days girls' clubs flourished on country dancing and raffia work. Then the schools started to teach both, and leaders raced in turn through Scottish, National, Scandinavian, mid-European and American square dancing, from raffia through canework to basketry and stool-making.

Hence, when people complain of the unimaginative nature of many youth programmes they do not always realize what a burden is placed on the leader who is at once expected to keep abreast with the work done in the schools, and also to think up 'new things to do in new ways'. Nor is it always recognized that ideas which are rare enough to come by, cease to be new all too rapidly.

Programme planning must also bear relation to the economic and social background of members. One of the most promising things about Circular 1486 (see page 91) was that it pointed out the interrelation of social and economic conditions. Employment and working conditions make heavy demands on the adolescent and influence enormously what he is willing and indeed able to do in his leisure time. Yet before the war one often visited clubs where the membership was largely composed of errand- and messenger-boys to find street-running advocated as a club activity; where the membership was largely composed of domestic servants and machinists to find an attempt being made to foster cookery classes and dress-making. Even recently I came across an attempt to foster health and strength classes among a group of boys already engaged on loading lorries in the daytime. All too seldom in programme planning is this question of occupation taken into consideration, or any allowance made for the fact that many young people are so physically jaded rather than tired that in sheer self-protection they are driven to passive rather than active entertainment. It should be obvious that boys and girls whose work is sedentary will profit from and enjoy physical activities in their leisure, while those whose work demands that they should stand and walk about, lift and carry, will need a different programme. But all too often 'that good idea' picked up at a training week-end is introduced, with little thought of its suitability to the working life of the neighbourhood. Yet a programme which does not consider the employment of the member is foredoomed.

Moreover it is well to remember that there is an *industrial attitude* which is even more important than industrial conditions. Young wage-earners in their first outfits paid for by themselves develop a tradition in activity and interest. Nowadays it is socially accepted that schoolchildren go to camp—hence the young wage-earner demands a different type of holiday. Certain games, such as netball and football, may be played by young wage-earners; others, and they vary in different parts of the country, may only be played by people still at school. The adolescents' dignity is affronted by being offered games or crafts in the wrong tradition, and there is often a local or neighbourhood pattern of games. In certain parts of England a boys' club without a skittle alley would be an empty thing indeed. In other parts it would be a waste of space. Shove ha'penny must be played in certain other districts to show you are of man's estate. Indeed, on these lines, a great deal of very useful experiment could be made concerning local crafts. In Lancashire, for instance, some attempt was made to revive the clog-maker's art and quite often the co-operation and interest of the parents and the oldest inhabitant can be secured on behalf of a dying craft as in no other way. In Lincolnshire ironwork was revived in youth organizations, in Wales coracle-making, and in Devon lace-making, with great success. Unwittingly, I once did my bit to keep poaching alive in Lincolnshire by mentioning in one club how fond I was of jugged hare!

With all this in mind, therefore, it would be fair to say that any adequate programme must aim at being diverse enough to cater for all ages, capacities and occupations. It must also be progressive enough to give fresh interests to the school-leaver and to the older age group. Many a club has killed its upper age groups because even the less intelligent will *not* do the same thing at the same level of attainment, for more than three years on end. A club programme must also be elastic enough to allow for shortage and sickness of helpers, and for those special events which are the red-letter days of the club calendar and which should be as frequent as those of the Church in the Middle Ages. Further, of course, in any consideration of programme planning, we must make every allowance for our premises, equipment and personnel, and how we can vary them.

Whatever type of group we are responsible for, our activities must grow out of the desires and limitations of the members themselves and *no* subject is more cultural than another. One of the great responsibilities of living in a democracy is that of educating people to be free judges of values, and the only way to do that is to start from what the member values and take him to see

Youth Group Activities I: Programme Planning

what we and others value, always remembering that our values are probably not ultimate and eternal values either.

Apart from that there is only one essential feature of programme planning. Human nature thrives on parties and no club can do without a party once a month and a really splendid shining high-light at least three times a year; it does not matter whether this is a concert, a Christmas pantomime, or a sports day—but the high-lights give us the courage to work quietly in the shadows for those hidden values of the less talked of activities—those imponderables —such as the 'word in season'. These can never appear on the notice-board, but without them the group never fulfils its highest purpose.

Moreover, it is important to remember in all our programme planning that, just as education should not stop at the end of schooldays, so it should not end at twenty. It is the job of schools to give young people a good start, it is the job of Youth Service to see that those aptitudes nurtured in the school are cared for and not allowed to die for lack of opportunity. But it is also the job of youth groups to see to it that young people are given an interest which shall carry over into adult life, either as something which they may pursue in their own homes when they make them, or something which they will carry further in adult organizations. It is the good youth group which accustoms its members to going to concerts and plays intelligently and which gives them some standards of selection in music or in radio and television. It is the good group which trains and passes on its members to such bodies as the Workers' Educational Association, the Women's Institutes and Townswomen's Guilds, adult Keep Fit groups and dramatic societies and adult classes in evening institutes. It is true that it is often difficult to find the right adult society for any given member —but we are not alone in experiencing the fact that but seldom do we find 'the time and the place and the loved one all together'. It is also true that many adult societies do not seem to pay any-thing but lip service to their desire for 'new blood', since com-plaints of their unwelcoming attitude to the young are too numerous to be completely ignored. But at all events we must try to encourage our members to lay in a stock, as it were, of interests which will serve them throughout adult life. We hear much about the problem of the old and the lonely. But their major problem is one which is seldom mentioned. In at least seven cases out of ten

156

Youth Group Activities I: Programme Planning

they are a misery to themselves and everybody else because they are so bored and so boring. Only too frequently they have no hobbies, they neither sew, paint nor read, they have never learned to listen with discrimination to the radio or to use television. They have never collected stamps or friends and are, therefore, thrown back on themselves; and all that is left for many of them is to dramatize sufferings and injuries which are frequently the product of an imagination starved of more interesting material to work on. After all, if by education we mean the act of assisting the growth of human beings to the full flowering of all their potentialities, we must not be unmindful of the necessities of providing for a fruitful old age. Education must teach people not only the necessary skills to earn a living but also the necessary skills to live a life. It must provide for all the wherewithal to live with some dignity and purpose. No man is fully educated who cannot adjust himself to the circumstances in which he finds himself. The classical scholar who lives the life of a hermit, the unskilled worker who works to sleep and eat and fill in football coupons, the lonely who waste their lives in envy and the old who resent and make life unpleasant for those who try to look after them, are all warped and, therefore, ill-educated human beings.

But however informal our approach may be, we must never underestimate the intelligence of young people, their keenness to use their minds as well as their bodies. We tend constantly to water down the milk of education when what is really needed is that it should be presented in a vessel of a different shape, in the adult cup instead of the infant's feeding-bottle.

It is natural that most people will wish to start where their own interest lies, or where they think the interest of their young people lies (unfortunately, this is not always quite the same thing). The music lover, the drama expert, think that theirs is the most urgent and pressing need, and that their work will make the finest contribution to the further education of the adolescent; the games or dancing experts feel that one must start with the fitness of the body in order to build on a solid foundation. Those who are politically aware feel that good citizenship is the essence of the problem; and those whose spiritual experience is most near to their everyday life feel that religious education must come first. The difficulty is, of course, that all these people are right, but we must beware at the outset of falling into the trap of regarding any subject as having any special intrinsic value. A great deal of harm has been done in formal education by this concentration on the subjects taught, by regarding some subjects as more valuable than others. It is still a common fallacy that classical scholarship is a method of training the memory when it is quite possible that the good classicist is the person who had a good memory before he started. It would be a thousand pities if the same error were carried into informal education, since surely the truth is that it does not matter much what subject we teach, it does not matter where we begin our informal education (as long as it bears some relation to where young people are), but it is of supreme importance how such a subject is presented. It does not matter whether our group is interested in navigation, which in Elizabethan schooldays was known as geography, or whether they are interested in domestic science, which we now call homecraft, or whether a group starts with drama and ends with a Passion play, which in many a club has been a religious experience of the greatest possible value. Youth leaders often yield to the temptation, or to the pressure put upon them by people who ought to know better, to show a varied list of activities, or to show a varied list of subjects for discussion groups. This often goes to quite absurd lengths, and one is shown with pride a vast list of subjects which have been discussed in the past twelve months. But nothing is explained by giving it a name, and a discussion group led by an adult who slams his mind into young people's faces is of no more value than any other type of study which is pursued but never effectively overtaken. Physical education, crafts, the economics and mechanics of adult life, civics, drama, psychology, philosophy, religion, are all of pressing interest. It is only when those who specialize in each of these subjects are wise enough to disclose the link to others that the chain of further and continued education is really forged. Young people are seeking after a wider experience and understanding than that afforded to them by their immediate surroundings and daily work, but even education is a means and not an end. Nothing in the world really matters very much except that which happens between mind and mind. Education is merely a means to this end. The end is not freedom because freedom is a condition; it is not democracy because democracy is merely an opportunity; the means, the ways, and the conditions of life are not life itself.

Youth Group Activities I: Programme Planning

Informal education is rather like a visit to the cinema—some people go in during the newsreel (the citizenship group), some people arrive for the Disney cartoons (the art class), some people arrive for the documentaries (the politically minded), and others half-way through the big picture (those who don't quite know what they want), but most of them, if their interest is captured, will see the whole programme through and it is only by seeing the whole programme of life through that we can most fully live.

In all this, of course, we must not forget the purpose of the whole exercise and allow 'activities', formal or informal, active or passive, to become, in our own minds, ends in themselves. They are, in fact, part of the means by which we try to help the young people grow in their mental, emotional and physical capacities to become more socially competent and able to manage their own affairs. They must be involved in the making of the programme and choices and decisions should be theirs, though they will need all the help a good leader can give them in order to learn to do this both realistically and adventurously. It is not normally the leader's job to determine the programme on his own, though sometimes in the early stages he may need to do just this in order to get things moving. At this stage, if the leader sits back and leaves the members to decide with too little help, there will either be a discouraging series of false starts, or the programme will go happily for a time with the things they already know and like, but after a time will go stale for lack of new ideas, and merely be adding to the problem of boredom. The adults, out of their wider experience, and with imagination informed by knowledge of the members' working conditions and social backgrounds, must be able to make suggestions in a way that will open up new horizons for the young people, and will educate their choices. Suggestions have often, perforce, to be of a subtle kind. One often has to disentangle inadequately expressed desires of members, and to start through casual conversations, or through a visitor, possibly introduced 'with intent'. One club took to playing chess with the Rotarians all because a personal friend of the leader was persuaded to play chess rather ostentatiously in a corner of the club for a whole week while members made friends with him. The enthusiast taught a few young people the names of the pieces and the opening moves and they were off! A series of travel talks started once because the corporation suddenly decided that the tenants of a

Youth Group Activities I: Programme Planning

certain estate could at last keep hens. A man of many parts came and talked to the fathers on Fathers' Night about poultry-keeping, and he was the sort of man who could begin with an egg and end with the history of China, and he did. The next week he came back with his slides and these had to be shown to the whole club; and he knew a fellow who had played his way through Spain and *he* had a film about it all. Naturally he put the club on to a man that had sailed the seven seas—literally sailed—and so it went on—but not for too long. In a club such as that was a series of eight or ten lectures or discussions is usually too much, and six is enough. A fine course of local government lectures once 'happened' all because the girls did not turn up to one committee meeting. A very good dance band started with one banjo being brought to a club and left about 'careless-like', and the encouragement of a boy with a mouth-organ led to the formation of a minstrel party. When Jenny made a fuss about losing her lipstick, someone said she didn't know how to use it anyway, and this led to a visitor taking a session on 'How to Use Make-Up' and going on to the 'Care of Hair and Hands' and ending with 'Personal Hygiene'. A quarrel about fashion and its eventual settlement by the leader led to a talk by a fashion buyer on 'Dress—how to Choose it' and later 'What is Worn'. Chatting about film stars, sometimes much despised by some of the boys, can lead to a session by an expert who will rapidly have the boys engrossed with how to use projectors.

Of course, this method takes time, but the skeleton programme of music, dancing, the coffee bar and easy chairs is meanwhile getting into the systems of the members, and it is better to be successful slowly than to fail rapidly. We need not expect to be the Complete Civilizing Influence in six months. It is better to have an activity that people want and enjoy rather than something that is going to be ineffectual everywhere except in the annual report. There is no special virtue in running classes which are better catered for elsewhere or very badly attended. Nor should short-lived activities that are enjoyed be thought valueless.

Youth Group Activities II: Games, Dancing, Camping, Holidays and Parties

✳

There was a time when people believed that a club could be kept together by a spot of English country dancing if it happened to be a girls' club, or a little of what was called 'football training' (mostly skipping) if it happened to be a boys' club. This was in the days when physical education in schools, except for the more progressive ones, was still called 'drill', and was a very dull business indeed. Gradually, as physical education in the school improved, a club had to look to other things for an attractive physical event in its programme.

In boys' clubs the football training became 'P.T.', and thanks to grants from the Jubilee Trust and a stray grant or so from the National Fitness Council many clubs became excessively grand and obtained a certain amount of gymnasium equipment, and in some cases even rose to the dizzy heights of showers. Boys' clubs have always been able to do a great deal for their boys through boxing, which after all is acknowledged to be a manly art, and if only a good instructor can be found, and if only the club handyman will make a pukka boxing-ring to add a touch of verisimilitude to the otherwise bald and unconvincing knock-about, boxing is often a major attraction.

Boys are always interested in personal achievement and, therefore, always like to feel that they are developing their muscles, and becoming strong. Girls, however, are seldom interested in

L   161

external achievement since by their very nature and training they are more personalized.

The Keep-Fit movement made a great contribution to physical education among women by allying it to music and dancing, by not being too proud to sugar the pill by encouraging the members of their classes to indulge in pretty frocks and bright colours, and by introducing slimming exercises and exercises designed to improve the carriage, slim ankles, remove double chins, and so on. Except for the more sophisticated, however, the school-leaver who has had good physical education at school often finds keep-fit work is neither vigorous enough nor exciting enough to hold her. What she needs is something strenuous, something that needs a certain amount of skill and above all something that does not take too long.

Fortunately the cumulative effect of the special dietary provision made for children during the war, improved health services and full employment has resulted in taller, heavier and far more robust adolescents than those of former generations. Most experts agree, however, that one of the first outward and visible signs of both physical and mental strain is bad posture.

The first few weeks of employment may produce the beginnings of bad posture due to fatigue, unaccustomed work and unaccustomed hours of work; this will respond to corrective treatment. Fortunately, under the guise of 'keep-fit', 'health and beauty'—or some such euphemism—girls can be persuaded to take an intelligent interest in their bodies, and every variety of dancing can be introduced with equally beneficial results. It is not as easy to help boys who, if they are interested at all, hanker after the more violent forms of exercise. This interest, unless carefully watched, may encourage them to indulge in activities involving a great deal of additional overstrain. The adolescent girl wants above all things to keep slim, and the keep-fit technique can help her to do this while preserving her charm and her health; the adolescent boy wants above all things to develop his manhood, his prowess and his muscles, and it is all too easy to overestimate and overstrain the strength of the growing boy. The average youth leader who caters for sedentary workers is too apt to imagine that any activity which will give the body a great deal of exercise must be good, and that in a group of heavy manual workers exercises using different muscles will necessarily be beneficial. The idea seems to be that the heart, having stood up to the best of its ability to one kind of strain, can quite cheerfully be transferred 'for a rest' to another kind of strain. Fortunately, perhaps, the heart is the first organ to show signs of over-fatigue, and contrary to popular superstition, the easiest to put right. It would be interesting, however, to have figures to support the theory tentatively advanced, that possibly many working boys have had latent tendencies towards tuberculosis activated by indulging in heavy daily work plus too much exercise.

Quite frequently too, the boy who longs to develop muscular strength is very depressed by his failure to do so. Someone tells him that two hours' P.T. at the club, the institute, or the Boys' Brigade will 'tone him up', and he tries it.

He looks an object stripped to the waist and in shorts, and he knows it. But he has set his heart on the glorious muscles of a boxer or the strength of a champion wrestler and with the optimism of modern times, he thinks that a few hours will cause him to fill out and cave in, in all the right places. Unfortunately, this seldom happens, perhaps it could never happen, but it certainly does not do so quickly enough for a speed-minded generation— he loses heart, he slacks off, and gives up altogether. Hence it would be a mistake to insist that an orthodox physical education class is one of the things one simply must have in a club. Even when we succeed in getting it, it may be a constant source of disappointment. One must never lose sight of the fact that young people join youth groups to enjoy themselves, and that doing good to themselves or anyone else is purely incidental. They come voluntarily and they demand, therefore, that they shall be entertained or given that type of 'physical improvement' which they feel *they* need. As they have been hard at work all day, as they have probably quite a lot of things to worry them, since all the minor upheavals of adolescence feel like earthquakes while they are undergoing them, they demand that they shall have fun. If they cannot get fun in the class they will get fun by breaking it up.

Young people expect personal example, personal interest, attraction, results and variety from physical education. Hence it is useless to expatiate on the virtues of cleanliness, hygiene, health and beauty, and insist on the spick-and-span turnout of the club member if the teacher looks as though his own apparel has been slept in for a week. It is also essential to establish a personal interest in the members themselves. It is not enough to watch the development of Willie's muscles, but we must know about Willie's mother's rheumatism. It is not enough to see that Winnie's hips are getting slimmer, we must also be interested in Winnie's new frock. No youth group can be held together on a basis of 'Hi, you, that fellow in the khaki shorts' or 'That girl in the third row at the back, with glasses'. Adolescents feel very strongly that when they have done us the honour of joining a class we should pay them the respect of learning their names.

Youth organizations of all kinds owe a great deal to teachers of physical education who take classes for them, very often on a purely voluntary basis. In particular they owe much to young teachers straight out of college who give up many evenings to such work after a very strenuous day's teaching—and the more informal methods of teaching which are now employed in the schools have greatly helped them in developing the technique required for youth work. But here almost more than anywhere else, to be expert is not necessarily to be effective. A rough-and-ready sergeant-major (old type) may succeed among a group of boys with the dullest-looking old-fashioned exercises where another man, an expert, knowing far more about the whole business, with a 'hail-fellow-well-met' attitude, will fail dismally. In girls' work, where keep-fit, however well and attractively taught, seems to have failed, the very same girls will choose musical drill or club-swinging as the thing they like best—and in youth work it is what people like best which is important, because it is only on that basis that we can proceed to give them something they will like better still. All youth workers are in the position of commercial travellers—if people do not like their goods they will not buy. A perfect gymnasium, perfect equipment, and an excellent teacher do not necessarily mean that we are in a position to provide a perfect class. It is the technique, the method of approach which counts more than anything else. Even with all the advances that have been made, it will do no harm to repeat that even though we have learnt that something between the sergeant-major's 'Form two deep' bark and the 'Will you kindly choose a partner and get into a straight line in front of me', is probably the best way of getting across commands, there are other matters to be taken into consideration. Adolescents often resent the manner of the expert, particularly the young physical education specialist whose standards are high (as indeed they should be) and who is accustomed to the ready-made class and good equipment. It is unnecessary to point out, either by manner or asides, that it is really impossible to do any *worthwhile* work on such a floor and with such inadequate equipment. Even if the room *is* dirty, dark, and otherwise inadequate, it is just possible that the club members are fond of it, and although they may not bat an eyelid they may deeply resent any adverse comment. One of the finest gymnasts I ever knew ruined a class in this way. When the class closed down the erstwhile members of the group said, with surprising venom, 'Now he can go and do his blasted hand-stands in his marble palaces.'

Physical activity, like patriotism, is not enough. It is the spirit behind that matters, and any form of physical education has missed its full and final purpose unless it develops in the group a desire for controlled freedom rather than a liking for too much rigid organization, an emotional stimulus to counteract the monotony and drabness of so much of the working day's environment, a craving for self-expression which can be found as much in making the body a beautiful instrument as in any other craft. Its purpose is also to foster leadership where leadership lies dormant. For too long we have tended to imagine that the person who is good at games is not necessarily good at anything else. But if we watch youth groups carefully it does not take long to realize (and the findings of American Surveys confirm this) that the leader in games is very often the good leader in other departments of life. Leaders of the country's higher policy may have been trained on the playing fields of Eton; the works foreman is often equally trained by the street-lamp cricket on any piece of open ground, or in the youth group sports club.

It would seem that one of the major difficulties about team games is that leaders are apt to be either much too half-hearted about them, or else much too enthusiastic. One knows only too well the type of boys' club which seems to be run for the benefit of the football team, and where everything is considered from the angle of the footballers. On the other hand one is equally often faced with the club where the netball team is regarded as a not very necessary evil. In team games, too, girls are much less well regarded and catered for than boys. Because the girl is less demanding than the boy her need for physical activities is ignored, and even if she has enthusiasms, little is done to encourage them. Club leaders who would be horrified at turning out a football team dressed like a crowd of 'Baker Street irregulars', will not bother about a uniform for girls 'until they show that they are really keen'. But how can you become keen if you are not given equipment to make you keen? How many people would become book-lovers, if they had to serve an apprenticeship of reading newspapers and magazines before they were allowed to read books? The club leader who goes regularly to watch 'his boys' ' football is but seldom observed at the girls' netball matches. Again, it never seems to occur to many leaders that the boys should provide supporters for a girls' match, though the girls are often expected to prepare the football tea for the boys.

'In this connection it might be well to remember that girls are not necessarily perverse or lacking in team spirit if they fail to turn up at a swimming gala or other athletic activity. In the interests of public health, if nothing else, girls should not swim in public baths during their menstrual period, and in spite of all calculations girls cannot always be sure that they will be fit to swim. The very excitement of a competition often precipitates menstruation—and is one of the reasons for much of the girl's so-called lack of responsibility, and team or club spirit.'[1]

Again, many clubs make no arrangements for the girls' privacy for changing for physical activities. One is often told that several attempts were made to organize Keep-Fit or Netball but that few girls attended and even the few dropped off after a week or so. In such cases the leader has frequently overlooked the complete lack of provision for the girls to wash and change, in either the club or games field. Few girls like to go through the streets 'looking a sight', and they need, and should have, more privacy than boys. It is not good enough to demand that girls should 'just muck in as the boys do'. We cannot at one and the same time accuse girls of being vulgar, bossy and self-assertive, and yet fail to provide them with those safeguards and comforts which are essential to decent and modest behaviour.

If the group is to take part seriously in team games a great deal of spade work is necessary, equipment is difficult to come by, it is expensive and its care demands constant supervision. Only too often teams are organized and flourish for a little while and then

[1] *Girls' Interests*, Occasional Papers No. 1, N.A.M.C. & G.C.

fade quietly away, or what is worse disintegrate with much mutual recrimination. The chief difficulty seems to be that the leader regards the team as an end in itself rather than a means to an end, or as something useful for keeping the more lively spirits occupied.

The truth is that games make demands on the leader and one must be prepared to face this or find someone who will act as a regular team games adviser and coach. By great good fortune team games also make demands on the young themselves and perhaps it would be worth while considering the many lessons which are learned by a well-organized team. The very existence of such a group depends on the young people's contribution of loyalty to the captain and adaptability to the other members of the team, an all-round spirit of give-and-take and, one of the most difficult lessons for the adolescent to learn, the sheer necessity of being reliable and punctual, the ability to turn up at a given spot at a given time on a given date. Quite apart from all this there is the elementary fact that each team will need a secretary and a committee, and the work of planning and making fixtures and selections provides excellent training in the art of self-government. Moreover the arranging of matches brings in its train two other valuable social skills—the art of looking after and being polite to visiting teams, and the even more difficult art of accepting hospitality politely and graciously and of behaving decently whether one has lost or won. Contrary to common belief the latter is much more difficult for young people than the former. Finally, games should teach young people how to look after their bodies when they are hot and tired, personal neatness with regard to underclothing, and that a little knowledge of elementary first aid is no bad addition to our general knowledge. This question of personal neatness and politeness is seldom fully appreciated. I remember taking a gang of young toughs to a collar-and-tie club to play the second round of a table-tennis tournament. The boys were brilliant players but they had scorned the necessity of washing or changing from their rather grimy working clothes. The fact that the team which had formerly visited them in their own club had been clean and well dressed, had only occasioned slight ridicule and conveyed no hint to them. They won their match and came back to their own club to be suitably congratulated. Not a word was said, at least not in my hearing, but on the following Tuesday when a further match was held, the members of the team had washed and put on their best suits, and the look in their eyes dared anyone to call attention to these phenomena. From that date onwards it became fashionable to 'wash and dress' for the club, and who shall despise the value of pride in one's personal appearance as one of the more valuable adjuncts to self-respect and to social living? Nor do we always have to play matches. There is much to be said for playing games simply for the sake of enjoying the game, and it has the great advantage of allowing all those who enjoy it to take part irrespective of their degree of skill.

Finally, to learn a game means to increase one's skill, and skill in any activity is something infinitely precious and valuable to us and to all men.

The difficulty of obtaining games' coaches is not insuperable. With a little determination it should not be impossible to secure all the help we need. Local education authorities' Organizers of Physical Education and the staff of the Central Council of Physical Recreation are all very willing to help. Most team games have National and County Associations and their officers are expected to give what assistance they can. Moreover all the major team games have their own national bodies who are always anxious to help to promote interest in their game among the younger generation.

Since we are a games-minded country, or so we are frequently told, it is a pity that the majority of schools have for so long concentrated on such games as football, cricket, netball and hockey, games which need fifteen to twenty-two players and at least a quarter of an acre of ground if they are to be played satisfactorily. When people complain that modern youth is content to watch games rather than play them, one is tempted to observe that it is truly fortunate, since if they all selfishly wanted to play these same games there just would not be room for them. Indeed there are seldom enough pitches in any town for those cricket, football, hockey and netball clubs which already exist. Rightly or wrongly, games in this country are not only regarded as something in which all right-minded people should be interested, but as social assets. Yet games such as tennis and golf, which *are* social assets which can be played with far fewer numbers, have only recently begun to be encouraged in schools and youth groups.

We have numberless rivers, pools, ponds, reservoirs and waterways in England, many of them navigable. Happily, swimming is being much more extensively taught in schools, and some of the same young people who learn to swim are taught to handle boats. Now that more interest is being taken in yachting and small boats, it is encouraging to see that many youth organizations have built their own boats and some have taken them on most adventurous journeys. Fencing, again, is an almost perfect physical exercise in the training of hand, mind, eye and temper. It can be taught to large groups at the same time, and it is encouraging to note that many youth organizations have taken it up extensively since the war, in spite of the initial expense of the equipment. Squash and fives are amazingly good exercise and do not need vast numbers to play them. Once the initial outlay has been made, the upkeep is practically negligible, but only our more expensive schools seem to teach either game. Again, one of the most remarkable features of post-war Britain has been the unusual interest in horsemanship. Happily, many of the older adolescents at all events are now able to pay for most expensive holidays, and equipment such as cameras and motor-bicycles. Hence in many areas there are club riding groups and pony trekking is popular. As girls nearly always go through a stage which can only be described as hippo-mania in their early teens, there is no activity more popular. Furthermore, like fencing and cricket, it has the inestimable merit of looking beautiful, as indeed it is. Most riding schools will give special help and perhaps block terms to a youth group which will ride regularly, particularly in the evenings, rather than at week-ends when they are apt to be over-fully booked. Skating rinks and bowling alleys offer similar opportunities.

There is no need for a formal class if young people get their physical recreation in other ways. (There is, after all, a great deal of virtue in outdoor activities.) Adolescents who would not be seen dead in a gymnastic class are often most enthusiastic cyclists or campers, and even the girl who would hesitate to walk a quarter of a mile will dance quite cheerfully for a whole evening, thus covering, on a conservative estimate, at least eight or ten miles often in high-heeled shoes! In many ways dancing is the perfect activity, combining music, movement, sociability and self-expression. It is only those who have not taken the trouble to learn properly who are unaware of the enormous scope for self-expression in modern jiving, rock 'n' roll, twist, shake and other 'off-beat' dancing. It increases self-confidence, and it is also, of course, the perfect mixed activity. There are dances which boys who have never danced before find it fun to begin with, probably because you do not even need a girl to do it with, if you go wrong it does not matter much, and hence, you can gain confidence and a sense of rhythm at the same time. It is true that Youth Service is meant to do other things as well as teach dancing, but to dance well means that one has gained a certain amount of control over one's body, a sense of balance, a sense of rhythm, a sense of give-and-take, because one cannot dance really well with anybody unless one is prepared to do this. Indeed, any really good dancer knows that it is very difficult to dance well with anyone with whom one is annoyed. All these things are not so undesirable that they can be swept away with a gesture of disdain, while the value of the dance as a form of emotional release is imponderable.

It is fortunate that the great popularity of American square dancing and Scottish national dancing in the 1940s has given a fresh fillip to really vigorous folk-dancing of all kinds. No one who saw Douglas Kennedy take a demonstration of English folk-dancing could ever feel that it was anything but the greatest fun to do. One of the best ways of interesting young people in national dancing of all kinds is to arrange for them to see, or organize a party to see, a demonstration by the English Folk Dancing Society or indeed any first-class team of dancers. Even boys who have gone determined to watch and scoff have often been begging to join in before the end of such an evening.

Walking, hiking and camping need, and have, books to themselves. Suffice it to say that here again one has to try to find a happy mean between over-organization and disintegration. The week-end or evening hike can be a dreary stroll, a grim trial of endurance or an exciting expedition. The trouble with most ardent walkers and cyclists is that they frequently become mileage hogs, interested only in the distance they cover. Once this starts in a group the weaker spirits are very easily discouraged. Hence, this is one of the few activities in which it is desirable to see that the members' committee do not override all discretion in their zeal to plan walks and cycles, whose main feature is their length. A great deal of help, advice and leadership can be obtained from the Youth Hostels Association and the cyclists' touring clubs, and these associations are always very willing to lend responsible leaders for youth groups. Climbing and pot-holing have also become popular among youth groups, and are not confined to those who live in the vicinity of mountains and moors since some excellent centres catering for week-end or longer-stay parties have been established. These centres, and some that provide for sailing and other water sports, also provide qualified instruction which is, of course, essential. Army Youth Teams are also able to give first-class help in mountaineering, rock climbing and pot-holing and are enthusiastic about doing so.

As one of the main objects of all youth work is to encourage young people to live in peace and amity with one another, one of the most valuable experiences is that of spending holidays together. To anyone who has worked in the industrial north or in other areas where they indulge in 'Wakes' or 'Trip' weeks, the most amazing thing is the amount of money that people spend as a matter of course on this one week's holiday. The week at Blackpool, or week of day trips, is saved up for steadily from Christmas to September, and during that week the savings are spent like water. People have, of course, the right to spend their savings as they themselves prefer, but the drawback to such holidays is that they are usually very poor value for money, and the holidaymakers frequently return from holidays not only 'spent-out' but also thoroughly jaded.

Before 1939 it was possible to take a party of young people to Paris for a week at the inclusive charge, including transport, of £5. A week in Holland could be arranged for £4 if one happened to live on the East Coast, and for a sum ranging between £4 and £7 10s. any country in Europe could be visited for a week. I shall never forget the sheer distrust evoked when I suggested the first club holiday abroad. In the first place I was told that Blackpool or Skegness had 'always been good enough'. In the second place, that it stood to reason that if it took at least £10 to £15 to have a really good holiday in either of these places, it was quite absurd to imagine that one could go abroad for such a small sum. It did not help when it was pointed out that this small sum only included transport, board and lodging, and one excursion; that if you felt you really must spend more money, there were still cigarettes, chocolates, and presents to bring home, to provide for. All my blandishments only succeeded in taking twenty-five people, but the effect it had on those people, and indeed on youth work in the whole area, was well worth the preliminary agony. The ones who decided to try this experiment asked to have French classes before they went, and although none of them were grammar-school pupils they all reached the stage where they could ask the more obvious questions and deal with money before arriving in France. This purely 'utility' French class was followed up during the winter by some of the keener spirits, who were at last convinced that there really were people who spoke in this extraordinary fashion, and they wanted to go back and talk to them again another year.

But such language teaching has to be done by someone who will use the direct method and encourage people to *talk* to one another. I can never understand why, when we have so many nationals of other countries in Great Britain, we do not utilize them in our youth groups. For six weeks (alas, I could spare no longer!) I spent two hours a week teaching a group of cotton operatives how to say certain things in French and German. It was not very good because I am fluent rather than accurate, but those boys and girls thoroughly enjoyed it, and five of them went on to evening classes the following winter. In another club situated in a town containing many Poles, the girls started to learn the language in this free and easy conversational way and, when last heard of, were seriously considering the question of Russian! Most of us do not want to read much in another language, and certainly do not want to pass examinations, but we do like to be able to talk, and there is endless room for experiment. But it is no good being 'precious' or pedantic about languages, they are meant to be spoken, not to be conjugated or analysed. If only an Englishman could realize, for instance, that when he says 'Yes, yes', he means anything from 'I agree' to 'Oh, do shut up, I want to go on reading', and that when the Frenchman says '*Oui*', he means yes—just that and nothing more—we might go a long way towards mutual understanding. If only we could once grasp that the German's love of academic thought, the Frenchman's desire for clarity and the Englishman's love of compromise, are inherent in their very speech, we might be just at the beginning of our preparations for the laying of the foundation-stone of international goodwill and peace.

Before 1939 there were those hopeful spirits among us who felt that these interchanges of visits with other countries were a very real step in the direction of increased human understanding and consequently a means of securing world peace, for such groups were meeting the ordinary people everywhere, not the intelligentsia, nor the cranks, nor the people with axes to grind. In 1939 many of us felt that, after all, this had been in vain, but perhaps it is safe to say that there has never been a war when there was so little Jingoism, and when any hate talks were directed not against the race but against the ruler. So perhaps, after all, something was achieved.

Happily, since those days, young people have more money to spend and the holiday abroad has become an annual event in many youth groups. Any leader who agrees to take upon himself the anxieties, and they are many, of such a trip is amply repaid by the number of added interests which it brings into the lives of everyone both in preparing for it and afterwards. But without adequate preparations, such holidays are as much of a waste of time and opportunity as Wakes Weeks, and after all no one ever pretends to organize these.

The camping holiday has an appeal for younger age groups, and may yet return to its former favour in the eyes of older groups. Moreover, week-end camping is an excellent spring and autumn activity and might well find a place in the programme of more youth groups.

The Guides and Scouts are probably the best campers in the world. They have raised the whole thing to an art and their standards are consequently very high. If, however, one is taking away a group of young people who have never been Guides or Scouts, it is wise to lower one's sights a little. There is probably nowhere where it is more necessary to temper the wind to the shorn lamb than it is in arranging a camping holiday for beginners. A canvas camp for those unaccustomed to camping is usually much too demanding as a first experience, and if people who have never camped before sleep in tents, it is certainly advisable to choose a site which has a permanent building of some sort into which they can be gathered if the weather becomes too difficult. Going back to nature is all very well, but many boys and girls are quite near enough to nature already, and are much more likely to respond to the joys of the sea and country if it brings them its message while they have time for sun-bathing, rather than in the wind and rain of a leaky tent. Really efficient camping is hard work and the sooner the ardent camper admits that it is not everybody's holiday, the better. As a rule it is courting disaster to take a highly urban-ized group of working boys and girls to a full-dress week's camp, run on strict Guide and Scout lines, miles away from anywhere. Having persuaded them to sample the delights of a quiet country or seaside spot, one should go half-way and arrange at least one or two trips to the nearby town, and one evening trip to a cinema; and one is well advised to sacrifice some of the law and order and some of the usual chores of camp life if one is to avoid a certain amount of understandable discontent and grumbling. One must, of course, be particular about sanitary arrangements, but there are many other things on which it is possible to relax, for although there may be a great deal in the theory that a change of work is as good as a rest, most of us prefer to rest. After a year or so we may be able to bury these same people in the heart of the country without any protests. If we try them too high in the very first camp we may never persuade them to come again. The Boys' Brigade always shows considerable wisdom in engaging really first-class cooks for their annual camps. In this way the boys are relieved of many chores and are well fed. It may be fun cooking one's own sausages, and no harm comes to one if they do fall into the fire and they are washed and started all over again. But this is not fun for seven days of the week, especially if one is normally accustomed to living out of a frying-pan.

Human nature flourishes on parties. No youth leader can afford to ignore this. Like the Church, the youth group must have its regular festivals, with occasional extras thrown in. These annual or monthly festivals should have grown up already in a club which has an established history and tradition. The Christmas concert, the summer holiday, the Good Friday hike, the Valentine's Day dance, all these in youth groups, as in private life, form the red-letter days of the year. It is as important that people should have the enjoyment of anticipating them as it is that they should enjoy them at the time.

Any party needs to include some reasonable eating and drinking, but some parties have these as their central features. Good supper and dinner parties are enjoyed by most people, especially young people, and they can provide excellent opportunities for growth in social poise and capacity to offer good hospitality. The 'slap-up' dinner party is a good way to mark a celebration occasionally. It takes a great deal of careful planning and offers opportunities for members to learn about budgeting, choosing menus, serving, inviting guests, looking after them, arranging tables and decorations, and so on, and so long as it is taken light-heartedly and care is taken to ensure that no one who cannot cope is 'put on the spot', it can include one or two brief speeches or toasts. Less ambitious, but still worth the trouble of doing well, is the barbecue, and as a complete contrast to the club dinner, comes the tramp supper. Socials and dances also require refreshments and these can be varied and interesting without causing vast expense. All these occasions and the regular refreshments at the coffee bar offer opportunities to help young people learn more about food and how to eat it.

People vary in their ideas of what a party programme should consist of. Most people of youth club age like 'off-beat' dances to pop music, but if older people are included in the party they are likely to prefer traditional ballroom dancing, and there is, of course, in most communities an Olde Tyme brigade. There are those who like to play games, those who like to perform, those who like to watch performances, and those who prefer background music and social chat. The solution sometimes is to mix various types of dancing with games, 'turns' and opportunities for chat. Another way to approach parties for people of varied tastes is to get a different group to be responsible for the programme each time. There is little point in attempting to force the shakers to do olde tyme dancing or the chatters to play games, but seeing each other enjoying their own choice without too much partisanship being allowed to build up (and preventing this is mainly a matter of leaders and helpers expressing a tolerant attitude all round) sometimes tempts people to try each other's pleasures. Those who do are often greatly surprised to discover that they enjoy the experience too, and thus people add to their repertoire of enjoyment. As one confirmed young twister said, after being inveigled into filling a gap for a set of old tymers, and who began with an expression of puzzled disdain, 'I suppose they did enjoy themselves somehow before our time!'

It seems a tradition that every party should have a number of prizes for both games and dancing, but these should be reduced to a minimum and it is usually a good idea not to announce which games and dances have prizes attached. Competition is perhaps a good and natural thing, but one needs to be wary of introducing too much competition into youth work. Experience would seem to show that it is youth leaders no less than teachers who often infuse into inter-school or club competitions that over-anxiety which insists on young people regarding a defeat as a tragedy. Of course people compete to win—it is sensible that they should. But an exhibition of extreme partisanship is not a pretty sight at a party, on the games field, or at the drama festival.

It is best to avoid those games which have too many properties and too many explanations. Both mean an extraordinary waste of time, and people get bored before starting or else do not listen. For instance, why will so many clubs play musical chairs, at great risk to chairs as well as limbs, when equally good versions can be played by using either arms, chalked rings, parcels, coloured ribbons, or even the floor, which is always there. Except in the more sophisticated group, paper and pencil games are usually a mistake and seldom make the grade.

It is essential that the programme for a party should be made well in advance, that it is discussed with the members' committee and anyone else who is going to be a steward or helper for the evening, and that the programme should be carefully timed, so that each item is stopped before people get bored with it. (The B.B.C. should have taught us much about the art of stopping a programme while it is still popular.) It should be so arranged that quiet and noisy games alternate, and that as many games as possible should be done to music. The programme should never be so rigid that it must be strictly adhered to, at the cost of acrimonious discussions at the next meeting of the committee, nor should it be so flexible that it is disregarded after the first half-hour. It should be a guide rather than a measuring-rod, but used intelligently is the only infallible way of keeping the party together.

Dancing, games, food and drink, the holiday and the party are the five-finger exercises of physical education in the club. But even if we have all these things, even if all our organization is perfect, even if that miraculous time comes when we are beginning to see some improvement in the general well-being and posture of our members, even when a few of them cease to 'walk like slaves', as one physical educationist puts it, even then we have only made a beginning. A strong and beautiful body under perfect control is a lovely thing, but it is not the be-all and the end-all of youth work. A beautiful body is, after all, only the temple of the spirit, and there is no need to become either sentimental over it on the one hand, or smug and self-satisfied on the other hand. True education is the development of the body, mind and spirit, or the physique, intellect and character, to their fullest capacity. It is quite possible to produce a number of really beautiful dancers, but this does not mean very much if they are merely selfish exhibitionists. It is possible to build up an unbeatable football team, but this means very little if they use the resultant glamour to bully the rest of the group. The marvellous class which wins every competition, the group which wins all its matches, secures its championship cups and is out for blood every time, will not shape the world. The boy who goes off on his own looking for birds' nests, or studying bugs and beetles, may be no less a devotee of the open air than the one who goes on the hearty hiking party. The whole object of all this 'keep-fittery' is in its purpose. It may be that to be fit is an end in itself, but those who ask 'fitness for what?' cannot be ignored. Through games, through camping, through countless other things, people can learn the team spirit on the one hand, and self-control and unselfishness on the other. Above all they can learn the arts of leadership in the small group, and this is the thing that will eventually shape the world, not the number of trophies on the shelf. We are still painfully learning that tyranny never abdicates and that life in a Welfare State demands a socially aware democracy, and this means putting a lot more into the latest dance than just the right steps.

12

Youth Group Activities III:
Music, Drama, Crafts and Projects

✳

How can we help young people to live more fully? How can we encourage those who retreat from life to come forward and take part in it? How can we encourage those who think of nothing but their own talents—or nothing at all—to sit back and form an appreciative audience when the talents of others are being displayed?

What we have to do is to provide opportunities for creative energy and demonstrate by the activity the fact that it is given to all to make or to appreciate, and that all may share in the joy of fulfilment and achievement. The achievement may not always be of an outstanding kind, but the value to the person concerned in the making is immeasurable. Who does not remember with a glow of pride the first present 'made by my own hands' which was given to Mother, or the first meal 'cooked all by myself'—or the first flowers and vegetables 'which I growed'?

It is important that all young people, particularly in adolescence, should learn that at least five things are necessary for the pursuit of any creative activity, self-control of mind and of body, tolerance, confidence and cheerfulness. All useful virtues and all giving life value and values.

For the most part any creative powers that they may have will not be used in their working hours, and now that education must perforce take what is known as a scientific bent, it is more important than ever that young people shall give at least some of their time to the humanities lest a future generation shall develop a scientific squint. The main channels through which the creative urge can be satisfied and the emotions both exercised and displayed in the youth group are through the forms of music, drama and creative work with the hands. How does one provide such emotional education within the rough and tumble of club life?

Like most other things in the youth group, the cultivation of an interest in music, drama and crafts must be achieved by providing —in the initial stages at all events—work in which it is possible to obtain quick results without too much technical skill. There can be no greater error than to imagine that adolescents will all be content to crawl before they can walk. We must show them the joys of riding first, even if it be on our own back, but having been taught the joys of the ride, many of them will show a growing interest and application in learning the mechanics of the thing.

MUSIC

In order to achieve music in youth groups it is usually mere foolishness to ask young people to work very hard from the beginning with scales, instrumental music, or voice production, but if we show them the fun that making our own music can be, many of them will be prepared to work quite hard on their own later on. In many groups, by virtue of the limitation of available rooms, the paucity of helpers and of expert helpers with the right technique, and because of the expense of such people when discovered, it is necessary that any given activity shall cater for a large number of people at the same time. This is why it is often pointless to discuss individual work. The youth group can take pride in the soloist, whether he is a vocalist, an instrumentalist, or an elocutionist, and give him what outside help he needs, but it has to concentrate on something for the majority. Consequently in any discussion of music it is necessary to confine oneself to three forms—choral singing, bands and listening to music.

It has become the fashion to call choral singing community singing, and under this name it has become both very well known and very badly done. It could be a splendid emotional experience, but it is only too often conducted by someone who cannot conduct, and accompanied by someone who cannot play, and the songs are sung by people who do not know the words. Often

179

pitiful attempts are made to 'have a little community singing' with no conductor at all, and young people who have suffered under much of this are rather apt to groan at the very suggestion of community singing. This is unfortunate because, with a really good conductor, who has some knowledge of music, who has an unfailing sense of time and rhythm, and who takes the trouble to make out a programme before beginning, there are few things more enjoyable. It has so many advantages. A Friday night sing-song helps to work off a great deal of youthful exuberance. It is only by hearing our members sing *en masse* that we are likely to find out which of them really have some talent for music, and in no other way is it quite so easy to educate people's musical taste. With a well-chosen programme it is possible to begin a musical half-hour with the latest film tune and to end up with 'Drink to me only'. It is possible to find out how many really good modern tunes there are, and to interest our members in other good tunes which have lived through the centuries, to point out similarities and differences and to interest them in discovering what they like best, and why they like it. Here the films and television have come greatly to our aid since they have demonstrated so often how singable so-called 'classical' tunes can be. It is possible to play, and get people to learn opera selections which they have heard from their favourite film-stars' or television-stars' lips when one could never get them to listen to an unadulterated course of six lectures on opera. Community singing, therefore, is not an amateur's trick for filling up an odd half-hour but a real opportunity to further musical education and to assess our members' ability. But one must have a really versatile accompanist and a conductor whose tastes are catholic; one must, too, devise some means of providing the group with copies of the words they are singing. If it is impossible, and it probably will be, to provide copies of everything we need, the old device of preparing a series of charts can be employed. Boys and girls interested in lettering can often be persuaded to letter charts of this kind, and very stout brown paper with white lettering is extremely effective. We can also use the back of old-fashioned wall-paper sample books, or best of all, secure long strips of yellow Lancaster cloth which can be lettered in black. Of course, it would be simpler to use a blackboard and chalk, but it is too reminiscent of 'old-fashioned' lessons, and unless one is a practised blackboard writer, in no other way can one more easily lose control of the group and ruin the atmosphere of a whole evening.

Naturally, owing to the time-consuming nature of chart-making, one only prints worthwhile songs, but this has its advantages since, as a rule, young people come to prefer those songs of which they know the words rather than the film or radio hit of the moment, of which they know only some rather silly lines and the melody.

Rightly handled, one can soon develop a concert party from a good community-singing group, and since there is nothing most young people like better than 'dressing up', one can produce some beautiful musical tableaux or a nigger minstrel troupe capable of singing anything from 'Home Sweet Home' via Scott-Gatty to Negro spirituals. This type of concert party is particularly suitable for adolescents because burnt cork and raffia are practically the only expenses entailed, and such costumes are among the few in which boys are unembarrassed.

No club should have a history of much more than six months without starting a band. Unless we have a few harmonica players and are the lucky possessor of a piano-accordion, this may have to start very humbly. However, since the skiffle band, which is, after all, nothing but a collection of improvised instruments, caught the imagination of young people, a band of improvised instruments and maybe some interesting original ones is easily formed. Many young people, too, are now the proud possessors of mandolins, guitars and piano-accordions and, eked out by a comb and tissue paper, whistles, basutos, triangles, washing-boards and the necessary thimbles, a cheese barrel and a broom, all the necessary ingredients of a good skiffle band are easily available. Let no one despise these humbler creative efforts. They satisfy a youthful need to make a noise; they give opportunity for team work. Large numbers of young people are teaching them-selves to play and one can introduce a certain amount of reading of scores with less difficulty than ever before. As soon as they have grasped the fact that in any orchestra there is a time for listening and a time for playing, they have learned two lessons—the lesson of giving and taking (you have to give in to the washing-board in order that you may take your opportunity on your beautiful cheese barrel a little later) and the lesson of listening to music itself. After the first flush of enthusiasm when everyone wants to play at the same time is passed, they soon learn that much pleasure can be gained by listening to the other fellow having a turn. In fact, as one of the most inspiring supporters of such bands once said, 'the curious thing about these bands is that the better the players the less they play'. Another proviso is necessary, one must use discrimination in the type of music which one uses. It is essential to begin with tunes people really know, and to proceed via 'D'ye ken John Peel?' to the 'William Tell Overture', via quite a number of other things, and we must be selective. There is something slightly ludicrous about an endeavour to skiffle or percuss a cradle song or *Träumerei*, though most ballads and work songs lend themselves readily to such handling.

Probably all the best bands must begin, in clubs at any rate, by a very informal system of 'nods and becks and wreathed smiles' from the conductor. In the early days of its formation almost anyone can run a band provided that he is the sort of person who can keep in step to a march tune, and it is fairly easy to get an unbiased opinion on this subject where it would be more difficult to get one on one's vocal attainments. Time and a sense of rhythm are essential, but too delicate an ear may be a disadvantage and, of course, the conductor must be without too tender a regard for his own dignity. It is better, of course, if one can play a more orthodox instrument oneself, but some extremely good work is done with gramophone record accompaniments. Thus we have succeeded in persuading people to listen to music without realizing that they are doing so.

All this may seem too simple to be entirely feasible, but the fact remains that all sorts of people, from children of play-centre age, ten-year-old boys who play in a gang-band, young men and young women, to Darby and Joan clubs, have all fallen victims to the thrill of a good tune to which they have themselves added something even if only with a rattle or a triangle.

Once people have enjoyed the excitement of such a band it is fairly easy to persuade those with a more highly developed musical sense to 'take up' an instrument. One boy who has learned to play his own instrument will often readily teach a few others, and one may develop, for instance, a harmonica band or a stringed orchestra from these improvised beginnings. Stringed instruments are, of course, much more difficult, and few clubs manage a string orchestra, but a great deal is sometimes done with recorders and

with their humbler brothers, pipes. A pipe band has a great deal
to be said for it, since one can here combine music with craft and
club members can be taught to make their own pipes. Unfortunately, however, the making of pipes always seems to be a long,
slow and utterly disheartening process which adolescents will seldom endure. Some youth groups have developed brass bands very
successfully. It is true that the noise they produce has to be heard
to be believed, but the pride and joy of the whole group when the
band 'almost gets third prize' at a local contest are well worth the
discomfort which we all suffer during rehearsal. A set of drums, a
piano-accordion and some harmonicas can make quite an attractive dance band, and there are always local amateurs who are
willing to train a young band of this kind.

Many young wage-earners have a passion for collecting their
favourite records and for listening to broadcasts of good jazz
bands, and jazz trumpet players have become the hero figures of
our age, in youth clubs as well as in fiction. No youth leader
should be unaware of the fact that any club which has a good band
will soon have a group of members who come just to listen;
therein lies another opportunity.

DRAMA

Drama has a long tradition of group work since it has been the
most popular method of using leisure from the days when our
Saxon forefathers, Brunhild and Wulfgang, sat at the back of the
great hall of the manor with the dogs and others of little account,
watching the jugglers and the tumblers and the mummers, through
the days when their great-great-grandchildren, 'Will the apprentice
baker' and 'Sally of our Alley', went to see the modern comedies
of Master Will Shakespeare at the 'Globe'; from the days when
Harriet and Herbert went to have seven-pennyworth of Harry
Lauder or George Robey at the Coliseum; and more recent days
when Tom and Elsie went weekly to see their favourite film stars
at the local Odeon, to the present when many young people are
'choosy' about television programmes and when films, being less
numerous but of higher average quality than they used to be, are
less of a habit and more of an intelligent interest to a great number
of young and older people. The young people in all these audiences,
no doubt, hold each other's hands in much the same way, and as

there is fascination in the magic of wide screens, so there was in the antics of those 'rogues, vagabonds and idle fellows' the play actors; and of course the Greeks did it long before that. A surprising number of people are exceedingly good amateur critics of the sort of performance which appeals to them, and it is just as important in introducing drama to youth groups to see that we are educating the audiences as well as those in the limelight. For those who are in the unfortunate position of being obliged to raise funds, there is no better publicity and no more certain money-making event than the production of a series of plays. This is perhaps a great grief to the purist, but after all, as no less a person than George Bernard Shaw said, there are few occasions when people are less harmfully employed than when they are making money.

The great feature of dramatic work is again that essential of all group work, the fact that so many people of differing ability can be usefully employed at the same time. No greater mistake can be made than to imagine that if a play with seven characters is chosen, only seven people will be occupied for the next six weeks or so. Indeed, it is as well to sell the idea to the dramatic group as early as possible that the most important people are not those who are acting, but the others. Those, for example, responsible for the lighting (it is as well to call them electricians, no matter how flattering this may be) are part of the show. Boys seem to know a great deal more about this than we sometimes give them credit for. Ingenuity and a few yards of flex, some old biscuit tins and some coloured gelatines, buckets of water and other contraptions can achieve most professional effects and frequently some most entertaining side-shows. Those who make tickets, posters and programmes, and the less fortunate people who sell these necessary commodities, those who sell chocolates and cigarettes on the night of the performance, are all essential performers. Moreover, if we have no stage and we feel we must have one, something can be contrived in the woodwork room, and once we have a stage we must have a stage manager. Immediately curtains become a necessity, and these have to be made and hung and pulled backwards and forwards (and curtains need not always stick). Someone from the crafts group must be called in to paint flats or to make portable mantelpieces and other reversible furniture. The sewing group must provide costumes and a wardrobe mistress.

All these people have to go into action at the very same time as the first rehearsal. Even the prompter ought to begin his work then and not, as often happens, at the final performance. The most dramatic pauses in a play need not then be spoiled by the under-rehearsed prompter who rushes in where angels would not have whispered, and only thus can one ensure that one has a prompter who will prompt in a low, clear voice and not in the sort of moan that can be heard everywhere in the house except on the stage. In the interests of prevention of cruelty to prompters, if one is appointed from the beginning, we can at least be certain that on the night he will not ruin the whole effect by falling from the steps on which he has been most perilously perched, or otherwise spend his evening knocking over scenery himself, or alternatively being knocked over by players as they rush on and off. Only if players have become accustomed to his presence, and know in which corner he is hidden, will they be prevented, if and when they dry up, from searching wildly round the stage for the voice which cometh not, or from ruining a tense scene by hissing, 'Speak up, can't you!' The fact that it is necessary to be seen in order to secure creative satisfaction has surely been killed for all time by the glorious remark of a club member who eagerly demanded of his rather seedy father who had been persuaded to come to see the final effort, 'Did you hear the ghost what groaned at the end of the first scene? Well, that was me!' And probably one of the best of prompters was a most retiring boy who never crossed a room alone if he could gain his objective by proceeding timidly along the walls.

The only expert necessary is the producer who should be experienced but not temperamental, who should have the patience of Job and the vitality of Puck, possessing the resilience and enthusiasm which one might associate with an unburstable rubber ball. These saints are hard to come by; a youth leader is well advised to choose, if choice can be made, not the drama specialist who has the most talent, but the one who has the most sense of humour. For in most youth groups unless we are merely going to produce a drama society of neurotic exhibitionists who only act because they think they can act, we must find someone who cares for adolescents more than performances. For unless our drama group can entice new people into the group, unless in some way or other it can interest every member of the group, unless it can

185

stimulate a team spirit and can afford people the opportunity of learning how to laugh at themselves, unless in fact drama can be both fun and purposeful, it has little place in youth work. That is why it is just as well not to begin by being too ambitious, or to be too set in one's ideas.

Until we know whether we have any talent in our group at all, it is best to begin gently with drama's poor relations the charade, now called 'improvisation', miming games, tableaux, and the potted tragedy or comedy, before we embark on set plays! All these are useful introductions to drama and all of them possess those three essentials of any youth activity—they are cheap, they are quick, and they are fun.

There are some extremely lively miming games, such as modernized versions of 'Three Jolly Welshmen', which some young people play with enthusiasm and never suspect that they are acting. In this way one can spot talent and proceed to more ambitious charades without words. In addition to enabling one to pick out the more promising actors, these dramatic games give excellent opportunities for self-expression to members who have no memory, or rather whose memory has remained untrained, and for those who are so bashful that the very thought of doing something before their fellows is sufficient agony without the additional one of having to remember words at the same time. Sometimes, too, such work can be developed usefully for outdoor entertainment. Miming is an excellent way of achieving good clear-cut action and teaches young people to show the audience what in fact they are doing.

A drama group can get a great deal of satisfaction out of nursery rhymes and historical scenes, Bible stories and ballads; and once we get to the ballad we can risk a reader or, more fashionably, a commentator or compère. In this way some members will learn to read aloud in a fashion an audience can find bearable. Later on, when they have become less self-conscious, it is possible to try improvising sketches with words. Here it is essential that they shall learn the art of constructing little thumb-nail plots for each scene; otherwise they will not know how to close each scene so that the characters do not scramble off in a huddle. A plot is essential, too, if such improvised work is based on the charade, so that only one player in each scene speaks the clue word, an elementary precaution which is so often overlooked.

Music, Drama, Crafts and Projects

In some youth groups it is possible to do a certain amount of play-reading, but this has to be handled very carefully indeed, and so has verse-speaking, which can only be done effectively, perhaps, under a really inspiring teacher. For the rest there are numbers of extremely helpful books concerning dramatic work in clubs, and as long as we are not afraid of experimenting, as long as our choice of play (when we come to that stage) is not so flimsy that they get sick of it, nor so heavy that they get tired of it, we really have very little to worry about.

We need not, however, worry about a stage or curtains—curtains are out anyway in many theatres—nor do we need to feel we should eventually arrive at the point where we produce set plays. This is particularly so if we can get a helper who is expert in dance drama. It can be done indoors or out, requires only a minimum of props, and no stage. It combines dance, miming, improvisation, expression, control and team work in a most satisfying way for the participants, and if an audience needs to be entertained, it can provide visual beauty, be highly amusing, or be very moving for the onlooker.

CRAFTS

The youth group should try to give scope for every interest of hand, mind and heart—in a word it should endeavour to keep its members fit in every sense. Handiness with tools and materials is a form of physical fitness just as definitely as soundness of wind and limb; it belongs not to the hand only but to the eye and brain as well. Working with materials cultivates accuracy of calculation as well as touch. It stimulates visual imagination and demands infinite forethought and patience. Such handiness has an especial value in an age in which mass production has substituted mechanical operations for the craftsman's skill. Moreover, much of the skill achieved in craft work spills over into everyday life, from increased happiness in the home (even the cutting of bread and the carving of a joint are easier matters for the craftsman) to the development of that patience and discipline which the handling of raw materials forces on one.

We are much helped in all this by television, for great as its dangers undoubtedly are it has shown a fascinated generation of young people beautiful things, lovingly handled and described, beautiful places visited, as well as the great skill of the ballet dancer, the artist and the actor.

A great deal of nonsense is talked about crafts; on the one hand there are those who feel that it is a dull business, especially devised for those who possess a lower type of brain—the manual workers —as though everyone who writes a book does not labour with his hands! On the other hand there are those artsy-craftsy people who make one connect crafts with pretty-pretty knick-knacks for bazaars—those people who feel that craft is 'artistic' and whose true artfulness is, perhaps, revealed in their absorbing passion for making everything look like what it isn't, those people who cannot see a piece of leather or wood or glass without wanting to paint it, who can't see a pot without wanting to cover it with a piece of paper or 'decorate' it with a bow. So it comes about that there is a great deal of self-consciousness about crafts and great conflict between those who will not do it because they think it is *not* clever, and those who will do it because they think it *is*.

We are told that 'there are nine-and-sixty ways of constructing tribal lays and every single one of them is right'. This is certainly true of crafts in the youth group. There are countless crafts and methods of teaching them, but no one can say which is right, and so few of them have even been tried.

One can choose a craft because it is popular or because there is a suitable teacher available. If our choice is determined by the latter, it is advisable to begin by arranging a small loan exhibition of suitable work carried out in this craft, either by the expert or by members of other groups, and during the course of the exhibition a demonstration should be arranged. But in most youth groups it is essential to avoid, as one has to in music and drama, anything which takes too long in its initial stages or any craft that requires laborious preliminary exercises and technical processes, since young people are creatures of moods and patience does not come easily to them. While teachers must sometimes place some restraint both on work that is not demanding enough and on over-ambitious projects, they must also place some restraint on their own desire for excessive law and order; the craft group is the place for conversation as well as work.

Its main purpose in the youth group is to encourage the appreciation of truth and beauty in the handling of raw materials and it is not designed to turn young people into expert craftsmen.

Music, Drama, Crafts and Projects

Neither is it part of the club's function to compete with the local education authority in providing facilities for technical training; such training needs more specialized equipment, more space, stricter discipline and more regular application than is either practicable or perhaps even desirable in a youth group. The job of the latter is to give young people a taste for craft or music or drama, or any other form of creative endeavour, and to pass them on to the expert later if they show desire and aptitude. One of the most remarkable advances in this field since the war has been a revival of interest in painting in youth groups. Perhaps it may seem offensive to some that this should be regarded as a craft, but the great artists would not mind. Here the expert is essential from the start, but it is a joy to see young people enjoy the release of playing freely with colour and design in such art classes; and where a skilled and sensitive teacher can be found the emotional value of such work both within the club and in the formation of outdoor painting and sketching classes is inestimable.

Another method of tackling craft in the youth group is to take as one's starting point some pressing need of the club or its individual members. It may be that new furniture, curtains, cushions, or bookshelves are needed; it is almost certain that redecoration is overdue, pictures may need framing or the dramatic group may need staging and dressing, or girls may want to try to make fashion's latest 'accessories'. From these needs a craft class can readily be formed. This method does not lend itself to the development of organized classes, but this does not really matter. The choice for most youth leaders usually lies between an informal class or nothing; and the leader has a primary duty to cater for the more casual groups who, maybe through the irregular hours of their employment, or maybe through their determination not to be 'improved', will not take kindly to anything resembling formal instruction.

This type of craft group, which takes on various jobs as they arise and whose intention is not to produce a work of art but to achieve a particular result in the most direct and effective manner possible, is often much the best approach and sometimes the only method of inducing members to attend. Here we are much helped by the modern cult of 'Do it yourself'. Coming to us as it has from America, a compound of financial stringency and the high cost of labour, it has given many people a high degree of creative satisfaction. Moreover, the 'Do it yourself' fashion has produced those innumerable and fascinating gadgets such as paint rollers, which are fun to use and give the adolescent an opportunity to use tools which in the home are commonly the playthings reserved for their parents who have developed the zest of children for splashing an infinite variety of colours on their walls. There is, after all, no special virtue in making things just for the sake of making them, and no reason why a club leader should be more proud of a group who are somewhat unwillingly making rather pointless samples of artistic felt-work, which they very sensibly aim to get rid of as soon as possible by means of a bazaar, than of a dancing class which the members come to willingly and where they are improving their balance and control and learning to walk better. Many young people have as yet found little purpose in life, but there is not much advance if we merely encourage them in purposeless creation. We are much too self-conscious about our creative work, and young people who have the imagination to see things as they really are, are not interested in making something look like what it isn't. The child asks why, the adolescent asks what for; a craft class which is started to fulfil some definite need answers this question and so gives satisfaction on the creative level which, after all, is really what craft is all about.

Having taken into consideration those three scarcities of club life, money, time and space, the only prerequisite we must obtain is a good, big, steady table; even a separate room for crafts is not essential, and not always the most successful way of dealing with the craft. The best equipment one can afford is always the cheapest in the end, but just as a child gets an enormous amount of pleasure out of a rag doll while other and more expensive toys lie neglected around it, so the adolescent often gets a great deal of satisfaction from makeshift equipment. This does not mean that we should be satisfied with this, but it does mean that one need not hesitate to indulge in crafts merely because one's equipment is not exactly what one would wish.

There are still surprisingly few people who get as much fun as they might out of making things. Life for the process worker and the office worker has become, as it has for the research scholar, a matter of knowing more and more about less and less. It is pathetic to witness the joy of many young people when they find that they are hand-brained, that feeling and touch are their natural channels of expression (this is why we ought to do more carving and modelling), that for them the world of ideas can after all be translated adequately in terms of things.

Since doing a job together is one of the best ways of promoting right feelings, a great deal of 'feeling one's way to thinking' can be conducted in the youth group through what has become known as the project method. But what is a project? One could hardly do better than use the Oxford Dictionary definition—a scheme, plan or course of action. Most groups could do with some planning and all adolescents like action. A secondary meaning of the word (as a verb) is 'To cause light and shadow to fall on a surface', and the surface can be regarded as either the programme or the minds of the member. It is an ideal mixed activity and is as useful a way of planning a programme for the one-night-a-week group with little in the way of premises and equipment, as it is for the large club with many resources. It is an active approach to learning, and assumes that *everyone* is interested in *something*. If one is interested in something, one can be encouraged to find out more about it, and the best way to find out is at one's own speed and in one's own way. It assumes that one will want to share what has been learnt, and that if there is some finishing point or climax, one will learn more quickly and enjoy it much more.

One of the best kinds of project in the club pattern is the pantomime. This has all the essentials of a project for it has to be planned, perhaps by the whole club. Then the work has to be shared out, therefore it is necessary to have groups who help one another, and the resulting climax is the show itself. Every youth leader is familiar with this, but they do not always see how the method can be used for other activities.

There are all sorts of ways of leading into projects; for example, seizing on national events (such as a Royal Tour), on a common interest (such as television or dancing), on a club event (this can be either a special week or birthday or group holiday). A project can be used to pep up committee work or a discussion group, to get people interested in current affairs or their neighbourhood. The river on which the town stands can be a 'centre of interest' and traced from source to mouth—a holiday abroad can be 'projected' into a wall newspaper, a log book, a group of dressed dolls, or an international evening.

Music, Drama, Crafts and Projects

The vitally important features of any project are that it should not last too long, that it should end 'with a bang not a whimper' and that as many as possible should be drawn into it. One of the most vitalizing forms a project can take is that of service to others. For a most important development of Youth Service since its inception has been that of the training in service to the community which has been encouraged among young people. Youth groups in common with other societies are usually all the better for adopting somebody or some good cause. The great advantage of helping others is that one gets to know their problems and so broadens one's sympathies and understanding. It is astonishing how many concerts and parties are arranged by youth groups for hospitals, the blind and the old, how many adopt a leper or a ship or care for a cripple or a spastic member. Moreover point and purpose is given to many a youth activity—the play—the craft work—if it is designed to help, or to raise funds to help, other people. But however laudable the raising of funds may be, it is the acts of *personal* service, the shopping for the old, writing letters to the lonely or to nationals of other countries, the visits to hospital, the reading to the blind, which are perhaps the most important things to encourage. In a Welfare State it is no mean thing if young people can be brought early to the realization that although material aid and succour are the State's business, no man can pay another to love his neighbour.

13

Youth Group Activities IV: Discussion, Radio, Television and Reading

✳

Duuring the first eleven or twelve years of his life the child is learning to use the tools of education. By the time he has achieved a certain facility with the use of these tools, he is plunged into the many and various changes of adolescence. He is busy coping with his emotional adjustments to life; he is groping his way through this emotional tangle and feeling his way towards thinking, which is why his idealism is lofty and his practical application often leaves much to be desired. He thinks that he is thinking, but what he is really doing is testing his feelings on certain subjects. Some people never pass beyond this stage, they never reach their way out of feeling, and all their adjustments to life are coloured by their emotional responses. Quite often, let us hasten to add, they reach the right conclusions, but their inability to sustain and follow any reasoned process remains. All youthful enthusiasm is inspired by feeling, and it is right that it should be so, but if constructive thinking does not follow, full adulthood is never achieved.

In the youth group, therefore, we should be much concerned with harnessing feeling to thinking. All can enjoy either music, drama or crafts, can be encouraged to make their own music, to employ themselves in their favourite craft, or to perform in some type of play, but the time comes when this joy in doing must develop into appreciation and discrimination. It is merely, of

N   193

course, repeating the history of childhood. At first the child is content to draw—he enjoys the feeling of covering his paper with scribbles; then he draws cups and saucers, and houses and trees; but later on, though he still enjoys the feeling of expressing himself in this medium, he discovers that his execution is poor. It is at this stage that he wants to know *how* to do it, or at least how other people do it. He is ripe then for some instruction in perspective, shading and all the tricks of the artist's stock-in-trade. In the same way, through the practice of democratic government in the committee, he can be brought to a realization of the difficulties of the government of the country. Through realizing the difficulties of managing the group's subscriptions and finances, he can gradually realize the importance of political economy. In the same way through drama, through music and crafts, the adolescent can be made ready for discussion on how the job is done, and there is no real appreciation without a sound knowledge of the technique and difficulties of any art. Indeed one might go further and say that one can never fully appreciate any art that one has not at least *tried* to practise. Love of an art and really full appreciation are two very different things, just as loving people does not *necessarily* mean that you fully understand and appreciate them.

Appreciation is merely more highly developed feeling—that is, feeling coloured by thought. The important thing at this stage is how adolescents feel about newspaper articles, books, talks and discussions; how they feel about the club library, about the film shows they see and the speeches they hear over the radio, or the television.

It is a field of great opportunity because the adolescent is very receptive to ideas that *feel* right to him—unlike the adult whose emotional entanglements have taught him to suspect his feelings since they always seem to lead him into some sort of trouble. It is one of the most exciting things in the world to sit round a fire or round a table, or in the bar of a public house, with a group of young people who are groping their way into the world of ideas, who are testing facts against feelings and trying to rationalize the whole process. Everyone has to work out his own salvation and his own philosophy of life, and adolescence is the time when all one's childish puzzlement about 'what is time?', 'where does tomorrow go?', 'which is the dream life and which is the reality?' —revive. But in adolescence the questions are more urgent and

194

demand an answer. The adolescent demands the truth, the whole truth, and nothing but the truth, and if, just then, one can so put him in the way of thinking (very few of us are big enough to do anything quite so presumptuous as to 'guide' people's thoughts), the sooner he will work out his own philosophy and the easier it will be for him to arrive at the conclusion that though, after all, none of us is great enough to perceive truth with a capital 'I', truth has many facets and it is given to all of us to

> *Follow the thing as he sees it*
> *And each in his separate star*
> *To draw the truth as he sees it*
> *For the God of things as they are.*

But that is where we hope to end. Where shall we begin?

Most people think of the 'discussion' group as the method *par excellence* of providing 'mental' activities for young people. The discussion method has become the new idolatry, but it is no substitute for factual information, as one realizes when one listens to discussion groups who have been provided with nothing to discuss but their own confusion. Indeed, it has great disadvantages over the now old-fashioned 'talk' since, though during the latter the attention of *some* of the group may wander, others actually *listen*. In many a discussion group, few people are really *listening*; they are largely preoccupied with what *they* are going to say next! Hence, one of the major dangers of the discussion method is that, unless it is very wisely handled, it encourages people to use their natural gift for *hearing*, but does not develop in them the art of listening.

In promoting any conversation or discussion with young people, it is essential to remember that they are predominantly self-centred. Their reaction to every new idea and new plan of campaign is 'What is the use of this to *me*?' They are unfair too. Like the Tudor Morton they tackle us with a two-pronged fork of objections, the utility and the futility arguments. This affects their responses to every variety of subject; they want to know the *use* of everything from religion to keep-fit, and having been convinced of the use of these things they want to be assured that their efforts to become more religious, more knowledgeable or more physically fit, shall not be entirely futile. 'Yes,' they say, 'I quite see that I ought to be a good citizen, I ought to know this and that, but even

195

if I am, what difference will it make? I can't of myself do anything, I'm not important enough and I don't know enough, and anyway Dad says it's just the same rates and taxes no matter what blinking government we've got.' Hence one of the most useful points of departure for discussion is the film and television, because this is familiar ground. Between them the films and television have probably the greatest impact on modern life of any kind of informal education, and we neglect the opportunities they present us with at our peril. Even a bad film or television show has its talking point, and there are many programmes which present sociological and moral problems of the greatest significance.

But one must proceed from the familiar, and nothing is too commonplace. Even on the basis of making-up and love-letters valuable discussions or a series of talks can emerge. Girls *will* make-up (and so do most of us—art usually transcends nature), so why not ask someone to show them how? If we are clever and get the right person we may be plunged into a short course on famous beauties of bygone days. On one occasion I happened to go into the sitting-room of a girls' club to find a group of seventeen to twenty-fives howling with mirth. It turned out that they were comparing love letters, handing them round and reading out the best bits—and very interesting it was. I was invited to make the minimum contribution of one letter to the pool, and though delighted that they asked for this, and that they should pay me the compliment of thinking that I lived a normal enough life to have a possible contribution to make, unfortunately I was much too inhibited to respond. However, from lovers and their ways we passed to preparation for marriage, and a short lecture course on parenthood and its responsibilities was the outcome of a very hilarious evening.

As long as one is not impatient, as long as one plans one's very nonchalance carefully, there need be no boundary set to the 'thinking' content of youth work—from make-up to psychology, from club committee to citizenship, from reading a newspaper to reading a play. Only two things are necessary, that we should be content to make an unhurried start where their interest lies and that we shall have a very clear picture of where we are asking them to go.

And where can we go? One can begin with what are rather loosely called visits of observation, from gas works to courts of law, from films to film-making, though such visits need far more careful preparation and follow-up than is usually afforded them; from visits to the theatre to making plays, from walking to map-making or to surveys. There is nothing quite like making a relief map of the district; it gives one all the fun of using those lovely messy materials such as plasticine, plaster of Paris, paint and papier mâché and twice it has taught me that adolescents have a very happy knack for modelling—that most neglected, so cheap, and yet so satisfying craft.

A study of the group's finances (can we afford new records and a football this month?) can end up in a series of lectures on 'How the Town is Governed', which sounds so much more practical than that curious thing termed civics.

The subject is not important, but one must get hold of the man on the job, the real expert. There are too many of the uninitiated talking to the uninterested in adult groups, and there is no need to inflict them on the adolescent. Speakers must be told exactly what they are up against and one must be prepared oneself to keep the ball of discussion rolling. Rotary Clubs, Chambers of Commerce, and so forth, are full of people who can tell young people glamorous real-life experiences of business life. Such people may not be platform speakers perhaps, but they are usually excellent at answering questions, and they will give many young people just the contact with the adult world that thrills them most. One of the most valuable workers in the service of youth that I have ever been privileged to work with is the manager of a large chain store; he can talk to young people—and to their fathers and mothers—on big business, on travels and on religion, and bring the house down every time. Why? Because he is a real person living a real life in the workaday world, and they can go into the store and see him at it. For the sake of the future of local government, one could wish that our councillors could be persuaded to give a little more time to their future constituents. If only they would come just to tell them electioneering stories; or if they would only help one to assure the young that they are not paid for the job it would help. (How many town councillors know that many people believe that they get a fee for their services?) If only the mayor could be persuaded to let them finger his chain of office, if the town clerk would come into the youth group, local government would become a fascinating and living thing in the eyes of

197

young people, instead of something which they feel concerns them not at all.

There are still many youth groups who do not take advantage of the willingness of cinema managers to come to answer questions about their work. They will often put one in touch with others who know about production and other aspects of the industry, and a whole course on films can well result—a course which, beginning with the lives of the film stars, can end with a study of scenario writing, or the history of photography, or the production of a play. One of the funniest things I have ever seen was a group which had been taking a course of film work and which produced for the Christmas concert a burlesque in dumb show of the old silent serial. If any of these young people had been asked to act, or join a drama group, they would have been frightened away completely.

For many young people the radio, the film and television provide just the help they need in their efforts to grow up. They are seeking to reconcile the eternal polarities of adventure and security. Their moods, interests and needs are changing almost from day to day, but they are self-conscious and shy of asking questions of people they know, and who know them too well! Hence, these impersonal media have advantages over others in illustrating and illuminating their personal problems, and it is part of the youth leaders' duty to bend the programme towards the satisfaction of their needs through discussions on films, radio and television programmes.

Many programmes make extremely useful and laudable contributions to the illumination of family problems, but it is absolutely necessary to pave the way for them and not to regard them as labour-saving devices designed to save one the job of finding speakers. During the first few months of the 'At the Armstrongs' series for instance, one rather noisy and very lively group, who listened in each week, produced in the end a burlesque evening which was a further instalment of the series acted and invented by themselves. From this a small drama class of no little talent emerged. The same thing was done in another group with the 'Archers' and 'Grove Family' serials.

It is not necessarily the programmes specifically designed for youth, or to air 'problems' that are the most useful for this type of discussion evening. A radio story told by a genius at story-telling, a piece of autobiographical experience, a short play, all provide gems for the club leader who will use the *Radio Times* intelligently, and even the poorish to bad play has its talking point, and the adolescent does less viewing at home than any other age group—for reasons which should be obvious. The club sitting-room with the easy chairs is the place for the listening group, where people can sew or mend while they listen, and where boys can go on fiddling with their models. It is right that the group leader should be helped by notes, but they are intended to stimulate ideas, and it should not be necessary to write them out. If one watches carefully the trend of the remarks afterwards, it is fairly easy to plan a campaign which starts with present interests. In all these lecturettes, discussion groups, what you will, it is essential to keep all the proceedings natural, to lead up to things gradually, and to begin from where the young people are. This cannot be said too often. One of the most important aspects of discussion groups (as indeed of music and radio groups) is not only the key to success in skilful and rewarding personal relationships; it is also one of the main tools by which we acquire education during our schooldays and afterwards.

This is why one is never happy about suggesting debating groups. The form is too artificial for most young people and is apt to mean that the more self-conscious and tongue-tied members of the group become discouraged. Moreover, one has to use all one's tact (often in vain) to prevent the member who is a born exhibitionist with the gift of the gab from monopolizing every meeting, on no matter what topic, with a further version of his ready-made remedy for every social ill. Quite often, too, a programme of debates tends to become artificial because the members' background is not sufficient to sustain a long debate on one subject. Therefore it is too easy to fall into the temptation of introducing frivolous subjects, of the 'Is it better to be a giraffe with a sore throat than a centipede with corns' variety, which really have very little value.

The Quiz sessions which have had a great vogue in some groups are open to the same criticism. Young people already have enough given to them in the way of 'bits and pieces', and although a Quiz evening has its part and place in the youth group, leaders and members would be better employed giving the same amount of time and energy to something more sustained and sustaining.

Discussion, Radio, Television and Reading

Such devices as the Jokes Evening, Sing, Say, Read or Pay Nights or an Inquiry Evening are more educationally sound and just as entertaining. The first two are almost self-explanatory. In the first, each member tells his favourite joke and the best is voted for and wins a small prize. This must be done by popular election. We must be prepared for a certain amount of shock and a certain amount of enlightenment as to what the adolescent thinks is funny, and it is most interesting to see how the brand of humour varies from county to county. The 'Sing, Say, Read or Pay' is the old-fashioned variation of a Talents Evening. They did it in Saxon times. Do you remember the cowherd who could not sing or say and crept from the hall? Our members merely part with a small fine. An 'Inquiry' night is a less highfalutin' way of talking about a commission. The group chooses a subject and inquires into it. For example, 'How did you get your first job?' 'A day in my job', 'Our house and how I would like it altered'. From these small beginnings it is possible to get people interested in local surveys and maps and even simple, elementary, but full-of-life instead of dry-as-dust economics.

Sometimes the technique of the Brains Trust proves useful. One must view it with a certain amount of disquiet, however, since it has become the fashion in some circles to form mutually elected Brains Trusts—a form of conceit which is wearisome— and partly because a good idea is none the better for being over- worked. As a method of dealing with religious problems it is excellent. Youth groups which hold monthly meetings of a Brains Trust presided over by a hand-picked selection of clergy- men have often proved it so. It is generally advisable for the questions to be placed in a box a week in advance of each meeting so that the clergy have a few days' notice of what to expect. To their eternal honour, most of them do not take advantage of this to prepare little pocket sermons. The Brains Trust technique, too, has the advantage of helping those who are knowledgeable with- out being eloquent enough to impart their information in other forms, but like the debate the Brains Trust can all too easily become debased.

Most boys and girls see a paper during the day, and a great deal can be done by using newspaper cartoons or headlines as a starting point for discussion. Every youth group ought, of course, to take one or two daily papers and it is quite a good idea to watch any

Discussion, Radio, Television and Reading

newspaper that is running a stunt. For in this way it is often possible to tie up the group's interests with the burning topic of the moment. Even a local murder trial can be turned to good account by discussing court procedure. Crime is always popular and one will not eradicate people's natural interest by ignoring it; but from this unpromising material a six weeks' course on the elements of English Law and Justice can be designed. A newspaper running a silly season correspondence on whatsoever form of adolescent behaviour is being castigated by the Press at any given moment, can lead to such things as a talk on the struggle for women's suffrage; a newspaper article on God and war may lead to another short series of talks on Comparative Religion.

A club which proves a little unresponsive can sometimes be helped in the direction of newspaper discussions by the much-despised competition. At one club, which was at the dance, darts and detached boredom stage, a beginning was made by a very simple competition. It was announced that on Saturday a simple newspaper competition would be held, based on matters of interest which had appeared in the newspapers of the previous week. Questions were varied so that everyone had an opportunity to answer at least two of them correctly. For instance, they were asked questions about a film star much in the news that week, about football, and even the current local scandal was not entirely ignored. Following upon this, at monthly intervals, various competitions were held and eventually a newspaper discussion group with weekly meetings emerged.

If one wishes the discussion group to be the point of departure for a series of talks, however, each talk should be complete in itself as well as having a definite connecting link with future work. In this way the casual dropper-in gets something that is of real value and no one gets into the habit of feeling that if they cannot attend for twelve weeks every Friday (so help them) it is not worth coming at all. It is true that there is a great deal to be said for the discipline of taking a course and *seeing it through*, but those of our members who have the time and talent for that sort of thing should be taking definite evening institute classes (even if they are held at the club). The boys and girls who are our *especial* care are the ones who have not yet developed the taste for long courses. Our job is to get them interested and to keep them interested. The people who need a solid meal must be directed to it,

201

but the youth group must keep an educational running buffet for the casual, for the timid, and for those who are still experimenting, and have not yet found an absorbing passion.

Story-telling, reading aloud and writing all play their part in providing material for discussion and in enlarging the content of adolescent experience. Reading aloud always sounds hopelessly mid-Victorian, but provided that we choose the moment it is surprising how much young people like it. I once worked in a club where there was a Friday night mending group. One evening I took in the newspaper, and sat down to read it. Then, having chosen the topic carefully, I started 'Just listen to this—'. 'This' was listened to and commented on by a few people, and then I went on reading to myself. As I had hoped, someone said, 'Is there anything else in the paper?'—and of course there was. I then strolled away and repeated the performance the next week; after a few weeks of this I went in with both a book and a newspaper. After my preliminary reading the usual question came, 'Isn't there anything else in the paper tonight?' I threw it aside after declaring there was nothing in it, and immersed myself in my book. I had deliberately chosen something that never fails to make me chuckle, and after a few of these chortlings the anti-cipated question came, 'What are you laughing at?' Then we were well away. For months after that the newspaper and readings continued. Some Fridays were deliberately missed; the actual readings never went on for more than twenty minutes to half an hour, but what fun they were, and what new worlds they opened to the group. Once or twice someone borrowed the book and finished it alone. I was asked if 'that feller had written any more like that'—and the books were obtained for private reading from the library. On the whole it is wiser to confine oneself to extracts rather than to read solidly through a book. The modern adolescent has a snapshot, or kinematic, mind, and the secret of success is to leave off while they are still interested.

After such an introduction it is possible to create an interest in writing or playing with words. One Friday I 'forgot' my book and mislaid my newspaper and told them some nonsense verse instead. On the first occasion it was limericks, and I then explained about the old-fashioned limerick competition—in which one is given four lines and makes up the fifth. Between us we made up a limerick about the group and everyone suggested last lines and promised to think of others for next week. A week or so later we tried a group ballad—there is no easier metre for beginners to work with. Then, because we got stuck for rhymes, we had a rhyming bee, much more fun than a spelling bee because it conceals one's inability to spell. One side says boom, the other tomb, and sooner or later you have to explain why bomb just will not do. In a very short while words have come to mean something more to them, they have been revitalized and are newly regarded. Even if we do not loosen the tongue of a potential 'mute inglorious Milton' we have probably found a versifier who can write a certain amount of doggerel, someone who can learn a stock of amusing verse, one or two perhaps who can read aloud well, and together we can make up new words to old songs, and most especially to new ones; and the English language becomes for some at least an adventure in human understanding and a delight in loneliness.

When young people have learned to talk, to versify, to tell stories, to be at home with words in fact, they often want to start a magazine. This would seem an activity to be hindered rather than helped, since it tends to become self-conscious and is rarely anything but the product of the few. Even the professional writer finds it difficult to produce something to order at a given date each month or quarter! A better alternative is to start a club log book or commonplace book into which we write our best efforts, favourite pieces of nonsense and beauty, and this can be enlivened with photographs and sketches.

The most powerful method of feeling one's way to thinking is still through the printed word and nothing is more important than encouraging young people to read. Perhaps a club library is the right approach but the two most unfortunate things about most club libraries, however, are that in the first place they frequently do not exist, and in the second place, if they do they are so limited. Sometimes youth leaders say, 'Well, of course, we used to get a box of books from the library, but no one ever used them!' After a little questioning, one finds that the box was kept under the stage or behind the counter of the canteen and practically no one knew it was there. More often the library consists of a dark cupboard, usually packed with an assortment of other articles, containing rows of books that no self-respecting adolescent would ever think of reading. Youth groups have suffered much from well-intentioned gifts such as *Dr. Dry-as-Dust's Sermons*, 1871–85 and *The Scientist at Home*, Vols. IV, VIII and X (pub. 1884). Many libraries contain row after row of those formidable works which collect the dust, and which no one dares to get rid of because they were given by a local worthy who might one day ask, 'Where is my great-Uncle Thomas's Sunday school prize which he won in 1862?' Good use can be made of the quite admirable Penguin and other paper-backed publications as a cheap, effective and up-to-date method of stocking youth libraries. Young people want to read good modern stuff and these books would seem to supply just what is wanted—good fiction, detective and mystery stories, biography, and more serious material. For £5 or £6 one can start with a good selection, all bright and new and clean. Moreover, if the members' committee can be interested in it, a great deal of useful discussion can centre round the purchase of further books, and the constant bogy of losses and replacements need not press too heavily on the librarian, while well-worn favourites can be replaced and *bound* by the crafts group before being placed into circulation again. A further important point is that such books are bright, gay, and take up very little room, and because they are cheap and easily replaced it might be possible to place a shelf of books in each room instead of having one room set self-consciously aside as a library. If, conversely, all the periodicals are then kept in the library, those self-conscious young things can be lured to the library itself, through a desire which any self-respecting tough guy might have to look at the *Amateur Mechanic*.

It is usually possible to come to terms with the public library over a constant supply of periodicals, and it is well worth allocating a weekly sum to the purchase of the more popular weeklies. It does not matter greatly if they do not happen to be *our* favourite weeklies—after all, it is quite fair if they come to the reading-room to read their choice and remain to read ours. There is much more likelihood of this happening if we consider their taste and what we liked at their age. The only golden rule about periodicals is not to have too many—to have bright and cheerful ones, to have recent ones and to throw them away when they get out of date. There is really no need to harbour a collection of periodicals for which a dentist's waiting-room is the only possible and generally accepted haven.

Discussion, Radio, Television and Reading

It is a sad reflection on the public respect for reading that many young people would rather be seen dead than visiting the public library, but if books are available in every room they will often take a book from the shelf and with studied nonchalance stroll to a corner and become lost to the world. It is true that a few books may get lost that way, but surely it is better that a book should be lost or damaged because Willie could not bear to part with it until he had finished it, rather than that books should get lost or damaged because Willie and his gang made a booby trap with them, or worse still, that they were not used at all.

There are two further points in favour of the paper-backed library. If members take the books home, they look like the sort of books other people are reading and they are a handy and convenient size for slipping into handbag or overcoat pocket for reading in the bus or train on the way to and from work, and in the lunch hour. A large number of young people have well over an hour's journey to and from work, and many of them maintain that they cannot take a library book because it is too bulky, because it makes them conspicuous, or because they are afraid of losing it and think themselves unable to afford the replacement. The paper book looks very little different from other magazines and they feel they can cope with paying for it if they lose it, though such is the strange way in which the young mind works that they seldom think of *buying* one for their own private consumpton.

A plentiful supply of good light literature in the club often guides the members in the use of a library, but they should be passed on to using the public library when they have learnt a little about how and what to choose. In spite of all that teachers have done and still do to encourage young people to make use of public libraries, there are still many who do not seem to know how to become members.

Before we deplore our young people's taste in reading, we might do well to inquire what facilities they enjoy for obtaining better. Because of the distance many young people travel to work, they are unable to make use of the local public library. In one borough alone, 209 out of 604 seventeen-year-old boys questioned were unable to make use of the public library since it was never open before they went to work and was shut again before they returned. A few said that mothers and sisters changed their books but none of them were entirely satisfied by this method. As one most unlikely devourer of travel books said, 'I like books about travel and last week my mother brought me a great thick book called *A Journey in the Desert* and' (disgustedly) 'it was all about love!' They do not seem to realize that they can often change their books at a library near their place of work, but this is not possible for all of them. Small wonder then, that many young people admit to being 'keen on books' and, when asked where they get them, say 'Oh, in the shop round the corner'. It is no good railing against the chain library—the 2d. library in the general store—and the magazine or 'comic', if it is so difficult for young people to come by anything better.

The question of 'taste' and so-called worthless reading material needs careful consideration. It is true that an astonishing amount of comics, Westerns and less desirable strip cartoon material is purchased and read by adolescents. But a shilling thriller or love-story is not of necessity or automatically any worse than a twelve-and-sixpenny thriller or love-story. Moreover, there is a danger of doing a great injustice to Jack and Jill's reading when we conveniently forget that in addition to all the good wholesome and possibly improving literature that we read, most adults also get through a great deal of rubbish too. We all have to lose our literary milk teeth. The trouble with omnivorous readers is that all is grist which comes to their mill. It is a consolation to find, therefore, that those who have done much exhaustive research into the method, manner and content of children's reading, assure us that the child who is literary-minded reads everything equally voraciously, good, bad or indifferent, and it does not seem to affect so much as to form his taste. But the tragedy would seem to be that many young people become the *victims* of their ability to read because when their taste for thrillers and the more luscious type of romance has been sated, they are unable to find a bridge to adult reading.

There are a number of adolescents who buy both a comic and a highly technical paper and enjoy both. In their stories they demand a blend of the realistic and the romantic, garnished with circumstantial detail and painstakingly and conscientiously up to date. During the war schoolboy and schoolgirl fiction provided a fifth column in the Fourth and a parachute landing in 'the hols'. Now it is space fiction and pseudo-scientific material that are demanded.

Discussion, Radio, Television and Reading

Mass communication now relies less heavily on words for our latter-day fairy-stories, and young adolescents and pre-adolescents consume a significant amount of their fiction from television and the printed strip-cartoon. Here heroes and heroines are all crudely conceived without an ounce of brains, intellect or reason. But the figure of superior power, the arbiter of destiny, is the scientist or professor—he is mere mind, poor drip, and the seductive heroine is not for him—but his is the all-powerful way of life. Obviously the majority are attracted by the strong-limbed, beautiful hero/heroine and identify themselves with them. But, as they do so they recognize they are still in the modern world, the playthings of mighty brains. Satanic scientists assault us with death-rays until their benevolent counterparts arrive with space rockets for escape. That these scientists are either malevolent or benevolent really implies that they have motives and, therefore, emotions, but these, when they appear, must be *made as impersonal as possible*—what is played out is a *vast abstract power game*. Thus, in these reams of lurid rubbish, we have the queer spectacle of disembodied intellect grotesquely re-embodied in sub-adult phantasies, and recognizable still. And always there is the dichotomy—the dissociation. Never does the egg-headed scientist marry the broad-hipped heroine or show so much as a flickering desire to do so. Reason and emotion, the life of the intellect and the life of the senses stand in absolute disjunction on either side of the road. *This is our modern mythology*. The modern Sherlock Holmes, no less than Conan Doyle's hero, still keeps clear of his Irene Adler (whom he 'greatly admired but felt no emotion towards akin to love!'). It was otherwise when Apollo pursued Daphne through the groves.

The comic strip-cartoons confront us with the spectacle of the Super Man, the Wonder Woman and the Pseudo-Scientist, who by their magical powers and appalling violence work their will for a crude version of good or evil on all who cross them, as indeed did the Good Fairy, the Wicked Fairy, the Prince and the Hobgoblin. Their common attribute is power—not the power of skill acquired through diligence or hard work, or of strong character developed from secure upbringing and self-discipline, or even of clever, ruthless manipulation, but the gratuitous magical power of a wand, a ray-gun, or an in-built supernatural personal attribute. Children who naturally feel lacking in power and see life in simple terms are attracted to and find satisfaction in fiction of this kind. Adults who have never really reached maturity, or who feel doubtful of their ability to cope with normal life, are sometimes tempted to seek refuge in identification with this kind of *deus ex machina*, and there are authors and artists willing to feed their desires. Perhaps this is especially true for inadequate adults who have no sense of the existence of a beneficent God. We have worried about the effect of the crudeness and violence of this kind of fiction on children. The fact that many of the ancient fairy tales were as crude and violent, though traditionally presented in word pictures, is sometimes forgotten, though this is no sufficient reason for ceasing to be concerned. We have also been worried about the effect on children of fiction in which the hero or anti-hero—the person with whom the reader is intended to identify—is himself anti-social or violent, because it might corrupt the child's values and standards of behaviour. The fiction seems scarcely likely to be more than a contributory factor to the development of a warped personality, and while we should eliminate any such factor we can, we need to look deeper for root causes. 'All the Plays and Diversions of Children should be directed towards good and useful Habits or else they will introduce ill ones,' says John Locke in his *Thoughts on Education*.

In earlier generations many clubs flourished on the teaching of reading (as do many clubs today in countries where educational opportunities are less than they are here), but the young people who were taught were usually those who had had little or no formal education. Today there are still some young people who leave school unable to read or read easily. They are mainly those who have not been cured of some particular disability needing skilled treatment, or those whose general educational capacity is low, but some are young people whose family backgrounds are such that even then they attended school—and attendance is usually erratic in their cases—the school's efforts impinged upon them very little. Because reading is so hard for all of these they often continue to entertain themselves with the same strip-cartoon material. Because this is so crude it tends to hold back their social development and the poor readers and non-readers continue to feed their self-confidence by identifying with magically powerful fictitious characters; and because they easily feel that life and society is against them they may readily identify with the strong

208

and powerful 'baddies'. All these young people feel inadequate and are likely to be problems as employees and later as parents. Their reading disabilities are frequently not their only difficulties. If not given the help they need, they may become criminal, but are more likely to become part of the group of incompetents whose lives are often miserable and who cost society so much. They seldom come to youth clubs or centres, and if the youth service is to help them it will be through workers making contact with them outside the orthodox settings, and having the patience and skill to gain their confidence through interest, understanding and helpfulness without making demands for membership or commitment. It may be a long time before any specific help with reading can be offered, and they may need help of other kinds on the way. Certainly they will need help through personal relationships with a trusted adult before they begin to see the world in less crude black and white terms than they have done before, and to begin to want to be more competent. If learning to read then has real point for them, direct help may be acceptable so long as they are not going to be 'shown up' by accepting it. One youth worker's path to this point was certainly adventurous. He had made contact with a small group of sixteen- to nineteen-year-old boys from highly problematic social backgrounds, who frequently 'slept rough', and who did not engage in regular employment. They did engage in 'dealing', and at one stage acquired a second-hand car that would go. They had seldom been far afield, but having acquired two provisional learners' driving licences, wanted to make a trip. They asked the worker to go with them because he had a full driving licence. Knowing they would probably go illegally if he did not, he decided to go and was brave enough to do so with one of them driving. They did not know the way, and the worker soon realized that none of them could read road-signs. Miraculously they survived the trip and were very pleased with themselves. The worker built on this feeling of achievement and was able to offer them the chance of being able to find their way by learning to read road-maps and sea-side brochures, and two of them eventually made an attempt on some travel stories. The record does not show what happened to the boys or the car after that, but new and richer horizons had certainly appeared to some of the boys. It is not always necessary literally to risk one's neck, but the kind of relationship and concern which made this worker willing to do so is very often the only foundation upon which more specific help can be mounted.

However, it is well to remember that seemingly most young people go through a craze for 'Comics' and there are some very good and well-meaning kinds published in this country. What we lack, however, is material for the less-skilled readers. Why are good authors not encouraged to write simple books for the adult whose reading pace is slow but whose desire to be entertained and educated has not necessarily come to a standstill? Are those who read slowly and less skilfully than others to be condemned for life to reading the tabloid press?

It is also comforting to remember that it is an established literary truism that there are only six different plots, the rest is but variation on a theme. A study of cheap literature reveals the fact that the content of the thriller is also ageless; in the 1940s the Atlantic convoy was surrounded by dive-bombers as Roland was outnumbered at Roncevaux, as Alfred was by the Danes, as Robin Hood was in the streets of Nottingham. There are still the three classical types of hero—Achilles, the man of prowess; Ajax, the man of strength; and Odysseus, the little cute one. Nearly always the strong man is in great difficulties with all the dice loaded against him, or if the strong man is in power he is almost invariably a villain. What could be more wholesome than this constant lesson that Might is not usually Right? All the more popular thrillers indeed constantly plug the virtues of truth and loyalty, courage and justice. The justice may be jungle justice, and very crudely applied. 'I never like to shoot a man when he is not ready,' says Dare-devil Daniel, but do you remember how often in Froissart the Knight waited for his opponent to retrieve his sword?

Girls were not as well served with regard to works of fiction until the sort of novel (like those of Monica Dickens) that takes the place of their brothers' adventure stories was published in paper-backed editions. Where they score, however, is in the wonderful selection of so-called 'glossy magazines' from which girls may, and do, learn to dress sensibly on a small budget, a great deal about new knitting patterns as well as make-up—and much about the art of personal relations. Most of these publications are written very well by sensible woman journalists who take their job of educating young women seriously. Girls need a good love-story and Cinderella is the best love-story in the world. It comforts many girls to read about the quiet girl who is 'put on' by the rest of the family and marries well in the end. The Beauty and the Beast theme is a good runner-up and the rest are variations on the tiresome mother-in-law theme which is, after all, the theme of more than half the ballads: a standard probably set by that shocking housekeeper who had not made her son's bed by evening, in spite of his reiterated entreaty of 'Mother, Mother, make my bed!'

All these tales, however, are quite competent and on the whole very well written. It is true that a study of 1914 war models gave the same basic content as the 1939 war models, and that the girl who in the 1940s married the Air Ace now marries her boss, but the stories of the Crusades and the wars with Troy are on the same themes. The reading matter which adolescent girls buy is impregnated with a wholesome if elementary, but quite distinct moral code; all that is wrong with it is that it is not enough, and that if Jack and Jill are not to tire of reading we must give them a richer diet.

What young people need is to be led through the excitement of reading a tale for the tale's sake to the more lasting joy of reading it for the sake of *how* it is told. This is the first and last lesson in literary taste! We want, therefore, to have plenty of books about, books which are 'better', not because they tell a different story, but because they have a richer and more varied characterization, a more subtle moral code and, even more important, especially in the face of strip cartoons and space fiction, books which display more humanity. After all the *Iliad* is probably the greatest book in the world because of the pity in it. And it is still the 'sadness at the heart of things' that is the key to much human endeavour and which has great motivating power in the lives of adolescents.

14

Religion and the Youth Group

✳

M ost of the older-established youth organizations were started by groups of people owing allegiance to one or other of the chief religious denominations. Many of them were started as an attempt by earnest young men and women from public schools and universities to justify their creed by works as well as by faith. The older uniformed organizations, many of the settlements and many of our largest clubs owe their inception to these self-sacrificing people who devoted their lives to this pioneer work. Gradually, however, a new spirit began to creep in and groups sprang up in which there were no closing prayers or Sunday services, and where the leaders, though certainly justified of their works, were motivated rather by ethics than by creeds.

Hence, between the wars (1918–39) we were perhaps at the mercy of two main types of leaders, those whose eyes were firmly fixed on the service of God and who somehow, in the excess of their devotion, lost grip of the young people they were trying to lead to see the vision as they saw it; and those whose eyes were so firmly fixed on the humanity they desired with their whole soul to help, that they lost touch with the fountain of inspiration, the God to whose feet they wished to lead that same humanity.

The perils and dangers of the 1939 war caused many people to return with renewed hope to the consolation of religious observance and to take an added interest in religious education. Evacuation brought in its train a spate of ill-considered letters concerning the alleged paganism of many schoolchildren and was another factor which caused the whole question of religious education to be reconsidered and reassessed. Much of that public concern was reflected in the 1944 Education Act which made an act of daily corporate worship compulsory in all State schools. Much of this concern has also borne fruit in that many more youth groups than formerly take it as a matter of course that the evening, or at least one evening in the week should conclude with a short Epilogue. These short services are often conducted by the young people themselves and a great deal of care and thought is put into them. Like many another human activity, its effect is imponderable, but in common with other human activities, these services can become a matter of empty form. In some youth groups they are very sparsely attended, in others all the members attend. Some youth leaders take the line that attendance at the Epilogue should be compulsory but, if this is so, it should surely be clearly understood by young people before they join that such religious observance is in fact compulsory. Most people, and certainly most adolescents, resent feeling that they have been trapped or tricked into taking part in something which they have not bargained for, and it would seem particularly distasteful that religious observance should be associated with trickery.

Since 1939 it would seem that church-going and church membership among young people are on the increase, certainly the Sunday School Movement has halted its decline in membership, and the youth sections of the Churches, notably the Methodists, have encouraged the growth of a large number of vigorous and flourishing 'open' and 'closed' clubs under their auspices. The keen interest displayed by ordinary men and women and young people in discussing religious topics, the frequent conferences, meetings, religion and life campaigns, and the stupendous attendances at the Billy Graham campaign (regardless of what may be felt or said about its lasting effect), all point to the fact that people are no longer satisfied with 'leaving Christianity to the parsons and the women'. Neither are they sure any longer that a good life is quite the same thing, and of quite the same value as a religious life.

It may be true that we live in an irreligious age, and probably true that never since the days of the early Christian Fathers have there been so few practising Christians in the world. Perhaps it is true, too, that England is practically the last stronghold of Christianity in Europe, the last country where both the government and the governed pay at least lip service to the Christian creed. But although it is open to argument whether politics, sex and religion are the three main interests of adolescents as the McNair Report affirmed, yet one has only to mix with young people to know that there is certainly no subject, with the possible exception of pop music, television, films and the pools, which is more often discussed than religion, if by religion we mean the problem of leading a good life and the problem of finding a meaning and purpose in life.

The attitude of many young people towards religion is, however, curiously ambivalent. At one moment they take the view that 'science has exploded all this religious business', but it is usually possible to persuade them that wherever science may be 'dizzyingly dancing' it is not away from a miraculous interpretation of the universe. At other times they take up a very strong position of attack when they assert that all religious people are hypocrites. This is very much more difficult to deal with since adolescents want to be satisfied of the utility of everything and therefore ask quite bluntly, 'What is the use of all this religion then, if it does not make people good?' They remain unconvinced unless they can be demonstrably shown results drawn from present-day life and not from what they dismiss as 'olden times'.

It is difficult, too, to reconcile the romantic and realist viewpoints from which they regard almost everything. The very same adolescents who will maintain with a wealth of reasoned argument that they have no use for religion—the 'Sez you' school of thought —will turn up a few weeks later wearing a small cross. The very young people who vigorously maintain that church-going is just superstitious nonsense will, the very same evening, seriously announce what the stars foretell for them this week, or what the fortune-teller told them on pay day. This curious mixture of cynicism and superstition has persisted since the war. In the 1940s, for instance, the managing director of one of the more popular stores reported that the sale of small crosses had increased by 300 per cent between 1939 and 1942. At the interviewing which followed upon registration, some interviewers were asked to take note of the number of boys and girls wearing such crosses, and in some cases it was sometimes possible to ask casually about them. The usual explanation seemed to be, that though they were not members of a church or Sunday school, they had a near relative or boy friend in the Forces—or they lived in a much-bombed area.

Religion and the Youth Group

The cross was a token worn with an air of 'Well, it may be a lot of nonsense, but at any rate it can't do any harm'.

During the war it was observed that whereas ordinary youth-group services were not well attended, a simple five minutes' intercession for the Forces was attended reverently by the majority. A service, asking for help for their friends or for someone they admired, meant something to them. The imminence of danger, the stark reality of the text 'in the midst of life we are in death', taught them—not to turn to religion, but to view it as something which they wistfully regarded as a problematical last straw in a chaotic universe.

One must be prepared for all kinds of slick and fashionable arguments about religion and, if necessary, one must make the slick answer. For instance, many young people take a great deal of trouble to point out why they do not go to church—those who assert that they are every bit as good, if not better, than those who do go; those who give the impression that they regard church-going as evidence of a want of faith in the Creator; and those who stay away because they fail to see the use of it and anyhow the parson and the congregation irritate them. A very telling method of pointing out the superficiality of these arguments is to say, 'Very well, let us take your reasons for not going to church and let us see if they could be regarded as equally valid excuses for not going to the cinema. It works out like this: I do not go to the cinema because:

1. My father and mother made me go too often when I was a boy.

2. No one at the cinema ever speaks to me.

3. Every time I go somebody asks me for money.

4. The man in charge never visits me and isn't interested in me.

5. The people who do go don't practise what the films teach them.'

It is not suggested that such arguments alone are enough to turn young people into ardent church-goers, but it does force them to consider how superficial their reasons are and to face the fact that they are not valid reasons at all but merely excuses.

Again, with the young would-be intellectuals—the bright stars very often of the discussion group—one can often take the war into their own camp by pointing out that much of the Bible can be turned into modern psychological terms and its validity remains unaltered. For example, take the well-known words of Saint Paul:

'Though I have the gift of prophecy and understand all mysteries and knowledge and though I have all faith so that I could remove mountains, and have not charity, I am nothing.'

This could quite easily become:

'Though I have full awareness of my situation and all my cognitions and beliefs are true, though I see all the universe in its proper proportions and am not inhibited or repressed in any way, yet if I have no outlet for my affections, I am not capable of living a normal life.'

Or again:

'Though I bestow all my goods to feed the poor, and though I give my body to be burned and have not charity, it profiteth me nothing.'

'Though my actions are all that could be desired and my code of conduct is perfect, yet if I am not fully integrated my personality is not well adjusted and has no absolute worth.'

Or the opening words of the Gospel according to Saint John can be given new meaning by changing it from metaphysical to utilitarian language:

'In the beginning was the Word, and the Word was with God, and the Word was God. . . .'

'In the beginning was the Purpose, and the Purpose was with God, and the Purpose was God. . . .'

Furthermore, although more things are wrought by faith than faith can explain, it sometimes helps young people to be told clearly that faith is not easy ether on which we can float away into religious ecstasy, but that each generation has to prove its own faith, and the clinching argument, the final faith, is to live a thing. Men have spent a great deal of time, energy and bravery in seeking new worlds, but the great thing to do is to create good worlds.

They are quick to appreciate that there is obviously something wrong in much of our political life, and with the standards of some of the leaders in their community, and their sense of decency and order is outraged. As a boy said once, 'If I kept my machine at work in the way God keeps the world, I should lose my job.' The only possible answer to that attitude is to ask, 'Do you clean your machine? For God relies on man to keep the machine clean for him and we, as a community, form the only body Christ has on earth. God relies on man to clean the world for him.'

But the essence of religion is that it should provide standards, a way of living, a way of choosing, and a purpose in life. Perhaps all one can do in this, as in so many other matters, is to condition the surroundings of our members so that they may be moved to make their own inquiries and to formulate their own philosophy and ethic. One has to remember that no one person is the sole architect of the universe, and that with youth one does what one can. Hence, the whole question as to whether a group holds services and prayers, or no services and no prayers, whether it is open on Sunday or whether it is not open on Sunday, has not necessarily any direct bearing on the spiritual value of that group to the young people themselves.

Therefore there is little that one can say about the practical side of how to cope with religious education or 'religious conditioning' in the youth group. It depends so much on the actual nature of the group itself and on the neighbourhood. Even the most superficial study of the new towns, large housing estates and overcrowded neighbourhoods, must have made it plain to most people that it is almost a necessity in most areas for a club to be opened for some part, at any rate, of Sunday. This, allied to the very fact that the peak period for juvenile delinquency is still four o'clock on Sunday in the country and six o'clock on Sunday in the town, would seem an unanswerable argument in favour of having something else for young people to do. To meet this need many brave and self-sacrificing leaders open their club for a sort of Sunday afternoon tea, and the rest of the evening is devoted to the ordinary activities which one would expect to find in a well-ordered home on that day. It is true that in most areas now, often with the tacit encouragement of the police and welfare workers generally, the cinemas have taken some of these young people off the streets and relieved some of the monotony of Sunday. The Sunday night television programmes are also of a quality and kind which encourages many young people to stay at home, if they have the sort of home in which their presence is tolerated. The whole question of 'monkey parading' and where to take your young man, and of how to cope on wet Sundays with that difficult period between after church and supper is something which bears very heavily on many young people. A certain amount of parading in fine clothes to attract the attention of the opposite sex is part of the normal development of the adolescent, and nothing we can do will discourage it; it is nature's problem, not ours. But the cold and wet Sunday is still a practical problem with which we might help.

One wishes there were many more places like the one where, every Sunday night after evensong, the vicar takes along his gramophone records to the church institute and starts off the dancing. This man feels with David that it is possible to 'dance to the glory of God', and his reward came on a Sunday, when he was laid low with influenza. The young people not only sent messages of sympathy to him, but in a formal resolution decided that he was not really having a square deal, and that since he was broad-minded enough to come to dance with them, they should be broad-minded enough to go to his evensong beforehand! His church now has an unusually large number of communicants between the ages of seventeen and twenty-five. Another Sunday club organizes a most attractive programme of 'personalities' for the whole of the autumn and winter session. Ballet dancers, celebrated musicians, poets and artists have been persuaded to visit this lively group which is nearly 500 strong. Many must have been as taken aback as I was on the first occasion I visited them to realize that the enormous queue which passed right along the whole length of the church, was not for the cinema at the corner, but for the church hall.

A great deal of help can often be obtained by calling drama and dramatic societies to our aid. In many clubs the beginning of religious observance has been made through the Nativity Play at Christmas or the Easter play, and one has only to see these performed, often very beautifully, in the presence of mothers and fathers to realize how deeply felt their message has been. Dramatic societies, or play-reading groups, can sometimes be persuaded to help a youth group on a Sunday evening. If such groups can be persuaded to use as part of their repertoire extracts from such plays as *Saint Joan, The Little Plays of St. Francis, The Passing of the Third Floor Back*, to mention only a few possibilities, such evenings can be a very real spiritual experience.

A well-arranged programme of music can also make a wonderful contribution to young people's feeling and thinking.

Above all, when we now call in the expert as a matter of course

218

for everything else, we should not take the attitude that anybody can take care of religion. It is no part of a club's purpose to overlap and to take to itself the responsibility of the parson. This was one of the things that killed many Sunday schools in the past. For many Sunday school teachers became too amateurish and too unprepared to hold the interest of their young people. It is true that here more than in anything else it is essential to get hold of the right person, but we do not always try hard enough—if at all. For instance, many young people need the help and sustenance of public worship and have a natural desire for the beauty of ritual. Most of these people are better off in a place where the beauty of ritual can be so much better performed. There are many more clergymen than is sometimes asserted who are well equipped, by training and temperament, for helping to prepare adolescents for church worship and to take occasional discussion groups. It is no part of our work to formulate a club religion. Too many churches are empty already. It is our business to help adolescents to find the right sort of church for them.

If, however, the majority of our club members have no allegiance to any church and do not attend because they will not or because they cannot (since there is still a feeling that a certain standard of dress and respectability is a *sine qua non* of attendance at church), if there is no chance of allying our young people to outside agencies, we have the precedent of Mahomet in our favour in bringing our religious service to the club. One knows from their conversation, from their doubts and their discussions, that they need to formulate a philosophy of life for themselves, and therefore it must be made possible for them within the club walls if there seems no other way. Just as one endeavours to satisfy them on a physical, emotional and mental plane, there is no escaping the responsibility of their spiritual needs. Nevertheless, in this more than in anything else, one should be sure that it is what *they* need and not what we think they need, since club members are not just imperfect creatures given us to alter. We must resist the temptation to try to give people our own spiritual values rather than to help them to theirs.

If we believe that the religious service is an essential feature of our work, then we must hold such a service even if very few of our members attend, and it may be that there is great moral force in making such a witness. But unless, as has already been suggested, it is clearly understood from the beginning that attendance is compulsory, we should avoid at all costs any attempt to make attendance at such services a matter of 'honour' or moral obligation. Moreover, we must not offer religion to adolescents as though it were a sort of insurance policy. Young people have no use for the cautious investor whether he is bargaining in terms of this world or the next, and the idea that there should be some sort of reward for worship—that it is a safe investment—seldom seems either truthful or attractive to modern youth.

However, the fear that a service or even community hymn-singing will frighten members away is often quite unfounded. The adolescent has a very strong sense of what is fitting, and is sometimes only waiting for us to make the first advances. Even if they are definitely antagonistic, there is no need to despair. We are giving them shelter on a Sunday and all we have to do is to be quite clear about what we want, and to lose no opportunity to achieve it.

It would appear to be generally recognized that if a club service is held on the Sunday, it should not be held at the same time as ordinary church services, and that it should be different in kind and character. Moreover, neither the Sunday service nor the Epilogue should ever become too formalized. For though familiar things are precious there is always a risk of building up a 'youth religion' and this has dangers, not the least of them being that of building up a poor imitation of the best that there is in church services, which is not really satisfactory for the full development of the boys and girls themselves.

Perhaps the best type of service is the very short one with practical and simple prayers, plenty of hymns and songs and a short period of readings, an address or discussion. This sounds very modest, but every part of such a service demands a great deal of thought and preparation. Hymn-singing needs particular care for although it is advisable to throw as much responsibility as possible for their selection on to the club members themselves, some guidance over selection and performance is vital. We must try to avoid too much of the sentimental clap-trap, bad poetry, and worse music, which still pass for hymn-singing. A certain amount of religious emotionalism can be fostered by using those doleful dirges and tinkling old-English waltz tunes which encourage a sentimental lump in the throat. It is done even better in the community-singing which precedes football matches, and which is shortly afterwards dissipated in blackguarding the referee.

The same thing is true about prayer. We must be prepared to explain why we pray. Boys and girls are often troubled about whether there is any justification for prayer, yet these same boys and girls are often extremely interested in the idea of the power of thought and the additional power of combined thought. 'The things, good Lord, that we pray for, give us grace to labour for,' is something that they all understand, but it is no use expecting members to pray for qualities and objects in which they are entirely uninterested. There is no virtue in sinking into an ugly posture of semi-somnolence over the knees while words are repeated which have no real meaning for the majority. Such prayers encourage inattention and true prayer demands concentration.

As long as the reading of the address or the discussion is related to everyday life and is spoken in a natural manner, it will not really matter where one starts. This natural manner, however, is very important, and it is one of the reasons why, if one uses scripture readings in the youth group, it is probably wiser to use a modern translation of the Bible. This is often a very real sacrifice to those who have learnt to love the Elizabethan translation, but one has so often been greeted with the surprised 'Oh, so *that* is what it meant!' that it would seem well worth sacrificing one's love of beautiful words for the real gain of proving that there is no really unbridgeable gap between the sacred and the secular. After all, Christ Himself spoke the simplest language and in broad country dialect, not even B.B.C. Greek, but Aramaic.

For the rest, if one is sufficiently alert, there are always opportunities for making the religious way of life apparent to young people. For instance the discovery that a leader who was a heavy smoker did not smoke in Lent had a profound effect in one group. The members were most impressed by the fact that he was giving up the thing that obviously meant very much to him for the sake of self-discipline and the fact that this self-discipline was a feature of religious life led to an interest in other festivals of the Church. It is often difficult to discuss and justify one's religious observances, but as Evelyn Underhill has put it so well, 'Religious experience is life at its fullest or nothing at all. If it is something valuable to us and we wish to pass it on we cannot keep our spiritual experience in a glass case or reserved compartment.' We

Religion and the Youth Group

Religion and the Youth Group

must step down from the pedestal of superior knowledge or out of the shell of religious reticence and listen very humbly and sympathetically to descriptions of life as they see it.

The sooner we admit to the young boy and girl that being a practising Christian in the modern world is no easy matter, the better it will be. If only they can realize that religion is something towards which we are all working and not merely a state of grace beneath which we shelter, the easier it will be to take them along the road with us. Religion has been too often represented to the young as the easy way out, as though once you believe, you know all the answers and are secure in this world and the next—no more problems, no more doubts, no longer do you say 'the good that I would, I do not, and the evil that I would not, that I do'— you are always sure, always right, always happy. For most of us this simply is not true as it certainly does not seem to have been true for the saints of God. Religious faith is not a soft option, but a standard to be attained and struggled for, it is a challenge to humanity, not an opiate, a prize or a bomb-proof shelter of the spirit. Always the Christian is crying 'Lord, I believe, help thou my unbelief', his great glory being his faith that even his inability to believe can be helped. It is not sufficient to be prepared to die for one's beliefs (all sorts of people have been found ready and willing to do that), it is necessary to be prepared to live for them and struggle towards them day by day. One must help them to learn that they can see God in the three imponderables of Goodness, Truth and Beauty—in the things they already love and appreciate. One can do a great deal by helping people to see that all real love is good, that is to say, of God, so that we cannot, even if we wish to do so, live a life disconnected from religion. The affection of a mother for her child; their own regard for their family; their devotion to their special friends; the attraction of a young man to a young woman, all these experiences of love, where they are selfless, may be shown as expressions of the one God of Love. The teaching of the good life, like the teaching of everything else, must be a gradual advance from the known to the unknown. Young people are quick to appreciate that religion, like America, is an undeniable factor in the world, whether we have seen it or not, and the visible signs of good working themselves out in social reforms such as the Factory Acts, the Education Acts, free medical attention and old-age pensions, can all be

222

shown as part of the same urge towards things of the spirit, which is part of the nature of mankind.

The desire to 'be good' is a fundamental part of each normal person's make-up. It may be overlaid by pessimism, camouflaged by cynicism or transformed by bitterness. The very inverted snobbery which makes the young fatalist deny the use of virtue or the religious view of life is sometimes a measure of his longing for reassurance. Moreover, in adolescence particularly, one must be alert not only to help those who are going through a phase of atheism, but those who are going through an emotional hotbed of religious experience. There are also those young people who wish to argue for the sake of arguing. It is a natural phase of their growth, but there are times when it pays to be ruthless, dealing with them rather in the manner of the young clergyman in the bus who was tackled by a fussy foreigner: 'I do not believe in Heffen,' he said, poking the curate in the ribs. The curate went on reading. 'I haff studied the matter and haff come to the conclusion that no such place as Heffen is to be found.' Still no reply. 'I tell you,' went on the foreigner, still more loudly and shaking the clergyman's arm, 'I tell you, Heffen does not exist.' 'All right, all right!' said the clergyman, very quietly but firmly. 'Go to Hell then.'

Of course, once we invite questions we have to be prepared for awkward ones, but religion is full of awkward questions, and it is much better that doubts and difficulties should come into the open than that they should be repressed and be a constant source of irritation and trouble. There is no longer any room for the attitude of the two old ladies who were discussing Darwin. 'They say', said one, 'that man is descended from monkeys.' 'How dreadful, my dear,' said the other. 'Let us pray that it is not true, or if it is true, let us pray that it may not become too widely known.' If we are honest we know that some of the questions asked will be unanswerable, that sometimes they will disclose a warped and twisted outlook on life, that sometimes they will be so forceful as to challenge the very foundations of one's faith. But young people are often much more fair-minded than adults. They appreciate an honest endeavour to answer difficulties, and will frequently help us out by stating what they themselves think. But we must decide where we ourselves stand, and make it clear to those who question us. One of the main reasons why a generation ago the Communist faith often gained such a hold on all sorts of young people is that it did give definite answers to their questions. If we believe in the Christian way of life and the Christian experience, we must be prepared to be equally definite when we are questioned. So many people in endeavouring to avoid being dogmatic have ceased to be anything but negative. When young people bring a problem to us they want a definite answer and they respect a straight answer given in all humility. 'Well, since you ask, this is what I believe,' is more honest, more helpful and much less harmful than the more fashionable, 'Well, there are a great many points of view concerning this. . . .' Mary Brown is not interested in the light that the journeys of Saint Paul may throw upon her travels in search of the good life, she is concerned with the journeyings of Mary Brown, and it is there we must help or not at all.

Nevertheless, we cannot hurry. All we can do is to try to direct all youth work in a real spirit of redeemed behaviour, until the time comes when the members know it and feel it and are conditioned by it. This is part of what is meant by 'the atmosphere' of a youth group, and it makes far greater demands on a leader's faith and character than the easier way of having set services. After all, what is all this Youth Service about? Why do so many people give up their evenings for little or no pay, for little or no very obvious results and for little or no comfort? Do we do it in order to organize keep-fit classes? One can be a perfect physical specimen and yet be just a selfish beast, and the life of the jungle is there to prove that this is true. Do we do it in order to play darts or to make rugs, or to have socials? There are other agencies who do these things far better. Do we do it for the purely negative object of keeping young people off the streets, or do we do it because we must, because the very existence of community life is a testimony to our love of our neighbours, a testimony to our faith which is so strong, that we can go on in the spirit of Mark Twain's celebrated remark, 'Faith is belief in what we know ain't so.' It seems to me that the whole motive power of Youth Service is this devoted 'betting your life' that there is a God. If our members see that we have no faith of this kind they will soon discover that we have no reserves to draw upon. It is a thing that cannot be provoked by services and prayers or evoked by lip service, or brought into being by inviting parsons of every denomination to the group. It is the very motive power of one's whole life—or nothing at all.

Bibliography

✳

Government Publications relating to Youth Service (H.M.S.O.)

Circular 1486: *In the Service of Youth.*

Circular 1516: *The Challenge of Youth.*

Circular 1543: *Youth Service Corps.*

Circular 1577: *Youth Registration.*

Circular 1603: *Pre-Service Training Organizations.*

The Youth Service after the War. 1943.

McNair Report on the Training of Teachers and Youth Leaders.

Education Act, 1944: Section 53, Part 2.

The Purpose and Content of the Youth Service. (A report of the Youth Advisory Council appointed by the Ministry of Education, 1943: published by the Ministry of Education, 1945.)

Community Centres: Ministry of Education pamphlets, 1945.

Ministry of Education Circular 133: March 1947 (dealing with Further Education).

Ministry of Education Memo. A.W.1: August 1948. Grants under the Physical Training and Recruiting Act, 1939, as amended by the Education Act, 1944.

Further Education: Ministry of Education pamphlet 8.

Early Leaving: Ministry of Education, 1954.

The Youth Service in England and Wales (Albemarle Report): H.M.S.O. (Cmnd. 929), 1960.

The Training of Part-Time Youth Leaders and Assistants (Bessey Report): H.M.S.O., 1961.

Half Our Future (Newsom Report): H.M.S.O., 1963.

A Second Report on the Training of Part-Time Youth Leaders and Assistants: Youth Service Development Council Review Committee (H.M.S.O., 1965).

Bibliography

Education in 1965: A General Survey: Department of Education and Science and Central Office of Information.

Education in 1966: A General Survey: Department of Education and Science and Central Office of Information.

Reports on Education: Department of Education and Science.

Immigrants and the Youth Service: Youth Service Development Council Review Committee (H.M.S.O., 1967).

General

Report on Terminology (words used) in the Service of Youth, issued by the Standing Conference of National Voluntary Organizations, in association with the National Council of Social Service, Inc., 26 Bedford Square, London, W.C.1.

E. Younghusband, *Employment and Training of Social Workers* (Carnegie United Kingdom Trust).

Youth Service Tomorrow: A report of a Meeting arranged by King George's Jubilee Trust and held at Ashridge in 1951; published by the authority of the Council of King George's Jubilee Trust (Odhams Press Ltd., 1955).

Citizens of Tomorrow: King George's Jubilee Trust (1955).

Ferguson and Cummison, *In Their Early Twenties* (published for Nuffield Foundation by Oxford Univ. Press, 1956).

Central Office of Information, *Education in Britain* (H.M.S.O.).

J. A. C. Brown, *Social Psychology of Industry* (Pelican).

H. Heginbothan, *The Employment Service* (Methuen).

P. L. Kitchen, *From Learning to Earning* (Faber).

A. E. Morgan, *The Needs of Youth* (Penguin).

Alec Rodger, *Youth Employment* (Bureau of Current Affairs).

Ed. David Cleghorn, *Training Worker Citizens* (Macdonald & Evans).

Advances in Understanding the Adolescent: Revised edition 1955 (published for Home and School Committee of the English New Education Fellowship).

Moral Foundations of Citizenship (chapter on 'Problems of Human Relationships in Youth Groups') (London Univ. Press).

C. M. Fleming, *The Social Psychology of Education* (Kegan Paul).

Adolescence, its Social Psychology (Routledge).

Lester and Alice Crow, *Adolescent Development and Adjustment* (McGraw-Hill Co., New York).

Bibliography

Pearl Jephcott, *Girls Growing Up* (Faber).
Rising Twenty (Faber).
Some Young People (Allen & Unwin).
Time of One's Own (Oliver & Boyd)
G. W. Jordan and E. M. Fisher, *Self Portrait of Youth* (Heinemann).
Berger-Hamerschlag, *Journey into Fog* (Gollancz).
Edward Blishen, *Roaring Boys* (Thames & Hudson).
Wm. Foote Whyte, *Street Corner Society* (Univ. of Chicago Press).
M. Lloyd Turner, *Ships without Sails* (Univ. of London Press).
University of Bristol Institute of Education, *Spontaneous Youth Groups* (Univ. of London Press).
D. H. Stott, *Saving Children from Delinquency* (Carnegie U.K. Trust).
Delinquency and Human Nature (Carnegie U.K. Trust).
C. A. Joyce, *By Courtesy of the Criminal* (Harrap).
John A. F. Wilson, *The Child and the Magistrate* (Cape).
B. L. Q. Henriques, *The Home Menders* (Harrap).
Club Leadership Today (Oxford Univ. Press).
P. H. K. Kuenstler, *Youth Work in England* (Univ. of London Press).
Voluntary Youth Leaders (Univ. of London Press).
J. Macalister Brew, *In the Service of Youth* (Faber).
Informal Education (Faber).
Girls' Interest (N.A.Y.C., 1947).
Hours Away from Work (N.A.Y.C., 1949).
Bryan Reed, *Eighty Thousand Adolescents* (Allen & Unwin).
Leslie T. Wilkins, *The Adolescent in Britain* (Central Office of Information).
L. P. Barnett, *Adventure with Youth* (Methodist Youth Dept.).
The Church Youth Club (Methodist Youth Dept.).
Lord Beveridge, *Voluntary Action; A Report on Methods of Social Advance* (Allen & Unwin).
M. Penelope Hall, *The Social Services of Modern England* (Routledge).
J. L. and Barbara Hammond, *The Bleak Age* (Pelican, 1947).
Lord Shaftesbury (Pelican, 1939).
E. Moberly Bell, *Octavia Hill; A Biography* (Constable).
C. H. Dobinson, *Technical Education for Adolescents* (Harrap).
Sir Richard Livingstone, *The Future in Education* (Cambridge Univ. Press).

Bibliography

G. M. Trevelyan, *English Social History* (Longman).

W. R. Niblett, *Essential Education* (Univ. of London Press).

A. N. Whitehead, *The Aims of Education* (5th ed.) (Williams & Norgate).

Kathleen Allsopp, *A New Deal for Young Workers?* (Zenith, 1966).

Michael Carter, *Education, Employment and Leisure* (Pergamon, 1963).

Into Work (Pelican, 1966).

Bernard D. Davies and Alan Gibson, *The Social Education of The Adolescent* (Univ. of London Press, 1967).

W. M. Evans, *Young People in Society* (Blackwell, 1965).

George W. Goetschius and M. Joan Tash, *Working with Unattached Youth* (Routledge & Kegan Paul, 1966).

R. W. J. Keeble, *A Life Full of Meaning* (Pergamon, 1965).

Joan E. Matthews, *Working With Youth Groups* (Univ. of London Press, 1966).

Frederick W. Milson, *Social Groupwork Method in Christian Education* (Chester House, 1963).

Mary Morse, *The Unattached* (Pelican, 1965).

Leslie Paul, *Transition from School to Work* (Report to King George's Jubilee Trust and Industrial Welfare Society, 1962).

M. Joan Tash, *Supervision in Youth Work* (National Council of Social Service, 1967).

Articles

Sir William Alexander, 'Youth Employment Service', *Education* (17th and 24th December 1965).

A. C. Burns, 'Newsom in Practice', *Times Educational Supplement* (8th October 1965).

A. Crichton, 'Youth and Leisure in Cardiff', *Sociological Review* (July 1962).

Edward Guinness, 'Training the Non-Apprentice', *Industrial Society* (December 1965).

Joyce Joseph, 'Attitudes to Work and Marriage of Six Hundred Adolescent Girls', *British Journal of Sociology* (June 1961).

Gerald Kaufman, 'Teenage Films', *The Listener* (23rd July 1964).

J. G. Harries, 'Helping Half Our Future', *Education* (27th May 1966).

Alan Little, 'The Young Affluents', *The Listener* (9th May 1963).

Bibliography

Pamphlets

Raymond Feather, *The Employment of Professional Youth Leaders* (National Association of Youth Clubs, 1967).
James Hemming, *Adolescents and Society* (Arthur Mellows Memorial Trust, 1967).

Youth Group Interests and Activities

Note. There is a wealth of material, much of it published by the various voluntary organizations, and no bibliography could therefore hope to be exhaustive. The following is merely a selection from this material.
Club Leader's Handbook (N.A.Y.C.).
Tony Gibson and Jack Singleton, *The Spare Time Book* (Gollancz).
Geoffrey Trease, *Tales out of School* (Heinemann).
Ed. Dr. John Burton, *Group Discussion* (Central Council for Health Education).
L. A. G. Strong, *A Tongue in your Head* (Pitman).
Kathleen Gibberd, *Politics on the Blackboard* (Faber).
Gordon Allport, *The Individual and his Religion* (Constable).
Edward H. Patey, *Religion in the Club* (N.A.Y.C.).
R. Selby Wright, *Asking them Questions* (Oxford Univ. Press).
Cyril Bibby, *Sex Education* (Macmillan).
Ed. J. M. Brew, *Occasional Papers No. 1—Girls' Interests* (N.A.Y.C.).
Occasional Papers No. 2—Projects (N.A.Y.C.).
Occasional Papers No. 3—Looking and Talking (N.A.Y.C.).
Occasional Papers No. 4—Things to Do (N.A.Y.C.).
Occasional Papers No. 5—Drama (N.A.Y.C.).
Know the Game Series (Educational Productions Ltd.).
First Aid and Home Nursing Series (Educational Productions Ltd.).
Planning a Mixed Club (N.A.Y.C.).
Planning a Village Club (N.A.Y.C.).
Club Canteens Joint Publication (N.A.Y.C. and N.A.B.C.).
Handyman's How to Do It Series, prepared for amateurs by craftsmen (Odhams Press).

Bibliography

A. C. North, *I Made it Myself (Toys, Models, etc.*) (Batsford).
Furniture Repairs and Renovation (Arthur Pearson Ltd.).
Plastics and Models (The Falcon Press).
R. H. Fuller, *Hobby Book* (The Falcon Press).
Rodney Bennett, *Let's Do a Play* (Nelson).
Pamela Blackie, *A Drama Teacher's Handbook* (Blackwell).
John Fernald, *The Play Produced* (Dean).
Frances Mackenzie, *The Amateur Actor* (Nelson).
Susan Richmond, *A Textbook of Stagecraft* (Deane).
Further Steps in Stagecraft (Deane).
Lyn Oxenford, *Playing Period Plays, I, II, III* (J. Garnet Miller).
John Wiles and Alan Garrard, *Leap to Life—An Experiment in Youth Drama* (Chatto & Windus).
D. Macmahon, *Youth and Music* (Nelson).
M. M. Scott, *What can I Play* (Quality Press).
Rex Harris, *Jazz* (Pelican).
Sid Hedges, *The Youth Song Book* (Nat. Sunday School Union, (words 5s., music 21s.).
Twice Forty-Four Sociable Songs (arranged and collected by Geoffrey Shaw) (Boosey & Hawkes).

Kay Gilmour, *Committee Procedure* (Methuen).
Boys' Club Accounts and Records (Nat. Ass. of Boys' Clubs).
Committees Work in this Way (N.A.Y.C.).
Management or Advisory Committees (N.A.Y.C.).
Attend or Apologize (N.A.Y.C.).
Members' Councils (N.A.Y.C.).

Index

✭

Activities, misapprehension concerning numbers of, 155

Adolescence, Adolescents (*see also* Youth Groups, Youth Services): the nature of, 17–40; ambiguous status in, 20, 39; girls in, 21–3, 28–9, 30–4, 166; physical handicaps of, 23, 24; sex education in, 24–6; glandular changes in, 26; increased emotional awareness in, 27, 48; and friction tion with parents, 20, 27–9; creation of 'gods' in, 33–5, 39; dress of, 35, 47; concern with religion during, 37–8, 212 seqq.; sense of guilt during, 37–8; out-of-home interests of, 47–51; leisure of, 43–4; and music, 45–7; and dance halls, 45–6; and the cinema, 44, 48; other personal-relationship problems of, 48; and longing for success, 48; aggressiveness of, 49–50; and work, 52–62; and espresso bars, 121; and 'repetitive work' fallacy, 56–7; and unregulated occupations, 59; and frustrations at work, 52 seqq., 74; and automation, 56; and 'work's leisure', 58; and 'creative work', 57, 58, 78, 178, 187–9; education in, 63–72; early working-life disappointments of, 52, 60; and grammar-school entrance, 64; and evening institutes, 66; youth work and, outlines of, 73 seqq.; overriding aims of youth service for, 76–9; organization of services for, 135–41; trend of interests of, 111; uniformed organizations for, 113–14; settlements and community centres for, 116–17; church groups for, 114–16; clubs and youth centres for, 117–18; mixed groups for, 118–26; 'special interest' groups for, 120–1; spontaneous groups and squads for, 121–3; 'In-and-out' clubs for, 123–4; unattached, 109, 124–6; unreliability and unpunctuality part of make-up of, 167; and 'value for money' knowledge, 145, 152–3; and adherence to 'tradition' in games, crafts, etc., 155; and bad posture, 162; and physical education, 163–5; and force of example, 167–8; and the full life, 178 seqq.; and personal

231

Index

Index

Index

Index

Saint John Ambulance, 96, 121
Salvation Army, 87
School-leaving age, raising of, 63, 68–70
School pattern, revulsion from, 153–4
Sea Cadets, 96, 114
Secondary modern schools, 65–6
'Self-programming' groups, 106
Shaw, G. B., quoted, 184
Shop Act, 1912, 87
'Silent Social Revolution, The', 69
Skiffle groups, 181–2
Smith, Sir William, 88, 113
Sokol, 90
'Special interest' clubs, 120–1
'Specialist' helpers, 140
'Spontaneous' youth groups, 121–3
Square dancing, degree of interest in, 170
Standing Conference of National Voluntary Youth Organizations, 112
Students, 41–2
Subscriptions, 144
'Summer Holiday', 45
Sundays, special problems of, 217–18
Sunday Schools, 213
Sunday School teachers, 219

Teacher-leaders, 133
Teachers, staffing ratios, 67; training of, 68
Team games, difficulties of, 165–8; girls and, 165–6; profit derived from, 167–8
Team spirit, 167, 177
Technical Colleges, 69
Teenage Canteens, 123–4
'Teenager', image of, 41 seqq., 102; market for, 42
Television, 45, 187, 196, 198

Tennis, 168
Topics of conversation, 44
Townswomen's Guilds, 156
'Trad' fans, 45–7
Training and Employment Act, 1948, 63
Twain, Mark, on 'Faith', 224

'Unattached, the', 109, 124–6
'Unclubbables, the', 124–6
Underhill, Evelyn, quoted, 221
'Untouched' youth and Circular 1577, 97, 124–6

'Visits of observation', 196–7
Vocational training, 55–6
Voluntary agencies, widely varying policies and achievements of, 103, 105; the future of, 107, 108
Voluntary and paid leadership, 133–4
'Voluntaryism', the era of, 86–91; and State partnership, 91–8; and post-1944 integration, 98–102; and post-1950 developments, 102–10

Wakes Weeks, 171
Welsh League of Youth, 112
West Indians, 46
Women's Institutes, 156
Workers' Educational Association, 156
Working wives, 21, 58–9

Young Farmers' Clubs, 120–1
Y.M.C.A., 118
Y.W.C.A., 112, 113, 118
Y.W.C.A./L.U.Y.C. Coffee Stall Project, 125
Youth centres and clubs, 117–18
Youth Councils and Parliaments (as Youth Advisory Council), 94

236

Index